THE PROTEAN SELF

THE
PROTEAN
SELF

*Dramatic Action in
Contemporary Fiction*

Alan Kennedy

Columbia University Press
New York 1974

Published in Great Britain in 1974 by
The Macmillan Press Ltd.

Printed in Great Britain

Library of Congress Cataloging in Publication Data

Kennedy, Alan.
 The protean self.

 Includes bibliographical references.
 1. English fiction—20th century—History and
criticism. 1. Title.
PR881.K4   823'.03   74–9792
ISBN 0–231–03922–0

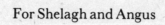

For Shelagh and Angus

Contents

Preface

In the Introduction I try to outline the way in which while engaged in literary criticism I encroached on the borders of Sociology. I have also found myself at the border with Philosophy and no doubt the awkwardness of my forays into alien territory will not go undetected by professional border-guards. I would like to be able to take some comfort in the belief that (according to Wm Righter in *Logic and Criticism*, 1963) the value of criticism is not in the conclusions it reaches but in the interest it arouses on the way towards a conclusion. Despite the fact that criticism is not like normal argument, and the additional fact that Art is not Philosophy, the critic cannot escape being a thinker and he must be prepared to accept the consequences of his own thought and its shortcomings. It must therefore be admitted that a concept of the nature of the Self emerges from the following study, and while it cannot be called a philosophical disquisition I naturally hope that this book will serve to reveal what the Self is like in some modern literature. Such information should be of interest to those whose task it is to construct systems of thought; and it could also be of some interest to those common readers of whom I am one, who like to think that on occasion creative literature has a 'philosophy' in the old-fashioned sense.

The concept of the Self I have called the 'protean self' and the reader, if he is the sort who reads introductions first will find some elucidation there. Others who read introductions as they are usually written, after the main text, but would like a short explication of the title will find the phrase from Coleridge that gives rise to it on p. 8.

I am greatly indebted to Alex Rodger of the University of Edinburgh, who not only provided a stimulus in the form of intelligent, wide-ranging conversation, but also carefully read

ix

and commented on this work in all its stages. I benefited also from a few brief conversations I was able to have with Sam Goldberg during his stay in Edinburgh. Frank Kermode was kind enough to read a draft of the chapter on Muriel Spark and make some encouraging comments. The financial support of the Canada Council gave me the time.

I am grateful to Walter Allen for reading and commenting on this book in its early form.

Acknowledgement is due to the following: the University of Texas Press for permission to use material published in an article on Cary's second trilogy in *Texas Studies in Literature and Language* (Summer 1974); the Bodley Head and Random House, Inc., for the extract from *Ulysses* by James Joyce; Chatto & Windus Ltd and Barnes & Noble, Inc., for the extract from *The Classical Temper* by S. L. Goldberg; Faber & Faber Ltd for extracts from *The Self As Agent* by John MacMurray; Faber & Faber Ltd and Random House, Inc., for extracts from 'Talking to Myself' from *Epistle to a Godson* by W. H. Auden; New Directions Publishing Corporation, New York, for 'The Desert Music' from *Pictures from Brueghel and Other Poems*, copyright 1954 by William Carlos Williams.

                                                        A. K.

As kingfishers catch fire, dragonflies draw flame;
As tumbled over rim in roundy wells
Stones ring; like each tucked string tells, each hung bell's
Bow swung finds tongue to fling out broad its name;
Each mortal thing does one thing and the same:
Deals out that being indoors each one dwells;
Selves — goes itself; *myself* it speaks and spells,
Crying *What I do is me: for that I came*.

Gerard Manley Hopkins

Only the counted poem, to an exact measure:
to imitate, not to copy nature, not
to copy nature
NOT, prostrate, to copy nature
                              but a dance! to dance
two and two with him —

'The Desert Music', William Carlos Williams

Our marriage is a drama, but no stage-play where
what is not spoken is not thought: in our theatre
all that I cannot syllable You will pronounce
in acts whose raison d'être escapes me. Why secrete
fluid when I dole, or stretch your lips when I joy?

'Talking to Myself', W. H. Auden

Introduction:
Fictions, Selves and the
Sociology of Role-playing

Although the prime intention of this book is to be no more than
literary criticism, or what is often called practical criticism, I
have found it impossible to be altogether practical in criticism
without being also a little theoretical. If practical criticism is a
method of 'close reading' – and the imprecision of that term is
revealed by asking what its apparent opposite, distant reading,
could possibly be – then it is a method virtually without a meth-
odology. Close reading is practical, pragmatic; and it yields
results. It is the ground of all worthwhile discussion of literature
and any merit that any of the following discussion of twentieth
century fiction may have is the result of an attempt to be as
'thorough' as possible in reading what is there in the text in
question. If attention is confined to any one text, perhaps it is
possible to be completely practical and focus only on the internal patterns of imagery and so on. To look at several texts,
however, and to find that similar patterns are being widely used
forces one on to questions that are not merely practical, but
which are demanding and important questions nevertheless.
And of course it would be the height of impracticality if the
effect of literature were to keep us forever circling around inside
the patterned confines of any one iconical text – and there, with
the word 'icon' we come upon at least the ideology of practical
criticism. We rightly expect literature to be practical in another
sense; to be of some use to us after we close the covers and start
again to go about the daily business of living. To have access to
this kind of practicality, it is necessary to pose questions which
are usually considered to be theoretical; questions such as,

1

What is the relation between fiction and life? What is the relation between literature and the society in which it is produced and what characterises the literature of any one period and what is the relation between that literature and preceding literature? In the midst of a literary 'tradition', or movement, what is the function of the individual artist? And most important of all for the common reader, What does this mean for me? or to put it in a more abstract way, What is the status of fictions in what we call Reality?

Practical criticism is in fact a technique of analysis which developed with reference to poetry; it is a poetics, in the restricted sense of the term. Perhaps then it is inevitable for the student of the novel, finding that the only method currently available is one most suited to poetry, to find also that he must push beyond what is merely practical. There have been attempts recently to formulate a 'poetics of fiction' or a 'poetics of the novel', and they are responses to one of the most exciting challenges in modern literary criticism, but the very phrase reveals the bias of present theory, towards poetry. The same is true of that offshoot of practical criticism, linguistic analysis of literary texts.* It is possible, and rewarding to do a linguistic analysis of short passages of prose, but it is not really practical to consider such an extremely close reading of a complete novel, and certainly not of a number of novels. Novels are big pieces of literature and they demand a wider view and need larger questions if they are to yield their meanings. Let me repeat, however, that such questions and theoretical considerations must be based on a sympathetic and linguistically alert 'close' reading of individual works. The modern scientific method is to

_____

* It seems to me that the attempt to apply linguistics directly to literature is destined to only limited usefulness in literary criticism, and at best the use of formal syntactic analysis elaborately confirms what good readers intuit. Sociolinguistics, with its emphasis on the way that abstract language forms acquire meaning *in context*, suggests a potentially richer furrow. The provocative problem is then to determine what is the context of the language forms of any literary text. It is not enough to assume that for any isolated language element in a text the context is the rest of the language of the text (this is Lodge's assumption in *Language of Fiction*). The context of the language in a literary text is indeed – to a greater extent than non-'poetic' uses of language – that of the surrounding language. But the virtues and values of the whole text cannot be appreciated without some attention being given to its context in reality: social, historical, and personal (in interaction with a reader).

propound possible theories and then set about searching for evidence to disprove the theory. The study of literature differs from science in its greater degree of adherence to what used to be called the scientific method. We still need evidence before we can move into the range of hypothesis. And until we do our facts lack life.

The fact that one encounters in reading much recent fiction is the widespread use of what for convenience I have called metaphors of drama. Now the mere recurrence of a set of metaphors, seen as inert fact, is admittedly not very exciting nor worthy of much attention – unless those metaphors seem somehow to be essential to what a book is all about. If the impact of the novel one is reading can ultimately be accounted for in terms of those metaphors, they begin to yield their opaque facticity. Metaphors of drama have some relevance to the Artificial, and the most artificial mode of acting is the way of Art itself. To have found that fictions, novels, are about fiction, or that the modern novel is reflexive, would perhaps have been minimally interesting as confirmation of ideas made current by Frank Kermode, who has repeatedly asserted that the novels that should most claim our time and energies are those which themselves treat with the subject of fiction. What is troubling about Kermode's theory – the value of which is not in question here, and has made no small contribution to my own attempts to understand the novel – is that despite his insistence it is sometimes difficult to see why a theory of fiction, or the necessary narcissism of novelists, should be of any interest to any but initiates of the esoteric practice of literary criticism. If I have been able to extend what Kermode has said about the nature of fiction it has been by repeatedly asking what fictions are for and by focusing on the way in which characters inside novels are themselves involved in the discussion and the creation of fictions. Fictions about fiction are not interesting because the neuroses of novelists are interesting nor because of some recondite principle of literary criticism. They are worth our attention because the characters in novels are interested in fictions; and the implication of this fact – in so far as characters in novels are like us – is that fictions are important in our own lives, not only the fictions we read but the ones we all make. The subject is interesting because we all, not just novelists, live by fictions. To summarise the theme as it occurs in the novels discussed in this study: characters in novels are presented, and conceive of themselves in dramatic terms; the novelist himself appears to us, as readers, in a dramatic guise, we know him only through his 'presentation' or *persona*. And in daily life we are all actors, we live in and by drama and fiction.

It is with the last consideration, that life in the world is a dramatic affair, a matter of roles, that Art overlaps with Sociology, that part of it at least which is centrally concerned with what is called role-theory. As I have said, my purpose is to do literary criticism, but one of the boundaries over which I cannot help encroaching ever so little, at least in this introduction, is that between Literature and Sociology. The sociologist crosses it of course with carefree ease, making what one is often tempted to call 'raids on the articulate', to adapt Eliot's phrase. The literary critic who tries to cross the boundary in the other direction often finds flaming swords of the profession confronting him. For the literary critic to be sociological is to be an apostate. From the social scientist's point of view it is an impertinence for the unscientific to meddle in that for which he is not trained. Sometimes the literary profession seems to fear being put out of business:

> In fact the disciplines of sociology and structural anthropology are generating theories of social organisation and development and of meta-cultural continuity in terms that implicitly challenge the special status of art that the idea of 'culture', in the traditional sense, and the existence of criticism depend upon. For if art comes to be seen as merely a manifestation of certain social drives, if it is reducible to data, then not only is the critic working in an absurdly private darkness, but the traditional disposition to locate value in an art-culture is a provincial sentimentality.[1]

But is special status more important than truth? If Art is a matter of 'social drives' we should know it. With a little more precision of wording, Philip Thody warns of the dangers for the critic, of sociological theories such as those of Lucien Goldmann. He warns that the literary critic 'cannot, without being unfaithful to his calling, allow himself to be absorbed into some general inquiry concerning the relationship between author and society'.[2] And one is compelled to agree with him, partly because of the force of that word 'absorbed'. Nobody wants to be absorbed by a theory; or to lose sight of the problems by disappearing into a solution. Nevertheless, it seems to me that the literary critic must be unfaithful to his calling if that calling is so narrow that it makes him turn back in contempt before essential matters. To put it another way, the critic must, without being unfaithful to his calling, to his sensitivity to literature, meddle with questions about the relationship between Literature and Society. As Leavis suggested, sociological questions about Literature are too important to be left to the sociologist alone, who too often has too clumsy a perception of literature:

> [No] 'sociology of literature' and no attempt to relate literary studies with sociological will yield much profit unless informed and controlled by a real and intelligent interest – a first-hand interest – in literature. That is, no use of literature is of any use unless it is a real use; literature isn't so much material lying there to be turned over from the outside, and drawn on, for reference and exemplification, by the critically inert.[3]

It is doubtful that the critically inert could make real use of anything, but it is just not true that literature can only be turned over from the inside. Apart from our internal experience of it, it is material lying there and if it can be rewardingly turned over from the outside, it should be. The real thrust of Leavis's point, however, is that the literary critic has a duty to turn his particular expertise to larger questions than those he might find within the confines of his donnish discipline.

It was clear to me from the start that some of contemporary sociology dealing with the subject of role-playing and the relation of the individual to society might be of value for an understanding of dramatic elements in the modern novel, but I deliberately avoided such an *a priori* approach in order to see what the novels themselves actually do reveal, if anything, about self and society. This *post facto* introduction offers the ideal place in which to look at the ways in which literature and sociology overlap, and the ways in which they differ in their use of metaphors of drama. There are of course other ways of using sociology to understand literature, but it is not my intention to enter directly into the debate about whether or not literary forms are products of a particular social base. I am more interested in the way in which both sociology and literature seem simultaneously to be approaching a subject of central interest, and the way in which they complement each other. This discussion of the relation of self to society does lead on to a few comments on Lukacs's theory of the way in which literary forms are related to society. Discussion of the views of individual sociologists will be preceded by a brief general introduction to the differing ways of sociology and literature with the idea of 'self', and by a short explanation of the title of this book which should also serve to emphasise the particular sense of 'dramatic action' used in the following studies. The concept as I use it differs significantly from the conceptions of drama often used in sociology and social psychology.

Imaginative literature grows out of the belief, and makes the claim that the world is 'selved', as Hopkins might have put it. It expresses a native sense of Self. Hopkins has been so much in my mind that I use this phrase as if it were my own; I read it somewhere recently, where I cannot remember. The belief that there are Selves in the world is not a surprising one either to those familiar with literature, or indeed to common sense and the belief is remarkable only when set against a contrasting belief that derives the existence of individual selves from social circumstances; which, that is to say, regards Society as the prime reality and 'selves' as functional, secondary formations whose task is to provide for the continuity of Society. This sociological point of view suggests to the literary intelligence that there are in fact no selves in the world since such 'selves' exist not from themselves, but only as functions of a social system. Sociological thought, at least one central current of it, must account for the origin of a 'sense of self' as a derivation from social facts and processes. It will not do for a science of society to begin with the hypothesis that there is a God who created us complete with souls, nor with the belief that there are naturally occuring complete individuals who at some time freely choose to relinquish their existence in a state of Nature in order to form a social contract. Modern sociology is post-theological (just as it is post-Rousseau and Hobbes) and when it attempts to account for the social genesis of the self it substitutes itself for theology. Modern literature is also post-theological, and the modern novelist cannot have Hopkin's confidence that there is a creator who is the ground of being. Nor do I mean when I say that literature asserts that the world is 'selved' that imaginative literature testifies to a religious ground for being. For modern literature, it is equally unsatisfactory to find the ground of being either in Society or in God, which are both external sources of the self and therefore both 'inauthentic', in the current terminology, accounts of the nature of being a Self.

In a sense, then, modern literature like Sociology sets itself the task of accounting for the genesis of the Self, although this is not its prime motivating energy. The central assertion of modern literature might crudely be put as, 'I exist whether or not God or Society exists.' Or, 'I exist in spite of God and in defiance of Society.'*Implicit in this hypothetical stance is, however, a question about the origin of this Self which exists in spite and defiance. One might be able to construct a 'Theory of the Genesis of the Self in Modern Literature', which would conclude that for the modern writer Self is *sui generis*, and is to be discovered by looking inward. If sociology derives a self from the existence of external forms of society, then modern literature derives a self from the inward gaze. Both of these positions as outlined are absurdly oversimplified, but the oversimplification serves to direct attention to a fundamental difference in attitude to which I shall recur.

Literature, then, expresses a native sense of what it is like to be a self and suggests to us that it is against this primitive sense of Self that any theories of the origin and nature of the Self are to be tested. In this way literature is concerned with what experience feels like and not with ideas or theories. It is possible, however, to speculate on what this primitive sense of self expressed by literature might, or should, be like by considering the circumstances under which this sense is created and communicated. The fundamental building blocks of any piece of literature are: a writer and language. It is naive to assume that a writer merely expresses himself when he writes, because that *himself* which is assumed to be internal is shaped by the act of writing; the dynamic situation is that of a writer with a 'vision'

* The main part of this book argues that such generalisations, however necessary they may be at times, are inadequate under careful scrutiny.

which is internal – and in its pure state incommunicable – confronting language which is external. The native sense of self expressed by literature is likely then to be comprised of a subjectivity confronting and being changed by an objectivity. The content of its formal elements is the way in which inner self is formulated in language to become Self. Of course it is not even as simple as that, since language is not only external; it is internal as well. The writer (like all people) finds language inside when he looks there, just as when he turns his gaze outwards he finds that he exists, as a Self, in an external world and that his public 'self' is as real a part of his integral Self as is the 'self' discovered by introspection. There is an interplay between inner and outer.

Language then, as both internal and external leads subjectivity to transcend itself; it leads on to new possibilities of experience which can be first suggested by language. As we know from contemporary linguistics, language is creative; it is capable of generating an infinite number of sentences. Language that is to say, like Proteus of old is infinitely capable of changing its shape (or at least its appearance, its surface structure). This protean quality of language is the most telling reason why the concept of self which emerges from modern literature, which has been so dominated by a close attention to the use of language – from Eliot's purifying the dialect of the tribe to the most protean use of language of all, Joyce's – is the concept of a protean self. The phrase itself I have adapted from a passage from Coleridge in which he compares the genius of Shakespeare with that of Milton:

> While the former darts himself forth, and passes into all the forms of human character and passion, the one Proteus of the fire and the flood; the other attracts all forms and things to himself, into the unity of his own IDEAL. All things and modes of action shape themselves anew in the being of Milton; while Shakespeare becomes all things, yet for ever remaining himself.[4]

The protean self, the self formed by imagination and acts (particularly acts of language), is dramatic, and while it can 'become' all things it is in no danger of losing its centre (or its 'deep structure' if you like). Shakespeare remains forever himself. In the rest of this book I try to outline how Romanticism-Symbolism deeded to the Modern movement a predominantly – which is not to say absolutely, nor to say that the Moderns passively accepted this inheritance – Miltonic conception of the self: imaginative and, like a vortex, drawing all inside. The inherent solipsism of this inner Ideal self is countered by the re-emergence in the novel of the twentieth century of the protean self. The protean self is capable of externalisation, of playing numerous roles; even the predefined roles of father, mother, brother, banker, lawyer, or even that role made the infamous epitome of bad faith by Sartre, the waiter, without being guilty of living 'in bad faith' or 'inauthentically'. The centre holds after all. The protean self is not primarily concerned, though, with playing the set roles of society (although the question Why not? is tellingly posed since inner freedom is still potentially safe), but with the more vital task of creating free and unique, ordered ways of acting out individual subjectivity. The protean self creates roles that are defined only as they appear and so, although they are dramatic and active and so perceptible to and comprehensible by others, are no predetermined part of any social structure. These unique modes of acting, these individual roles, are appearances of the self, and as appearances they testify to a reality underlying, but they do not by any means give the whole of that reality. They are economical means of expressing a truth. They are fictions of the self; and not lies about the self. These fictions *realise* the inner man, and guard against the solipsism of subjective idealism.

The dramatic impulse that informs the protean self is similar to that energy that activates the 'world stage' of Shakespeare, but not identical to it. The protean self as it appears in literature, is evidence of a belief that there *is* a fundamental urge in man which is a dramatic or mimetic urge: the need to 'play' which is irreducible and not identical with any supposed desire to imitate, in the sense of copy. For his study of culture, Huizinga in *Homo Ludens* finds it necessary to posit a play element that is basic to human life. Civilisation, he says, 'does not come *from* play like a babe detaching itself from the womb: it arises *in* and *as* play, and never leaves it.' Of the Shakespearean and Renaissance (and Medieval and earlier) *theatrum mundi* he comments, 'On closer examination this fashionable comparison of life to a stage proves to be little more than an echo of the Neo-platonism that was then in vogue, with a markedly moralistic accent. It was a variation on the ancient theme of the vanity of all things.'[5] The play element has a more enduring vitality than that says Huizinga, and surely Shakespearean play is more than he suggests. Nevertheless, his differentation of 'playing' (the sense of drama is of course punningly present) pure and simple from the stoic acceptance of one's place, or role, in the great plot is a valuable one. Equally valuable from the point of view of the present study is his suggestion that 'play' is one of the roots of 'illusion'; play, or *ludic* activity, is at the centre of 'illusion' which is cognate with *inlusio, illundere*, or *inludere*. This is a direct parallel to one theme of this book which links dramatic self-enactment to the making of fictions; to play, to act out, is to make fictions. And the novelist, who must be among the most protean of creatures since he publishes any number of fictional appearances of himself, is almost inevitably, as a maker of illusions, going to be interested in the nature of the protean activity itself.

One recurring theme of *The Protean Self* is that much of contemporary criticism of the Novel relies almost instinctively on inadequate assumptions about the nature of Society and the relation of self, and literature, to Society. This belief in the existence of Society as a thing, the reification of an abstraction, seems to have been picked up by literary critics from traditional sociology. It is interesting to note that there is a new group of contemporary sociologists in reaction to reification in social theory just as I have reacted to it in literary criticism. Aaron V. Cicourel, whose *Cognitive Sociology* is of more suggestive value than the headlong jargon of some of his prose might indicate, is one of the new social interaction group (also tongue-twistingly styled 'ethnomethodologists'):

> So long as we continue to reify terms like 'social structure', 'culture', and 'language', we shall miss the contextual and cognitive significance of everyday social organization.[6]

The grand source of reification in social theory is Emile Durkheim with his dictum that one must regard social facts as things.[7] For Durkheim society is a thing which cannot be derived; it exists *sui generis* and its powers can be seen to be manipulating even so apparently individual and anti-social an act as suicide. A sociologist who is influenced by Durkheim but tries (not altogether successfully) to find an existential way out of the deterministic implications of his thought, is Peter Berger, who gives the following concise summary of Durkheim's conception of the way in which man exists in Society:

> If we follow the Durkheimian conception, then, society confronts us as an objective facticity. It is *there*, something that cannot be denied and that must be reckoned with. Society is external to ourselves. It surrounds us, encompasses our life on all sides. We are *in* society, located in specific sectors of the social system. This location predetermines and predefines almost everything we do, from language to etiquette, from the religious beliefs we hold to the probability that we will commit suicide. Our wishes are not taken into consideration in this matter of social location, and our intellectual resistance to what society prescribes or proscribes avails very little at best, and frequently nothing. Society, as objective and external fact, confronts us especially in the form of coercion. Its institutions pattern our actions and even shape our expectations. They reward us to the extent that we stay within our assigned performances.[8]

Berger makes not only a very frightening case of the way in which Society makes us prisoners by means of external coercion, but also a very interesting and persuasive one. He compounds the disturbance by going on to describe how Durkheimian sociology pictures the way not only that man exists in Society, but also how Society exists inside man. Society does not usually have to resort to its capacity for physical violence to coerce us, because we have 'internalised' the values of Society and are willing prisoners. We have developed a sense of self by means of casting inside an image of what we find already there as we grow into the world of Society; and for that reason, what we call our 'self' is comprised of internalised social facts and values.

Berger relies on metaphors from the drama to make his point, a development of the idea of 'performances' already mentioned in the earlier passage:

It would, however, be missing an essential aspect of the role if one regarded it merely as a regulatory pattern for externally visible actions. One feels more ardent by kissing, more humble by kneeling and more angry by shaking one's fist. That is, the kiss not only expresses ardour but manufactures it. Roles carry with them both certain actions and the emotions and attitudes that belong to these actions.[9]

By performing the externally defined role, a feeling of there being an interior self develops. Berger borrows from the social psychology of G. H. Mead, who is the origin of most sociological use of dramatic metaphors to illustrate the development of the self.* For Mead the self is itself a social creation, arising first of all on the organic level in a dialogue of gesture, such as we see in a dog-fight or in a boxing match where one combatant gets the message of the other's gestures and begins to prefigure future gestures. A self-consciousness is potentially there as soon as one combatant begins to plan future gestures, such as feints for instance. The genuine self is born when the organism begins to adopt the role of the other, perhaps in the strategic attempt to prefigure what one's own gestures might mean to the other. From the adopted position of the 'significant other' (one's close contacts) one can look back, as it were, on oneself and so begin to conceive of one's Self as an independent entity:

In so far as one can take the role of the other, he can, as it were, look back at himself from (respond to himself from) that perspective, and so become an object to himself. Thus again, it is only in a social process that selves, as distinct from biological organisms, can arise – selves as beings that have become conscious of themselves.[10]

Both Mead and Berger try to find some way beyond Durkheim's imprisonment of the self by society in a concept of a present or existential act,[11] but the net effect of their thought is relentlessly to reduce man to a social function. Perhaps the most telling objection that the subjective self is forced to make against such theories is that that is just not how it feels, subjectively. Subjectively it seems that anti-social actions are pos-

---

* And Mead seems to have borrowed from William James, at least the use of the terms 'I' and 'me'. Perhaps there is a useful way of approaching Henry James here.

sible, and from Mead's system it is not at all possible to see how such a feeling, let alone such actions could be possible since the motivations of the self are all social. Maurice Natanson (see note 11) tries to find a way out of this difficulty by developing the latent concept in Mead's thought of the difference between the self and the body, or organism. Anti-social behaviour is then sensual, or organic, and while this is a suggestive possibility it does threaten to reduce all critical or radical activity, and thought, to the level of animality, of bestiality.

One's subjective reaction to theories of the social derivation of the self receive some corroboration from the modern novel. In so far as there is a theory of the genesis of the self in twentieth century literature it is, as I have suggested earlier, that the self is found by looking inward. Certainly Joyce Cary gives special importance to the full development of the inner, romantic, subjective imagination – and then goes on to show the dangers inherent in that very subjectivity. Muriel Spark insists again and again on the fact that the self is primarily that internal source of fictions; fictions which must be made public according to certain rituals in order to avoid becoming fascistic. What is most surprising about modern literature, in face of the sociological attitude we have just been considering, is its testimony to the extreme moral effort that attends the very attempt to admit that there is a world beyond inner subjectivity that could be copied and internalised. It involves moral effort to see that there is a world other than the one we imagine, other than the fictions we create.

The difficulty for such subjectively oriented ideas of the nature of the self is solipsism, or the problem of knowing that which is external. The pragmatic solution that seems most able to bridge the gap, the one used in this study, is that action itself necessitates a field of other actors. By acting one sees the necessity for a field of agents in which to act. This is to play fast and loose with some of the problems of the philosophy of action, but free action is seen to be a necessary hypothesis for any understanding of man's nature that emerges from modern literature. There is one other possibility which the social theorists seem to overlook when they discuss the way in which the self is formed by playing at being an other. It is not strictly necessary for the organism to play at being either a 'significant other' or a 'generalised other' if all that is necessary is some external standpoint from which to look back and conceive of oneself as an individual entity. The subjective mind is faced with the possibility of contemplating its own mortality and this perception of potential absence gives extreme definition to the nature of the individual existing self. Bergson finds one of the sources of morality and religion in the perception of death;[12] the imagination immediately compensates for this shocking perception by structuring an after-life. Similarly the perception of non-being is potentially one of the sources of the conviction of personal individuality.* Obviously this perception of mortality depends on the ability to recognise the reality of an external world in which mortality occurs to other beings, and then to generalise from that experience – or rather to particularise from it – to oneself. The universal awareness of Death as one imaginative source of individuality does not, however, necessitate a social system since Death is Nature's child; nor does it reduce the anti-social, or a-social self to the level of animality.†

Berger, like Mead, toys with a notion of necessary existential freedom which can overcome the 'bad faith' of life in society. In fact Berger, somewhat perversely, sees in the possibility of bad faith the clue that suggests that we need not live by enforced disciplines unless we choose to do so, or unless we willingly acquiesce in our imprisonment. Unfortunately this idea is not systematically developed, and Berger turns his attention to the ideas of Erving Goffman. Berger sees in Goffman's conception of 'role-distance' some sociological evidence that the self is not confined to its role. Role-distance is signalled says Goffman by the gestures, facial and verbal expressions used by a role-performer to indicate an attitude to and distance from a present role. A twelve year old child on a roundabout will signal his distance from the role of 'young child on a roundabout' by a certain slouching, elegant contempt which allows him to go on

* This idea comes out in the discussion of Muriel Spark's *Memento Mori* in Chapter 4.

† Owen Barfield in *What Coleridge Thought* (London, 1972) reminds us of Coleridge's forcefully made point that the human mind is the only 'subject' that can be an 'object' to itself. If it is in the nature of the mind itself to overcome the gap between subject and object, then no 'external' standpoint is necessary for the development of the Self.

riding while clearly conveying the impression that he is not merely what he appears to be.

> That is, the dramatic model of society at which we have arrived now does not deny that the actors on the stage are constrained by all the external controls set up by the impresario and the internal ones of the role itself. All the same, they have options – of playing their parts enthusiastically or sullenly, of playing with inner conviction or with 'distance' and, sometimes, of refusing to play at all.[13]

This is perhaps as close as science can come to describing freedom. Berger puts it this way, 'it is impossible *a priori* to come upon freedom in its full sense by scientific means or within a scientific universe of discourse. The closest we have been able to come is to show, in certain situations, a certain freedom *from* social controls. We cannot possibly discover freedom *to* act socially by scientific means.'[14] With the possibility of the 'freedom *to* act', clearly, we move beyond social science into the realm of Art and it should be clear that Sociology does not offer the least threat to the special status of literature and criticism. In fact it helps us to understand more exactly what the nature of Art is. Art allows us *a priori* to come upon freedom.

Unfortunately for Berger's analysis of freedom within the universe of science, Goffman's interactionist sociology does not really offer any escape from a role-bound situation. With his own particular sardonic delight, Goffman pursues the concept of the so-called free individual until he has him back in his cage:

> We cannot say, however, that role distance protects the individual's ego, self-esteem, personality, or integrity from the implications of the situation without introducing constructs which have no place in a strictly sustained role perspective. We must find a way, then, of getting the ego back into society.[15]

Whereas Berger reluctantly leaves freedom out of his account, Goffman is only too willing for purposes of playing his role as social analyst to jettison extraneous 'constructs'. Social scientists capable of role-distance are likely to be those of most interest it seems. Goffman gets the ego back into society by arguing that the signs for marking role-distance are in most cases functionally built into the role itself. Thus a head surgeon may play at being just an ordinary, friendly sort of fellow in order to make the junior members of his team relax and so perform more effectively. Role-distance makes the surgeon a better surgeon and not less of a surgeon. For the purposes of Goffman's analysis the existence of a self is irrelevant, for he is interested only in the interactional system and the gestural signals (he is heavily indebted to Mead's notion of gestural language) that make up the stuff of social interchange. And there is little doubt that at times Goffman reveals us to ourselves in the way that we behave in society, even if he can say little about the way we *act*.

A concept of the self does, of course, emerge from the social science dealing with role theory. For Goffman there is no room, no need, for a subjective self, since life is all the managing of impressions. Life in society is the art of the great con and the self is totally 'other-directed'; that is, the human units act, or behave, not with regard to truth or even sincerity but only in order to make a good presentation and to come off best in any social 'transaction'. Being a self is nothing more than playing at being a self. The concept of the self that emerges from sociological role analysis is inevitably that of the self which is 'nothing more' than the sum of the disparate roles one is forced to play in society. Once again, Berger usefully sums up:

> This view [role theory] tells us that man plays dramatic parts in the grand play of society, and that, speaking sociologically, he *is* the masks that he must wear to do so. The human person also appears now in a dramatic context, true to its theatrical etymology (*persona*, the technical term given to the actors' masks in a classical theatre). The person is perceived as a repertoire of roles, each one properly equipped with a certain identity.[16]

For those not willing to limit their understanding to a single perspective, the novels studied hereafter provide a refreshing alternative to the limits of such sociological dramatism. Sociology posits roles, or social constructs, and argues that these dramatic roles can make selves. Literature posits a self, a protean self, and shows that it can make drama, make fictions.

Even in the line of social theory, however, we can see that there is not really a necessity to stop short of the concept of freedom. The symbolic interactionist school of role theorists tends to identify 'self' and 'performance' (giving rise perhaps to modish literary critical theories of a 'performing self'). A more formalistic and less psychological approach to the subject of role, defining it as a set of rights and duties, can find room for free choice. R. S. Downie[17] for instance, argues that whereas persons play roles, to be a person is not in itself to play a role. To try to put 'person' into the class of 'roles' is to distort both terms. He insists that while individuals play roles, they are as persons free to choose what roles they play. The person is beyond role, but plays roles.

The cognitive sociology of Cicourel mentioned earlier also valuably urges the necessity of being careful with potentially misleading terminology. The title of his recent collection of essays, *Cognitive Sociology* gives a key to his most interesting (from the present point of view) idea. If, as it is often assumed, individuals in society behave according to the norms of established roles, then, Cicourel says, there must be a cognitive centre which allows the individual to learn how to play roles, or behave according to norms. There must be a centre of cognition, of knowing, which Cicourel calls the 'deep structure' (borrowing his terms from modern linguistics) which gives rise to the various 'surface structures' of norm-bound behaviour in society. This is very close in general import to the comments made earlier about the way in which language itself, by reason of its 'creativity' is the informing genius of the protean self. A deep structure, or cognitive centre, or subjective self (Cicourel does not go this far) necessarily[18] externalises itself and in doing so it produces a number of surface structures. Because the passage from deep structure to surface structure involves some degree of 'transformation', it is not immediately possible to perceive the deep structure from the appearance of the surface structure, and yet there is a necessary relation between the two (linguistics of course has a series of transformational steps for generating surface structures, or for deriving the deep structure). Similarly, what I have called self-generated dramatic roles, or formulated appearances of the private self in the public world, are fictions of the self in the sense that they are incomplete evidence of what the deep self is like, but without the appearances it would not be possible to know at all what the deep self is like. The surface structures of the protean self are artificial transformations of the deep self and although they may betray by their partial nature, they also *realise* the deep structure. And here we come upon that ever-recurring revelation of Art, there can be no reality without appearances.

In Cicourel we see linguistics usefully coming together with Sociology to help us see through reifications. I believe that both linguistic theory and sociology come usefully together with criticism and with the art of the modern novel to give us a much more adequate (if not so satisfyingly simple and reductive) conception of the way in which self is related to society. One of the most interesting of recent publications which points the way beyond the limits of traditional (if one can speak of tradition in a discipline so young) sociology of literature is the anthology by Elizabeth and Tom Burns, *Sociology of Literature and Drama*.[19] Anyone interested in the way in which several disciplines can usefully combine for mutual clarification should take a look at this collection. The editors espouse a critical sociology and in their introduction welcome the new trend in sociology which seeks to move beyond functionalism (the positivist and Durkheimian heritage). I cannot hope to survey the contents of this volume, but I would like to refer briefly to some of the ideas in an essay, newly and ably translated by Tom Burns, by the sociologist George Simmel: 'On the Theory of Theatrical Performance'. Although Simmel begins by speaking of the art of the theatre actor he concludes with some comments that seem to me to come very close to the concept of dramatic action which I have tried to elaborate as a tool for literary criticism. Although Simmel begins, as I have said, with the conventions of the theatre itself, he concludes by denying that the art of the theatre is radically different from the art of living, and by denying also that the art of the theatre is slavishly to copy life:

> The actor's performance is, in terms of art, itself the end point, and not a bridge one has to cross in order to reach some more distant goal. There is a fundamentally theatrical attitude, a creative response of a specific kind to what life presents, in exactly the same way as there is for the painter

and the poet. Nor is this anything like a completely independent process; it is something involved in the manifold presentations and affairs of everyday life. To play a part, not just as hypocrisy or as deceit, but in terms of the involvement of the individual's life in a single expressive form which is entered upon in some pre-existing, pre-determined way, is part and parcel of the way in which our everyday life is constituted. Such a role may be appropriate to our individual self, but it is nevertheless something other than this individuality and not an intrinsic part of its innermost and unitary being.[20]

Simmel seems to accept the necessity for pre-defined social roles, but he attributes the desire to play them to some primitive dramatic attitude that inheres in human being and is similar to Huizinga's notion of *homo ludens*. in Chapters 1 and 2, I make the argument that such play-acting is in fact the way to 'unitary being' and try to show that in modern literature the self is not merely that 'innermost' self, but is a unity of what that inner self *is* and what it *does*.

What is most immediately suggestive about Simmel's ideas though, is the constraint he feels himself under to show that dramatic self-presentation is something that is part of the realm of authentic individuality and is not mere hypocrisy (a word whose root in the theatre needs no elaboration):

In the same sense, therefore, in which we are poets and painters, we are also play actors; i.e. culture endows every aspect of life with this characteristic. Without being in any sense false or hypocritical, the personal existence of the individual is metamorphosed into some pre-determined guise which is of course produced out of the resources of his own life, but is nevertheless not merely the straightforward expression of his own life. The possibility exists for us to assume such appearances, even strange ones, and nevertheless remain consistent with our own nature. We are harnessed into this paradox at all times. And this constitutes the prototypical form of theatricality.[21]

Here Simmel's paradox has its source in the idea that the forms of dramatic appearance are 'pre-determined' and yet somehow originate in the inner self. Perhaps this apparent contradiction arises because Simmel tends to see the forms available as those offered by Society. I have tried to avoid this particular paradox in the following text by a conception of conscious and controlled action (the opposite of 'blind action') which originates in the self and is 'figured' or 'determined' as it is acted out, having its origin and continuance in the knowing subjective self, but is not in any sense 'pre'-determined or 'pre'-figured by Society.

The notions that I have been trying to outline in Sociology, and the ones I try independently to develop in the remainder of this book, are highly speculative and certainly no more than tentative. It is the task of scientists and philosophers to solve all the problems of terminology. I have merely tried to show how this very rewarding dramatic attitude, which has received virtually no attention from literary critics, is of central importance to an understanding of the writing of our time. If any of this present discussion of sociology and literature leads anywhere, perhaps it leads to another tentative statement about the relationship of fictions to society. The conclusion is a simple, though contentious, one. Fictions do not passively hold a mirror up either to Nature or Society. They are creative. They do not so much show us how men do act in a present society, as create new possibilities for acting which transcend both Nature and Society and suggest the possibility of a human universe.[22] To make fictions is to engage in an act of surpassing importance to the way in which we live our lives daily. And to read fictions is to face the possibility of having one's own imagination, one's own source of fictions, activated. By no means are fictions 'escapes' from reality in the way that they have been often considered. They are perhaps ways of escape from older and inadequate fictions which have become reified into system.[23] Fictions, that is *novels* whose name testifies to the need to make anew, are in themselves new actions and they evidence the human capacity to act beyond expectation. The capacity to be a self, and to make fictions, is something more than a functional reflex of social facts.

I believe there is an implication here for the Marxist approach to the sociology of literature, which I would like just to point to without elaborating fully. If fictions are evidence of the way in which individuals can act without reference to a social base, then it must be inadequate to attempt to understand literary forms as expressions of a social or economic substructure. Lukacs for instance, argues that 'The novel's aim is to represent a particular social reality at a particular time, with all the colour and specific atmosphere of that time.'[21] Lukacs differentiates between the characters of stage drama, who must be 'directly and immediately typical' and the more complex characters of the novel. He stresses the idea that because the novel goes beyond the merely dramatic it can include the totality of a social situation and so become a kind of 'prose epic', or the 'bourgeois epic'. The special sense of drama suggested by Huizinga, Simmel and the novels studied hereafter indicates that the genius of the novel is not after all epical, but dramatic. And if it is not epical, the novel's genius is not therefore passively to recreate, copy, or imitate or reflect, Society or social 'conditions'.

Having thus dramatically overstated the case, one must of course admit that novels do have a relation to society and that some forego the creative effort entirely and do attempt to reflect social conditions. It is possible, for instance, to consider the novel by Anthony Burgess, *A Clockwork Orange*, as a type of epical reflection of Society* – which it is despite the surrealistic and misdirected manipulations of language. The dichotomy of the title is echoed in the limited choice open to the central character Alex. He can either be free, romantic, violent and an individual, or he can become a socialised automaton. It may be that the intended effect of this dichotomy is to produce in the mind of the reader an awareness something like: 'This is the way society is now, or is soon going to be and unless we are increasingly conscious of our circumstances we are doomed.' But the novel itself is limited to pathetic recognition. Because it limits itself to 'showing it as it is', and because it chooses to perpetuate inadequate ideas about the relation of Self to Society, it cannot go beyond what are taken to be social conditions to show how it could be if its imaginative focus had been free activity. Our awareness of our circumstances may be increased by such novels, but our freedom to act is not. We are shown the terrible grinding dichotomy between Self and Society and it is not suggested that there is a way out of the split. The fact that read-

---

* It should perhaps be said that what is being copied is not 'really' society, but an institutionalised fiction of what Society is. See the discussion of the 'social construction of reality' below.

ers, or cinema-goers since it is from the film that the novel is most known, go to fictions for new patterns of action is evidenced by the would-be imitators of the clockwork orange group, and by a killing said to be carried out in imitation of the film. Since the novel passively reflects a dilemma, it can only – in so far as it serves as a pattern for action at all – serve to reinforce the very pattern it abhors. By limiting itself to copying or analysing 'social reality' the novel limits itself to pathetic documentary and the moral realm of fiction is unapproached. There is perhaps some justification to questions about the social value of novels, despite the fact that those who raise them seldom known what they are talking about. We need not only to know our dilemma, we need to be able to put our knowledge into new actions. The social sciences, and even literary criticism can inform us about our dilemmas. Only creative art can aid us in devising ways of acting imaginatively and freely that take us beyond stifling paradox and crippling dichotomy.

It is necessary to emphasise the way in which fictions do relate to our life amid other men without falling back on traditional reifications about society nor the habitual idea that fiction is an escape from reality. One more theory from modern sociology cannot be resisted therefore – a theory, new as it is, that is fast becoming the orthodox sociological view. In the course of the ensuing critical analyses of the novel it is argued that the self can *safely* make fictions (that is, without violating the integrity of others) and that it is *necessary* to make fictions if we are to live as free and full individuals. And although I argue throughout that pre-defined Social roles do not, cannot, give rise to a unified and free Self, I do suggest that it is possible for the fictional roles, the invented roles, to mould the Self. That is, fictions can remake the individual; we can and do become what we pretend to be. Fictions, that is to say, can and do become institutionalised social realities. This is clear enough in the novel, which must always be searching for new forms since the old forms no longer serve. This idea that fictions become social reality is comprehensively put by Peter Berger and Thomas Luckmann in a book called *The Social Construction of Reality* (Penguin 1971). Essentially, they say that we can be free from the apparent determinism of society since society, and social reality, are man-made. The apparent solidity of society and all its fixed institutions is after all fictional. Society in so far as it exists is a fictional construction which we take to be reality.

Rather than attempt to quote piecemeal from a book which needs to be swallowed whole, let me offer an extract from a very clear paraphrase of Berger's sociology:

> Sociology, by emphasizing the 'fictional' nature of much social behaviour, provides the basis for seeing human behaviour as a 'construction'. It is not something immutably determined by 'human nature' or our genes. The hope exists that with greater knowledge, man can create social systems which offer greater opportunity for the full expression of human life and consciousness. He can modify the set of fictions which surround him and bind him. But to do so, he must sense the possibility of escape. It is this sense of possibility which existentialist thought offers.[25]

The belief in existentialist promises of freedom is characteristic of 'construction' sociologists since the basis of their thought is the philosophy of Phenomenology (particularly that of Alfred Schutz) which is at the centre of Existentialist thinking. A reader of modern literature cannot be altogether comfortable with existential promises nor with phenomenology, which is compelled to call that which appears 'real'. The novels available to us stubbornly insist that an appearance must be an appearance of something; and one of the difficulties of Berger's and Luckmann's book is the strain it puts on the word 'reality'. Nevertheless, a new freedom is gained by recognising that the reality of Society is only apparent; it is the sum of reified fictions. And the way to be free from outdated, hypostatised fictions is to make new ones. Which is not to say that one must *always* be making new ones. It is enough to be able to make new ones when necessary. The ability to make fictions is thus the guarantee we need that we are not necessarily prisoners of our systems. Fictions may, then, be an 'escape', but they are an escape from fictions, and delusions, and so an escape into freedom.

To conclude, I would like to pay tribute to a book which, had it appeared sooner might have had a great deal of influence on some of the themes of this one. It is particularly satisfying to see that Lionel Trilling's *Sincerity and Authenticity*[26] corroborates my own intuition that protean dramatic activity is a subject of central importance in the attempt to comprehend the culture of our time. Which is certainly not to say that he would agree with what I have to say. Trilling displays his characteristic ease with a wide body of knowledge and he provides a stimulating and unsettling commentary on modern modes of thought and morality. Trilling traces the cultural displacement of sincerity, which is characterised by a coincidence of inner self and external appearance (or by a coincidence of self and social norm) by authenticity, a more contemporary way of speaking of the ideal of the self; an ideal which defies Society and seeks total alienation and disintegration of consciousness as a road to the achievement of a truly individual spirit. Trilling's first text is Diderot's *Rameau's Nephew*, which he considers in light of Hegel's comments on the Nephew in *Phenomenology of Mind*. Two brief quotations from Trilling will have to serve to show that the protean self is not of recent advent. Trilling asserts that the prime intention of Diderot's work (he does not say if the intention of the work is identical with Diderot's intention) is to reveal society itself as the source of alienation. As he puts it, 'It is social man who is alienated man.'

> The theory of society advanced by the Nephew rests on the recognition of the systematic separation of the individual from his actual self. The social being, he tells us, is a mere histrionic representation – every man takes one or another 'position' as the choreography of society directs.[27]

The fact of having to play many parts is a sign of the way in which the authentic self is duped by society. The thrust of Trilling's tone and argument demands that we see the protean character in this light.

He does, however, admit that there is a second intention in the work, which is delight in play and mimesis. He refers to the episode in which the Nephew defends new operatic forms against old:

> The episode issues in his most elaborate mimetic display, for he proceeds to *be* opera, to impersonate the whole art – this musical Proteus, or perhaps he is to be called Panurge, sounds all the instruments, enacts all the roles, portraying all

the emotions in all voices and all modes. The astonishing performance proposes the idea which Nietzsche was to articulate a century later, that man's true metaphysical destiny expresses itself not in morality but in art.[27]

Trilling says that this second intention is what 'chiefly engages us' in *Rameau's Nephew* and 'constitutes the genius of the work'. Nevertheless, it is only the 'second intention' and we must not allow it to interfere with our perception of the first intention, the making of a moral judgement on man in society. I shall refrain from sniping at a critic I so much admire (a restraint which is allowed to slip a little in Chapter 1) and simply say that Trilling's sense of cataclysm and apocalypse transcends my own. The intensity of the moral imagination as it contemplates apocalypse is what gives Trilling's writing its special force and virtue. It is perhaps also the source of his tendency to oppose morality and art and to undervalue the 'creative element'. In the two passages on Diderot and in *Rameau's Nephew* I would find yet more evidence that the attempt to live by free dramatic action, to play freely created individual roles, is the attempt to come between capitulation to the roles of society and complete subjective isolation, or solipsism. It is perhaps because Trilling's goal is precisely to point to the solipsism of the Modern that he neglects the seeds of its transcendence in the attempt to find a way of ritual action which is both sincere and authentic.

Trilling provides also a useful discussion of Jane Austen's *Mansfield Park* (and more besides), particularly of the dramatic elements therein. That he does points to the limitation of my purpose. The subject of elements of drama in western culture is certainly not going to be finally resolved either by myself or even by Lionel Trilling. I shall be satisfied if I have been able to point to what Trilling's work convinces me is an important subject. What is needed is more close study of individual texts along the lines indicated. If the following pages have any validity, then the type of drama that comes in the middle, as it were, between alienated subjectivity and inauthentic objectivity, could have an important task in a reassessment of the way in which the Novel – particularly the nineteenth century English novel, which abounds in the use of metaphors from the drama – deals with the subject of Man in Society. My own first intention has been to draw attention to the fact that a large number of recent novels draws on one set of metaphors. My second intention has been to try to suggest why and in what way these metaphors are meaningful. It is my hope that one indirect result of these two intentions will be some general increase in conviction that the literature written during our own time is not only worth reading, it is worth reading carefully and with the same effort usually given to literature sanctified by age.

1 Dramatic Action, the Modern and the Post-Modern

'One of the troublesome facts of life is that my inside is always in contact with other people's outside. I am always inside myself but outside of others. The world of many a novel turns on this point of interaction between an inner and an outer world.'[1]

I

Perhaps the main reason for studying the recurrence of metaphors of drama in recent fiction is simply because they are there; the sort of reason usually given by people who climb mountains. Climbing over a mere catalogue of facts is not sufficiently interesting in itself, however, and there would be no justification in studying such a recurrence of dramatic metaphors if one did not believe that around the phenomenon of their appearance there lay a number of important and interesting problems that are at the heart of much of the best literature of our time. Anyone who has spent any time worrying about 'literary problems' will readily realise that they are not merely of esoteric academic interest, but that in fact what is problematical in our literature is of central interest to our lives. One of the most important metaphors from the drama which occurs in twentieth century literature is that of 'role-playing'. The meaning of role-playing in society is now such a central topic for social scientists that one of them, Erving Goffman, can say that the 'realm of face-to-face interaction' has 'become one to do battle in'.[2] It is perhaps no accident that social scientists should reflect the novelist's concern with this important question of the roles people play in their everyday lives and the

27

meaning for the individual of such 'play-acting'. It is not, however, my purpose to engage in the application of socio-logical concepts to the study of literature. While there is certainly room for cross-fertilisation between disciplines, I believe that there is much to be gained by approaching literature from the standpoint of the literary critic – by which I mean the assiduous common reader. I shall focus, therefore, on the way in which metaphors of drama actually function in specific novels and indeed part of my purpose is to show that a too-ready recourse to ill-defined abstractions such as 'Society' vitiates much of contemporary criticism of the novel.

What then is meant by 'metaphors of drama'? Simply, I am concerned with situations in novels in which characters are found to be 'playing roles', 'posing', 'putting on an act', being 'stagey', or creating a 'scene' as if they were 'actors on a stage' and as if 'all the world's a stage'. The central subject is those characters who engage in 'dramatic action'. In general, the 'scene' or 'setting' is important for my purposes only in that it is essential for the character who is to be a dramatic agent to admit the reality of a world beyond his own imagination or mind. I shall be interested in both halves of the term 'dramatic action'. It is important to consider the meaning (the philo-sophic import) of action, and the implications for the self of the choice of action and being an agent as against inaction and being passive, or being a 'patient'. I wish to consider dramatic action, then, as a form of 'action', but it will be equally neces-sary to consider the implications of the *dramatic* nature of the action. Briefly, 'dramatic action' will be considered as if it were a *form* of action for philosophical purposes;* in fact, it will be regarded as 'formal' action: ritual or ceremonial, or consciously planned and controlled action. I shall not, that is to say, be cen-trally concerned with the action of a novel† (although I shall find it unavoidable at times to make use of this pun on the two meanings of the word) so much as I shall be concerned with the action, the choice of conscious and ritual action on the part of

---

* The philosophical problems of 'action' are discussed in Chapter 2.

† In one sense, though, I regard the novel itself as a type of 'symbolic action'; that is, as an 'enactment' of 'reality' rather than a description of it. The novelist's relationship to the everyday world, through his novel, is then that of a 'dramatic agent'. The form of his 'act' is provided by language.

the characters who find themselves entangled in the action, or plot of the novel.

Although the philosophical implications of consciousness and action will be dealt with later on in this chapter and then much more fully towards the end of Chapter 2, it might be as well to indicate here that 'action' is an important subject in Modern literature because it is intimately related to the Modern concern with the relative value of the inner as opposed to the outer world. One of our most ready generalisations about the Modern period* is that, on the whole, it chooses the inner world of subjective imaginings and 'vision' as opposed to the harsh realities of the 'outer' world of capitalist, industrialised Society. There is reason to be wary of this proposition in that it implies that the Moderns were not at all interested in the reality of the external world. One implication of the belief that the inner world is the only real one is that the external world is only what I imagine it to be – which is the essence of solipsism. Another is that action is not only not necessary, it is impossible.

Eliot's poem, 'The Love Song of J. Alfred Prufrock' provides a keen insight into the relationship of inner and outer worlds, and the inevitable, concomitant problem of action. Prufrock *is* a highly sensitive, intelligent *consciousness*, and the more his mind is filled with images of elegance and art, with talk of Michelangelo, the less able is he to make his inner self act in the world. His whole effort seems to be to bring himself to the point of accepting the reality of the external world and asking it some enormous question, but he cannot. His too intense consciousness keeps him trapped inside himself and he can do nothing else but wonder to himself if he dare disturb the universe by acting, by rolling his trousers, or eating a peach. An intense innerness makes action impossible, and there is the implied question: Does action (or 'would' it) in the world make a heightened state of inner consciousness impossible? In 'The Love Song of J. Alfred Prufrock' consciousness and interiority are not necessarily held up as unquestioned ideals so much as they are the problematical core of agonised attempts at self-

* There is now a fairly well-established body of opinion that the literature of the period, roughly, 1900–25 represents an identifiable 'movement' in the history of literature. I am not here interested in the problem of the validity of 'periodisation'. I wish simply to discuss current generalisations about the nature of the revolutionary literature of the early part of this century.

definition. It is well to bear this qualification in mind when we encounter the generalisation that the Modern is unqualifiedly for the inner.

Given such a qualification then, one can say that the Moderns choose interiority, but look, with difficulty and little apparent success, for a way of acting in the outer world without losing any of the subjectivity which guarantees personal integrity or identity. If we were to try to summarise the post-Modern period (or contemporary literature), at least in the British tradition, we might say that it is no longer so concerned with the depths of the individual life. Instead, it occupies itself increasingly with the surface of life; it is 'superficial'. I use the word in a neutral sense because I happen to believe that the 'superficiality' of much contemporary literature is a sign of its significance and of the way in which it continues the exploration begun by the Modern revolt, and is not by any means a sign of its lack of interest, meaning, or value.

For instance, the 'concrete' prose of the writers of the *nouveau roman* school is concerned absolutely with the surface of *things*. It is superficial in that it focuses all our attention on observable phenomena. It does not, however, despite this apparent 'objectivity' sacrifice subjectivity; as Robbe-Grillet says, 'The New Novel aims only at total subjectivity':

> As there were many objects in our books, and as people thought there was something unusual about them, they didn't take long to decide on the future of the word 'objectivity', which was used by certain critics when referring to these objects, but used in a very particular sense, i.e. orientated towards the object. In its usual sense which is neutral, cold and impartial, the word became an absurdity. Not only is it a man who, in my novels, for instance, describes everything, but he is also the least neutral and the least impartial of men: on the contrary he is always engaged in a passionate adventure of the most obsessive type – so obsessive that it often distorts his vision and subjects him to fantasies bordering on delirium.[3]

Robbe-Grillet is an extreme example of the post-Modern phenomenon in which I am interested. He insists so much on the objectivity (the 'object-ness') of the external world, however, that it no longer seems 'real'; it begins to take on the hue of nightmare. By so subjectivising objectivity, his writing cannot deal with an important matter: the preservation of one's subjective life and the coincident recognition of a 'real' external world which contains real *other* people. It is part of Robbe-Grillet's purpose (or simply the inevitable result of his technique) that face-to-face encounters are impossible, and so too drama and dramatic action are impossible. He carries superficiality too far, one might say. The novelists whose work I am going to discuss have also an intense interest in the reality of the external world. They have, however, preserved and carried on the Modern emphasis on interiority and it is the interplay of inner and outer that is expressed in dramatic metaphor.

The contemporary writers with whom I am concerned, then, are 'superficial' in the sense that they insist on the reality of the external world because they believe in the necessity of acting in the world. They do not, however, sacrifice the inner world of subjectivity. Instead, they are more and more focusing their attention on the moment when 'vision' and imagination are externalised and fulfilled in the 'act'. The moment when what is merely potential in the mind or consciousness is transformed into what is 'actual' in the external world, is the dramatic moment. Metaphors of drama occur in profusion at this critical moment, when a highly subjective, imaginative and creative individual recognises the reality of a world beyond himself. Both Modern and post-Modern writers who direct their attention to this central question of action are expressing a moral concern. To admit the reality of the external world is to find oneself capable of action, and it is, much more important, to avoid the greatest of evils: the denial of the reality of the *other* person.* Once the reality of another individual is admitted, the inevitable consequence is 'drama' of one kind or another.

The foregoing discussion has been an attempt to indicate

* It might seem that a simple reference to the subject of 'personal relations' in Modern literature would solve a lot of problems here. Personal relations can, however, too easily mean a sentimental, undemanding acceptance of accommodation and compromise, of 'getting on well with others'. To recognise the reality of the other person is a pre-condition to any significant 'personal relation'. Such a recognition leaves open the possibility that relationship with the 'other' can be rejected. A recognition of 'otherness' can mean polar opposition, as we see in much of D. H. Lawrence's fiction.

briefly the potential value of studying 'action' in twentieth century literature. I would now like to turn briefly to the *dramatic*
aspect of 'dramatic action'. The chief form of dramatic action is
of course 'playing a role' or 'putting on an act'. The very
phrases reveal the suspicion we have about drama in life: it is
artificial, not natural or spontaneous. To 'play' at being something that one is not is to deceive others and to risk one's integrity as a human being. Inherent in this objection to 'playing a
role' is an objection to Art itself. Plato made the characteristic
objection to poets: they are liars, they ask us to believe that in
fiction we can find truth. So too the person who willingly plays a
role gives himself up to fiction and illusion. Anyone given over
to the mystic belief that only the inner world is real will believe
that action is illusory because it accepts the reality of the external world. This sentiment is reinforced by the 'dramatic' nature
of the action. To believe in drama is to believe in lies. So, writers
who are interested in the moment at which the inner potential
becomes an external actualisation, and are therefore concerned
with drama and dramatic action, will find themselves deeply
involved in the question of the value of fiction, including their
own.

An author, for instance, who believes that 'playing roles' is
evil, will find himself in the curious dilemma of having to justify
the role he plays as a novelist. To write a novel is to adopt a role,
or pose, or mask, or persona; to do so for the purpose of attacking 'role-playing' will involve the thoughtful novelist in a
searching questioning of his own art. Not surprisingly, those
novelists who believe in the value of their own fictions (novels)
as means of pursuing the truth, will, if they are consistent, be
found to be investigating the value for their characters of playing roles or adopting masks in their lives in the novel. Con-
versely, we should expect those who are critical of 'role-playing'
on the part of their characters to reveal a similar critical attitude to the novel itself. As we shall see, characters in novels will
find that playing roles is justified so long as freedom of will is
not lost; that is, so long as they control the role they play and do
not surrender themselves to the role and disappear behind a
series of automatic gestures. The role is safe – it is more than
that of course, it is a creative way to self-realisation at best – so
long as it is consciously held and to an extent draws attention to

itself. The consequence of such a theme for the form of the novel is that increasingly novels call attention to the fact that 'this is a novel you are reading'. The fictiveness of the fiction is no longer a thing to hide since fictions are safe and useful if they are consciously recognised.[4]

One reason to be suspicious of 'roles' then is that they threaten destruction by illusion. Another reason is the one hinted at near the end of the previous paragraph. Roles, dramatic roles, occur in plays and plays have plots and worse, scripts in which all the words and actions are set out. To play a role then is to surrender one's freedom to some 'external' authority (or author). It is in David Riesman's term to be 'other directed.'[5] In life we tend to think that the 'roles' we play, as banker, fireman or solicitor, are part of the play called Society. To accept such 'role-playing' is to accept the determination of one's life by a set of institutions which dictate how and what we shall do. Society becomes for the Modern writer, at least so we are told, the supreme illusion and the greatest evil. A complex problem arises at this point, however. It arises when we question the adequacy of a term like Society. Just what does it describe? What is the effect on the individual of 'roles' in Society? How rigidly are they defined and enforced? If the analogy of Society to a play holds, where then is the author and who can possibly be the audience? Most important, how many people must one have before one can speak of a 'Society'? Are two enough? As we have seen earlier, the writer concerned with the preservation of subjectivity and yet anxious to admit (and have his readers admit) the reality of an external world – which means admitting the reality of at least one other person – will be found to have natural recourse to metaphors of drama; and role-playing will have the function of preserving personal integrity and of admitting the reality of the other. But if role-playing is seen in terms of 'Society' and predetermined roles, then there is a danger of obscuring a recurrent and very important theme in twentieth century literature with an abstraction which is at best of questionable value, and at worst, when the abstraction begins to take on an autonomous reality, can be dangerously misleading.

The danger lies in the belief that it is only Society that can create roles. As I have suggested, the importance of dramatic action is that it necessitates the reality of the external world and leads to self-fulfilment. To admit the reality of one other person is, in a sense, a social* act. It is, in fact, an ur-Social act. Having once admitted the reality of another person, one is then free to 'act' in relationship to him. This dramatic action is social because it involves two people; but it is not 'Social' (with a capital 'S' and the full force of abstraction) because it is free and not institutionalised or codified. The presentation of self to another can be a free *and* ritualised act and needs no mechanism of pre-ordained Social institutions to make it possible. The free dramatisation of self can easily be confused with the acceptance of a role from Society and this fact perhaps gives rise to the many misdirected theories about the Social nature of the novel which are discussed in Chapter 2. The most important fact about the novel (in general, but especially about the post-Modern novel) is not that it is Social, but that it is ur-social; that is, it centres on a subject which precedes and subsumes all mere 'Social' matters.

One important point about 'dramatic action' needs to be strongly emphasised. From the time of the Romantic period there has developed a belief in passionate activity which is meant to be a spontaneous expression of the authentic self. 'He who desires but acts not, breeds pestilence,' as Blake says; and 'Sooner murder an infant in its cradle than nurse unacted desires.' A myth has grown up around the man of action and by action is usually meant the spontaneous, uninhibited expression of subjectivity. Action is by definition the antithesis of thought. The categorising, theoretical and calculating mind is inherently 'inauthentic' and insincere. 'Liberty consists in doing what one *desires*,'† says John Stuart Mill, and the Sartrean existentialist insistence on the value of the unpremeditated action, *l'acte gratuit*, is well known. It must be made clear from the outset that this is not the kind of action with which I am concerned in this study. If romantic action is spontaneous, it is to that extent 'informal'; it is not thought out, systematised, ritu-

---

* I must rely, in this passage, on this use of lower-case 'social' and upper-case 'Social' to distinguish between free acts between two or more persons, and codified behaviour demanded by institutions.

† See the *Essay on Liberty*, Chapter 5. My italics, to emphasise that free action is so often seen as the direct result of desire, and not thought or consideration.

alised or intentional action. Dramatic action on the other hand
is all of these things.

Dramatic action is formalised action. It is not necessarily
spontaneous nor need it be sincere. Action belongs to the realm
of the everyday life of men, dramatic action belongs also to the
realm of art: it is artificial and artistic. The use of dramatic
metaphors in contemporary fiction, then, is directed to all such
problems: the value of consciousness, of thought, of activity,
spontaneity, formalised action and the value of fictions. Above
all perhaps, it is concerned with freedom for the individual. The
tradition of romantic activity asserts that only in blind action is
the full unrepressed self set free. The 'classical' Modern and
post-Modern phenomenon which I propose to study, investigates the possibility that to set free the passions is only further
to be enslaved, and that only in intentional action is the full integrity of the actor and of other *agents* preserved. Freedom for
the individual is dramatic self-realisation (or fulfilment) in a
field of agents.

The dramatic metaphor includes the possibility that to be
free means to be free to be insincere. Fictions of the self are not
lies; they are one mode of the self in action. They are not the
whole of the self, but appearances in the world are 'realisations'
or 'actualisations' of potential. If fictions of the self are a central
subject for the Modern writer, this fact has important consequences for our assessment of the importance of fiction, that is
of novels, in our culture. To be free is to be able to create fictions, and also to be able to be free from fictions – that is, to distinguish between fiction and reality. The language of fiction
may be unnatural, but then, man himself is unnatural as Rémy
de Gourmont suggests in his comments on the origin of language: 'L'expression animale des émotions n'est pas un langage, car elle ne saurait fendre: le langage vrai commence avec
le mensonge.'[6] Freely translated, 'The animal expression of
emotions is not a language; true language begins with the lie.'
Or, we might say, if man is the language animal, then he is also
the dissembling and fiction-generating animal.

The remainder of this chapter will concentrate on a number
of theoretical statements about the nature of the Modern
period, and in particular on the claim that the Modern is essentially (by nature) anti-Social, and anti-social. The purpose is to

go behind such statements in order to draw out some of the
themes mentioned in an abbreviated way above. A large part of
what follows will be concerned with a consideration of the
meaning of action and dramatic action in the work of W. B.
Yeats. Although this turn to poetry might seem a little out of
place in a study dealing with the novel, it does provide an essential clarification of the concept of dramatic action and should
also reveal that the Modern period has at its centre at least one
major writer who believed in the value of the inner vision, but
did not therefore give up a belief in the reality of action in the
external world. Chapter 2 looks at another, James Joyce. It
should come as no surprise that a theme from poetry should
find full expression in the novel, for the Modern period has wit-
nessed even further blurring of the already indistinct borders
between poetry and prose. John Wain believes that we are
seeing the establishment of a 'poetic novel'[7] and the following
passage from an essay by Virginia Woolf (1927) seems to have
predicted its development:

> It will be written in prose, but in prose which has many of the
> characteristics of poetry. It will have something of the exalta-
> tion of poetry, but much of the ordinariness of prose. It will
> be dramatic, and yet not a play. It will be read, not acted. By
> what name we are to call it is not a matter of very great
> importance. What is important is that this book which we see
> on the horizon may serve to express some of those feelings
> which seem at the moment to be balked by poetry pure and
> simple and to find the drama equally inhospitable to them.[8]

II

I wish to look critically at certain assumptions which may be
getting in our way as readers when we look at a novel, or indeed
may be acting as blinkers for novelists who adopt these assumptions. They are:

1. The assumption that the Modern period is anti-social, or
anti-cultural;
2. that the post-Modern British literary scene is social – not
'socialist', but in general tending to support Established
Society;

3. that the Novel as a genre is social.

We may note that the first and third assumptions combine in an interesting way, so that the anti-social Modern period should find the 'social' Novel an impossible genre, and indeed we see that Stephen Spender speaks of 'poetic Moderns and prose Contemporaries' in his *The Struggle of the Modern*. We may also note that basically there are two possible evaluative attitudes to these assumptions. One can believe that the anti-social Modern period was heroic and therefore that the 'social' post-Modern period represents a loss of creative nerve. Or one can be convinced that the anti-social Modern period represents a scabrous interruption of the tradition of English literature which some few sane post-Modern writers are attempting to overcome. If the Novel is taken to be 'social' then one can believe that it is one of the most important forms of literature working to preserve the very fabric of civilised human existence, or alternatively, with the same premise one can castigate the Novel as the regressive, bourgeois genre *par excellence* whose very nature prevents it from having any human, experiential relevance.

I propose that there is a more fundamental question that should concern us in the literature of the twentieth century, particularly in the novel. The aim of this critical consideration of analytic terminology is to open an avenue to understanding the recurrence in recent fiction of the question of role-playing, self dramatisation, masks. I want to try to account for this recurrence without admitting that the post-Modern novel is entirely in 'bad faith' in that it counsels capitulation to established, external, Social order. Some novelists do counsel just this, of course. They represent what Yeats calls 'primary man' who feels the necessity to cease from self-expression and 'substitute a motive of service for that of self-expression'.[9] Primary man is characterised by an 'enforced Mask and Will' which are 'code, those limitations which give strength precisely because they are *enforced*.' Antithetical man, on the other hand, is *free*; he is free to improvise his roles against the background of 'an inherited scenario, the *Body of Fate*'.* The antithetical man, in playing

* Although I am borrowing freely a number of suggestions from Yeats, I would not wish to be responsible for the full weight of his system – for the purpose of this discussion I am only a part-time Yeatsian. It is the 'antithetical' type that I am interested in. *The Body of Fate* is, roughly, the circumstances in

roles, achieves formal self-expression and yet remains free,
unlike the primary man; 'Personality, no matter how habitual,
is a constantly renewed choice, varying from an individual
charm, in the more *antithetical* phases, to a hard objective dramatisation; but when the primary phases begin man is
moulded more and more from without.' To believe that the
post-Modern with its emphasis on role-playing, is 'Social' is
equivalent to saying that it is the era of the primary man. I
believe, however, that there is an important body of literature
which is still very much concerned with the antithetical man,
who can be free and still play dramatic roles.

If there is a preponderance of opinion that the essence of the
Modern is that it is against Society and for Alienation, some of
which we shall shortly look at more closely, there is a similar
tendency to believe that this means that the Modern is against
all forms of order, that it is subjective to the point of solipsism,
that it is despairingly and desperately trapped inside a stream-
of-consciousness. There is a limited sense in which all this is
true, and we shall look at that as well. The position that I shall
try to establish, however, is that although the Moderns find
themselves in this *state*, in this *stasis*, of consciousness that they
inherit from Romanticism via Symbolism, their dynamic is a
search for a way out of the prison of consciousness without for-
feiting the value of being conscious. Clearly, in the Modern
period we can see a battle between Art and Society. Society
offers a set of prefabricated forms, which can be passively
accepted. For creative freedom, it would substitute order, tradition, continuity. Art too offers forms,* but the forms, at least
in the Modern period, are new ones, generated from within,
and if the ideal of the Modern period is every man his own
artist, or artist of himself, then its ideal is also every man the

---

which a man finds himself over which he has no control. For example, date
and place of his birth, physical deformities with which he must contend, etc.

* By 'form' here I do not mean quite the differing 'genres' of literature. I am
referring to the idea that the individual work of art imposes a form on unordered experience. Each poem, or each novel, then, is a formalisation of experience. Similarly the 'self' which is presented to the world is a 'formal'
selection from the host of possibilities open to one. Modern art has rejected
many traditional notions of what form in a work of art is, and also the individual no longer finds a position in established Society quite so necessary to establish order in his personality.

originator of his own forms. We can see Eliot hovering between the two kinds of order in 'Tradition and the Individual Talent', and choosing finally a third order.

There is a danger though, that Art can be made to mean the absence of form; that its value can be seen to lie in randomness or in the 'dérèglement de tous les sens' as Rimbaud puts it. The danger for the individual who founds his life on art, on fictions, on the 'self-born mockers of man's enterprise', is of collapsing into a narcissistic, passive privacy. A personal form which no one else can recognise or accept, which has no public validity, cannot really be called a form at all. If the essence of the Modern is its assertion of the value of the internal, then it risks denying the validity of the external. The post-Modern British novelist is reasserting the necessity for 'form' in the 'self' but one need not believe that in doing so he is asserting the necessity for the pre-existing institutional forms of Society and he is not necessarily in reaction against the Modern in this.

Both the Modern and the post-Modern (and here one would perhaps have to include all other periods and all literature) are in search of something fundamental, which Yeats calls Unity of Being. Unity of Being is to be found on some middle ground between Alienation and Capitulation to Society. The middle ground need not be compromise nor the acceptance of 'limited freedom',* the traditional *via media* of the liberal. Dualisms cannot be overcome by a mechanical compromise between extremes of opposition. It is perhaps possible to glimpse a way in which the dualism of Alienation versus Society, which so plagues novelists and critics, might be overcome by means of a consideration of the meanings of Action, Dramatic Action and Mimesis, something which at least some of the writers of the Modern and post-Modern periods have already begun to do. The value of such terms is not that they are new, but that despite their antiquity they can still yield important insights if some care be taken to consider their possibilities. Towards the end of the second chapter, for instance, we shall consider how, by a judicious play on meanings, a 'form' can be seen to be an

---

* For instance, a chapter of Angus Wilson's novel *The Old Men at the Zoo* is called 'Limited Liberty'. The novel as a whole toys with the idea of the need for a liberal compromise and seems to conclude that the essence of life is not sincerity, or authenticity, or freedom, but 'administration'.

'act'.* Further, whereas a consideration of the 'Social' message
of literature cannot accommodate aesthetic matters, terms
such as 'mimesis' keep us within an aesthetic framwork and yet
offcr a way of seeing how literature can be 'about' life; the life of
a single man, or of men in groups called for convenience societies.

I shall begin by looking at the way in which Stephen
Spender, whose ambition seems to be to remember continually
those who were truly great in the Modern period, chooses to describe the literature of the twentieth century. In *The Creative Element* he suggests that there has been a steady decline in the
quality of the literature produced since the end of the Modern
period and acknowledges that, 'The great experimenters in
writing at the beginning of this century remain my heroes.'[10]
He analyses the work of Rimbaud, Rilke, Forster, Yeats, the
early T. S. Eliot, and D. H. Lawrence. Spender claims not to be
attacking the tendency of more recent literature to be unadventurous. He claims merely to be drawing attention 'to some of
the questions the new writers of the new orthodoxies do not
raise.'[11] Such a disclaimer is an unfortunate and indeed an un-
necessary attempt to establish objectivity and impartiality,
since no one who speaks in one breath of his heroes can convincingly in the next breath plead his uncommittedness.

Spender's analysis opposes 'individual vision', which he
finds in the work of the great experimenters of the Modern
period, to 'orthodoxy' which is the state of all other subsequent
literature in English. Individual vision is the 'creative element'
which had been overlooked in his earlier book *The Destructive
Element*:

> The main impulse of the whole great 'modern movement' has
> been the individual vision of writers who, out of their intense
> realization of the destructive element of modern society, have
> isolated and perfected that vision. The 'creative element' has

* There are two ways in which this can be understood:
(1) The creation of individual yet publicly viable forms is the artist's mode
of action in society. He acts by creating forms which make sense (to him,
and hopefully to his reader) of how we live.
(2) For the individual, to act is to give form to oneself. It is to choose from
amongst the myriad possibilities open to the mind, and commit oneself
publicly to one way of being. (1) is really a specific example of (2).

been the amazing release of individual vision *without any allegiance to society*, which allowed writers to think that in their art they were exploring primal values of aesthetic experience.[12]

While he does not provide any precise definition of 'vision', Spender is emphatic in his insistence that their opposition to society was the source of the greatness of the Moderns. After the demise of the Modern period there has been a return to one of three main forms of orthodoxy: Marxist politics for the writers of the thirties; a cultural orthodoxy of the BBC and the British Council or in North America the universities; and thirdly religious orthodoxy, Anglican and Roman Catholic. The three phases of twentieth century literature are, firstly the phase of 'highly developed individual vision; secondly that of anti-vision and despair; thirdly that of a return towards the orthodoxy which had been rejected by the writers of the first phase.'[13] The historicist position is fully revealed with the comment that 'the present tendency to return to orthodoxy seems to me inevitable.' One obvious result of such an end-stopped theory of literature will be a slowness to recognise the particular values of a post-Modern literature because it does not fit into one's fixed ethical co-ordinates.

Because he does not try to define precisely what he means by 'vision' and 'society', Spender's repetition of these terms, while it may convince us of the force and sincerity with which he holds a point of view, serves ultimately to make them almost meaningless. The vision of the great Modern writer is 'isolated and perfected'. What the Moderns share is a 'centre of isolated creative individuality'. The creative element is 'the individual vision of the writer who realizes in his work the decline of modern values from the context of society.' He maintains that it is not any particular society, or stage of society which is to be rejected; it is the *condition* of society as such:

So perhaps, the 'destructive element' was not, as I thought, capitalism, fascism, the political mechanism which produced wars and unemployment. It was simply society itself. Genius had renounced, or moved outside, society, and any acceptance of a social concept which threatened individual isolation was destructive to its unique vision.[14]

If it is not institutions of politics, or industry or economics, or even bourgeois society which Flaubert felt it the duty of the artist to reject, that Spender says the visionary artist must isolate himself from, it becomes difficult to see just what he does mean. Similarly, the vision of the visionary must be nothing more than an elaboration of what he finds in his mind and not of what he finds in the external world. By definition then, this vision must be incommunicable since for those to whom it might be communicated it is external, not internal, and therefore not real. If a vision is to be communicable or comprehensible, it must be a vision *of something*; in literature and particularly in the novel we would expect to find that the 'vision' is in fact a vision of other people. We tend to believe that the vision implicit in a work of art serves to take us beyond the limits of our own ego and lead us to perceive that there are others besides ourselves in the world. In this way then, the vision of the novel must be a vision of society, since society is basically nothing more than a group of people. The implication of an unqualified acceptance of Spender's point of view is that language itself must be a violation of the vision since language belongs to a community of men. The implicit solipsism of Spender's position makes it impossible for him to account for the way in which 'vision' becomes embodied in language as poetry.

Spender's attitude to the Moderns is certainly not a crude one and his enthusiastic support of them is all the more necessary perhaps, when one finds oneself so often confronted with crude dismissals of them. It is necessary though to draw out the dangers inherent in his choice of terms. It is unfortunate, for instance, that his emphasis on the opposition to society could be taken as adding weight to such irresponsible attitudinising as the following:

> In one sense, the Modern Movement is ancient history by now. A scholarship of the subject is in hand, which has stressed the awkwardness, the scabrousness, of its major writers.

> Committed to everything in human experience that militates against custom, abstract order, and even reason itself, modern literature has elevated individual existence

over social man unconscious feeling over self-conscious perception, passion and will over intellection and systematic morals, dynamic vision over the static image, dense actuality over practical reality.

In another sense, however, the Modern Movement is still about, with its 'anti-cultural bias' very little impaired.[15]

The really disturbing thing about this passage, the general inadequacy of which needs no underlining, is that its internal quotation is from the introduction to an invaluable source book on the Moderns written by 'well-respected' (and also, one must suppose, 'well-meaning') scholars. There is little doubt that there is an 'anti-cultural' bias current among some of the members of contemporary society, but it is little short of intellectual blindness to attribute this bias to the Moderns. A well-meaning overemphasis on the Moderns as 'in opposition' then, can give rise to monsters.

Curiously, we can see that another critic can use an almost exactly similar description of the Moderns and yet have a diametrically opposed evaluation of the period. Lionel Trilling too is very much concerned with the 'social' content of literature, particularly of the novel:

The novel, then, is a perpetual quest for reality, the field of its research being always the social world, the material of its analysis being manners as the indication of the direction of man's soul.[16]

Trilling tries to account for the 'loss of interest' in the novel in America by pointing out a coincident loss of interest in the observation of society and manners. One is tempted to ask the obvious question: has there really been any loss of interest in the novel? Either among writers or readers? One might be depressed by the profusion of badly written novels, but that profusion is hardly evidence of a demise of 'interest' in the novel. One must admit that there is much in Trilling's position that is both illuminating and suggestive. Any novel by Henry James, for instance, is obviously informed by some sort of 'social observation'. It is still necessary to ask, however, to what extent it is of the essence of all novels to be social observation.

Any definition of the novel should be able to account for 'romance' as well as for 'realism' and *Wuthering Heights* poses a serious problem for Trilling's theory. We might all agree that *Wuthering Heights* is a quest for reality, and that its subject is the direction of man's soul, but would we be willing to say that its essence lies in its research into the nature of the social world, or in social observation, or even realism?

In a more recent work, *Beyond Culture*, Trilling would seem to have allowed his conscientious reading of texts to alter his theory in the direction indicated by his title. Despite the apparent distance between them indicated in the idea of 'manners' and 'social observation', Trilling is here echoing Spender, although he is not so delighted with what he sees as is Spender:

> The author of *The Magic Mountain* once said that all his work could be understood as an effort to free himself from the middle class, and this, of course, will serve to describe the chief intention of all modern literature. And the means of freedom which Mann prescribes (the characteristic irony notwithstanding) is the means of freedom which in effect all of modern literature prescribes. It is, in the words of Clavdia Chauchat, '*se perdre et même . . . se laisser dépérir*', and thus to name the means is to make plain that the end is not merely freedom from the middle class but freedom from society itself. I venture to say that the idea of losing oneself up to the point of self-destruction, of surrendering oneself to experience without regard to self-interest or conventional morality, of escaping wholly from the societal bonds, is an 'element' somewhere in the mind of every modern person who dares to think of what Arnold in his unaffected Victorian way called 'the fulness of spiritual perfection.'[17]

If Mann's novel can depict an individual freeing himself from society, then either the novel is not essentially social observation or social observation means something drastically different from what it appears to mean. Trilling's explication of the moral dilemma of modern literature is challenging stuff for the literary critic. His spelling out of the 'chief intention' of modern literature is the work of a literate as well as ethical consciousness. Any yet, a doubt lingers on, a doubt to which Trilling's own dilemma points.

As he says of the teacher of modern literature, 'if he is committed to an admiration of modern literature, he must also be committed to this chief idea of modern literature.' This is perfectly plain and acceptable, provided only that one is willing to accept that the multiplicity of the Modern period (or of any *literature*) can be reduced to a single *idea*. He continues, 'I press the logic of this situation not in order to question the legitimacy of the commitment, or even the propriety of expressing the commitment in the college classroom, (although it does seem odd!), but to confront those of us who do teach modern literature with the striking actuality of our enterprise.'[18] Now this does seem odd indeed. How did Trilling get into this cleft stick? If he is right about modern literature, how can he be committed to it? If he himself is committed to this 'chief idea', how can he maintain a moral stance? How did he come to admire an idea which is so repugnant to him? How can *anyone*, we might ask, be for long committed to a literature which is nothing more than antisocial and amoral? The answer to these questions must be that Trilling has not yet fully recognised and accounted for what it is that he really does admire; or that his formulation of the 'chief idea' leaves out much of the essence of modern literature.

We can hear another critic, Jonathan Raban, echoing with confident assumption this belief in a 'chief idea':

If modern fiction has one overwhelming common theme, it is that of the conflict between the individual sensibility and the alien world outside. With such a subject only one point of view is possible – that of the sensitive, and usually suffering hero.[19]

The operative word of course would be that introductory 'if', but its rhetorical function is made plain by the following 'overwhelmingly'. If we refuse to read the 'if' as merely rhetorical, then Raban is raising an interesting and important question, one which has not been adequately answered. Raban has many valuable things to say about individual works of fiction. His theoretical interpretation is weakened, however, by a too ready adoption of widespread assumptions, such as that the individual and society are separable and are in conflict in all major modern literature. The critic often seems to adhere to the belief that 'individual' and 'society' can somehow exist independently of one another almost as self-contained units. It is the attribution of this belief to all modern and contemporary novelists that gives rise to misunderstanding. Raban borrows a term from Trilling to try to bridge the gap between the units:

> Manners equip the novelist with a bridge, over which he passes from talking about the individual to talking about society.[20]

It is as if 'manners' could exist somehow on their own, apart from any specific embodiment in an individual behaving socially. If manners are important in the novel, then they must be more than a convenient device for allowing the novelist's commentary to range from individual to society.

The question of the 'social' nature of the novel will be taken up again shortly, but I would like first to concentrate on the question of Modernism. Despite his claim that it is a Modern invention, Trilling's 'chief idea' probably originated in the Romantic period. Certainly a Romantic influence is noticeable in many post-Romantic writers, but it is misleading to suggest that twentieth century literature is nothing more than a repetition of Romantic themes. Giving oneself up to an experience to the point of allowing oneself to perish is a fair summary of what we find in Keats's 'Ode to a Nightingale':

> Now more than ever seems it rich to die,
> To cease upon the midnight with no pain,
> While thou art pouring forth thy soul abroad
> In such an ecstasy!

It is well to remember, however, that the fancy cannot cheat so well as she is famed to do and that the Romantics themselves were never more than 'half in love with easeful death'. One must be careful of taking an apparent desire for death too literally. On the one hand we find seventeenth century puns on 'die' and on the other hand the ambiguity of the Christian injunction that it is necessary for the ego to die in order to be reborn in spirit. A type of spiritual death and rebirth is common in much literature and an apparent desire for death may simply be a mask for a desire to be reborn.

Although it is possible that Spender and Trilling are both too extreme in their emphasis on the anti-social quality of Modernism, they do usefully draw our attention to a theme which often recurs in Symbolist and Modern literature: the favouring of the inner subjective state over the external world of phenomena. This valuing of the internal state over the mere mechanical objectivity of the external world stems from the Romantic idea of the power of the imagination, and the power of the eye as it alters, to alter everything that is seen. With the Romantics, 'vision' becomes not so much a matter of optics as a way of life. The logical extreme of subjectivity is 'subjective idealism' which will admit the reality of nothing beyond the sentient self. A complementary theme is the inability to act in the world (this theme can also appear as an assertion of the absolute lack of necessity for acting, since the external world is not the *real* one).

In his study of the legacy of Symbolism, *Axel's Castle*, Edmund Wilson provides some useful examples of this theme. The most well-known passage in the book is the one which quotes and discusses *Axel* by Villiers de L'Isle-Adam, but Wilson also refers to a very interesting passage from Pater's *Marius the Epicurean*:

> Those childish days of reverie when he played at priests, played in many another day dream, working his way from the actual present, so far as he might, with a delightful sense of escape in replacing the outer world of other people by an inward world as himself really cared to have it, and made him a kind of 'idealist'. He was become aware of the possibility of a large dissidence between an inward and somewhat exclusive world of vivid personal apprehension, and the unimproved, unheightened reality of the life of those about him. As a consequence, he was ready now to concede, somewhat more easily than others, the first point of his new lesson, that the individual is to himself the measure of all things, and to rely on the exclusive certainty to himself of his own impressions. To move afterwards in that outer world of other people, as though taking it at their estimate, would be possible henceforth only as a kind of irony.[21]

Wilson draws our attention to the ideal inherent in this passage of the 'withdrawal of the individual from society'. The rejection of society here, though, is not a passionate principled objection to society so much as a passive consequence of a choice of subjectivity. The value of society is potentially at issue, but the fundamental concern of the passage from Pater is with the potential richness of the inner world. Marius and Pater seem willing to risk the consequences of their dualistic attitude to life; the world is well lost for the pleasures of the imagination one might say. This is the sort of passage on which Trilling and Spender might well base their conflicting views of the Modern period. But if Pater is not aware, or does not choose to be aware of the solipsism of 'idealism', need we assume that the Modern is also therefore unaware of it?

We must ask the same question of the other important passage used by Wilson, the one from *Axel*. In the play, Sara and Axel have discovered the hiding place in Axel's castle of an enormous treaure and have discovered also their passion for each other. Sara conjures up as in a vision, all the delights of life that they will be able to have with their new-found fortune. Axel, however, refuses, after such a full imagining of delight to submit himself to mere physical experience and urges Sara to join him in suicide before time can tarnish the beauties they have tasted in expectation and fantasy. She is at last persuaded by Axel's forceful urgings:

> Live? No. Our existence is full – and its cup is running over! What hour-glass can count the hours of this night! The future? . . . Sara, believe me when I say it: we have just exhausted the future. All the realities, what will they be to-morrow in comparison with the mirages we have just lived? . . . The quality of our hope no longer allows us the earth. What can we ask from this miserable star where our melancholy lingers on save the pale reflections of such moments? The Earth, dost thou say? What has the Earth ever realised, that drop of frozen mud, whose Time is only a lie in the heavens? It is the Earth, dost thou not see? which has now become the illusion! Admit, Sara: we have destroyed, in our strange hearts, the love of life – and it is in REALITY indeed that ourselves have become our souls. To consent, after this, to live would be but sacrilege against ourselves. Live? our servants will do that for us . . .[22]

Then, as a gesture of supreme contempt for the external world, they drink poison. The theme of suicide as a result of submerging oneself in a subjective vision is an important one, and the ramifications of such a doctrine should cause us concern. But ought we to treat either *Marius the Epicurean* or *Axel* as anything like 'doctrines'? What is the logic and meaning of a work of literature in a social situation? Ought we all to commit suicide after we read *Axel*? Perhaps after reading Pater or Villiers de L'Isle-Adam we would find ourselves, at least temporarily, accepting life in the 'outer world of other people', 'only as a kind of irony'. There is, though, a curious kind of self-negating principle at work in these idealist 'doctrines'. If the contemplation or imagining of an experience is so superior to the experience itself that we can forgo the actual experience, then the contemplation of renunciation of the external world, or even of suicide, in favour of the inner subjective world, eliminates the need for our actually committing suicide. The gesture of contempt for the external world is thus complete and the symbolist work of literature is not really, as they say, something which is meant to effect change in the outer world. It is a form of words and nothing more; and nothing less. If we are interested in the social effect of Modern literature, we must ask if the Moderns themselves were so willing to forgo all action, all commitment, all ability to have their works produce some sort of external effect.

If there are questions to be asked about the implications that Wilson sees in Symbolist literature, there are apparently serious questions to be asked of his general interpretation of the movement itself. Wilson believes that the Symbolist writers, 'who have largely dominated the literary world of the decade 1920–1930', were in 'reaction against nineteenth-century Naturalism' and that Symbolism was a 'second swing of the pendulum away from a mechanistic view of nature and from a social conception of man' which tended 'to make poetry even more a matter of the sensations and emotions of the individual than had been the case with Romanticism.'[23] Of this Charles Feidelson has the following to say:

This has become the official view. But the truth is that the centre of symbolism is not in private feelings any more than in the objective world of science. Eliot's 'peculiar and unexpected' forms, whatever difficulty they may present to the reader, belong to the public medium of language, not to the private world of the poet. The aim of literature for Mallarmé, as Valéry says in a passage that Wilson himself quotes, was 'to emphasize, to conserve, and to develop the forms of which language is capable'.

For the symbolist, both romanticism and naturalism are uses of language that place the focus of reality outside language – romanticism, as Allen Tate puts it, is 'not qualitatively different from the naturalism it attacked, but identical with it, and committed in the arts to the same imperfect inspiration.' In both cases, from the symbolist point of view, the literary process is weighted by an ulterior motive, and the writer's eye has a cast induced by a conflicting habit of mind. Symbolism is neither one nor the other but a new departure, a revision of the literary question.[24]

Despite the weakness of Wilson's theoretical consideration, he has isolated an important theme in his references to Pater's and Axel's 'idealism'. It is a theme picked out also by A. G. Lehmann who argues that the very early Symbolists eagerly adopted any philosophic stance which would help to explain and justify their intuitive rejection of 'positivism'. In particular they found comfort in 'idealist' and solipsist versions of Hegel and Schopenhauer. Lehmann quotes the following passage written by Rémy de Gourmont 'at a time when he himself would not have refused the label' of idealist:

Une vérité nouvelle est entrée récemment dans la littérature et dans l'art; c'est une vérité toute métaphysique et toute d'*a priori* (en apparence), toute jeune, puisqu'elle n'a qu'un siècle, et vraiment neuve, puisqu'elle n'avait pas encore servi dans l'ordre esthétique. Cette vérité, évangélique et merveilleuse, libératrice, et rénovatrice, c'est le principe de l'idéalité du monde. Par rapport à l'homme, sujet pensant, le monde; tout ce qui est extérieur au moi, n'existe que selon l'idée qu'il s'en fait.[25]

Now, the fact which Lehmann goes to some pains to demonstrate is that this idealist and solipsist position was current only in the very early days of the Symbolist movement. In fact, Rémy de Gourmont radically revised his own views about the ideality of the world. As Lehmann puts it, he later 'tramples on the view that mind is in any way independent of material forms – with a violence that suggests the irritation of a man slightly ashamed of his own past assertions. . . .'[26] Lehmann offers a statement by Baudelaire to indicate the way in which the Symbolists themselves moved away from an excessively subjective interpretation of art: 'Qu'est-ce que l'art pur suivant la conception moderne? C'est créer une magie suggestive contenant à la fois l'objet et le sujet, le monde extérieur et l'artiste lui-méme.'* If the Symbolists themselves cannot be characterised as solipsist and idealist, one must ask to what extent it is justifiable to suggest that the Moderns can be.

To believe in the 'ideality' of the world is to believe in 'vision'; the external world exists for the individual only according to the idea which he constructs of it as de Gourmont says. Spender seems to be saying that the Modern is the 'idealist', and the solipsism implicit in this term may be the source of Trilling's despair about the nihilism of the period. However, we have seen that the Symbolists themselves moved from a belief in 'vision', in 'idealism', to a saner modification of this extreme position and recognised the independence of the external world. In so doing, and by admitting the reality of other people, they must also be admitting the possibility of society, if society means simply an active life in an 'outer world of other people'. This is not to say, of course, that they were not opposed to 'institutionalised' Society, or to all known manifestations of Society. There is a sense in which such a critique of Society is not at all 'anti-social'. What we want to know about the Moderns is whether or not they adopted this later position of the Symbolists and if they were alert to the negative possibilities of 'vision': its tendency to solipsism and a resultant inability to act in the world. The question about Society may be an important one, but it is a secondary and derivative one.

We cannot hope to provide satisfactory answers to enormous questions about the nature of Modernism, but it may be possible by considering Yeats to show how the Symbolist aesthetic was used by at least one major modern poet, and also perhaps

---

* Baudelaire as quoted by Lehmann, p. 85. It is interesting to note how close Baudelaire's definition of *l'art pur* is to the definition of Joyce's 'epiphany' given by S. L. Goldberg, which will be considered below.

to reveal an important strategy for bridging the gap between private vision and public expression. Frank Kermode's book *Romantic Image*[27] takes Yeats as a central subject, and one of his aims is to counteract the predominance of 'symbolist criticism' in our time. He concludes with a hope that we shall see a renewed appreciation of *Paradise Lost* which he calls 'the most perfect [*sic*] achievement of English poetry, perhaps the richest and most intricately beautiful poem in the world.'[28]

If the praise seems somewhat strained, it may be that general estimation of Milton is still vitiated by Romantic-Symbolist tendencies, or it may be that the praise *is* a little unconvincing precisely because Kermode himself seems at times to be more of the devil's party than he is of Milton's. For instance, he believes that Yeats's poetry is directly in the Symbolist ethic. As a man, therefore, Yeats embodies a negative criticism of the Symbolist tradition which he stands for as a poet.

The 'romantic image' is the image of the dead or mask-like face; in another form it is the 'dancer' and the 'dance'. It is closely coupled with the belief in the isolated artist and Kermode believes that it has dominated poetry from the time of the Romantics. Kermode's discussion makes clear the origin of the belief that the Modern is somehow committed to a life-denying subjectivity. The value of his approach is that it lifts the problem beyond the restriction imposed by the 'anti-social' approach. To be a poet, a man must relinquish his need to be active in the world of everyday affairs and, donning the mask of poet, he must pursue the stasis of the vision of the image:

To be cut off from life and action, in one way or another, is necessary as a preparation for the 'vision'. Some difference in the artist gives him access to this – an enormous privilege, involving *joy* (which acquires an almost technical sense as a necessary concomitant of the full exercise of the mind in the act of imagination). But the power of joy being possible only to a profound 'organic sensibility', a man who experiences it will also suffer exceptionally. He must be lonely, haunted, victimised, devoted to suffering rather than action – or, to state this in a manner more acceptable to the twentieth century, he is exempt from the normal human orientation towards action and so enabled to intuit those images which are truth, in defiance of the triumphant claims of merely intellectual disciplines.[29]

Kermode develops the point by reference to Pater's search for the 'beatific vision'. The achievement by the artist of this vision 'demands an intense individuality, a cultivation of difference and indeed conflict with the world at large.'[30]

Access to the image is gained only at great cost and the poet must choose either to be fully a poet and work for the 'perfection of the work', or he can be fully alive and give himself to life rather than art. This dichotomy is apparently unbridgeable for the poet under the Symbolist influence.

Kermode seems to believe that Pater's idea of the isolated artist is fully embodied in Yeats. He discusses the conflict in Yeats between the poet and the man of action and he suggests that Yeats was never able to overcome the gap in himself between these two roles. Kermode's terminology does, however, reveal some inconsistencies. In the passage referred to above, for instance, although he is discussing action in the world as opposed to the 'passion' (suggesting stasis and suffering) which is supposedly the source of the image and therefore of poetry, almost inadvertently Kermode reminds us of the 'full exercise of the mind in the *act of imagination.*' If the poet gives up action in the world – as politician, bank clerk or schoolmaster – he does not seem to give up action as such – not even in poetry – and the vision is not passively recorded. Instead it too is the result of an act. One might have wished for a clearer discrimination of kinds of 'acts'.

Although Yeats is seen as an embodiment of the romantic image, Kermode's admiration for him springs from the fact that he is something more. Yeats, we are told, 'accepted isolation, but also accepted the duty to communicate beneficially . . . tormented at intervals by the fear of a growing privacy, as if the necessary imperfections of the life were on the point of invading perfection of the work – a perfection which certainly entails a morally valuable act of communication.'[31] Starting as he does with an inheritance from the Symbolists, then, of idealism and extreme subjectivity, there was a danger for Yeats of slipping into incomprehensibility and solipsism, but he was aware of the danger and worked against it. Yeats could see himself as a 'smiling public man', at least some of the time.

Thinking exclusively for a moment of the Romantic poets, one might ask how helpful it is to say that Romantic poetry, the source of the 'romantic image', necessitated an abstention from action. The poems themselves may have been written in a somewhat passive state similar to Wordsworth's 'emotion re-collected in tranquillity', but we need only remind ourselves of Wordsworth's early fascination with French revolutionary activity, and Byron's active involvement in Greece or his need to try himself physically against all sorts of challenges, to recognise that the Romantic poet's relation to action is far more complex than the dogma of the passivity of the romantic image might suggest.

Almost as an aside (characteristic of his method), Kermode comments that Baudelaire 'remains true to a central Romantic tradition in abstaining from any attempt to alter the social order. . . .'[32] If that is what action means, attempts to alter external order rather than by contemplation or pursuit of the image to establish inner order, then we might agree that Kermode is right, at least about the later Romantics after they had become disillusioned with the Revolutionary cause. As the revolution became the Reign of Terror it must have become obvious to the Romantics that as far as external social order is concerned, *plus ça change, plus c'est la même chose*. From there it is only a short step to the conclusion that the only way to make any significant change in the social order is first of all to make a change in the inner man.

And what of other modern writers, is there an obvious abstention from action amongst them? There are certainly many men of action amongst modern writers, far too many is what Wyndham Lewis seems to believe. In *Time and Western Man* he speaks of the evils of unbridled 'Romance':

Fatally and intimately connected with this [i.e. Romance] is the gospel of *action*. This doctrine has, in the form of the romantic energetics of war, already made a living melo-drama of the Western World. The last ten years of *action* has been so overcrowded with men-of-action of all dimensions, that they none of them have been able to act; and what has been *done* on this doctrinal but terribly real field-of-action, has brought us to our present state of inaction, in due course.[33]

Lewis is discriminating between kinds of action here; between blind action which seems to be a concomitant of the romantic attitude to life (and of the romantic image?), and *effective* action which at the very least cannot be the denial of the mind and reason. Conrad though seems to fit Kermode's insights very neatly, since he turned to literature only after giving up the active life of sea-captain. And *Lord Jim* is a study of the way in which excessive imagination interferes with an ability to act in an emergency. Jim dreams of being a hero and on two occasions when he has the opportunity of acting he is incapacitated by his romanticism. His 'second chance' in Patusan is marked by momentous action, beginning with the leap over the fence. We have already considered Eliot's Prufrock. There is perhaps a more recent example of inaction in Beckett's *Waiting for Godot*. Vladimir and Estragon have no idea what they are waiting for, but they cannot move; they keep waiting, unable to act. There is perhaps a similar theme in Pinter's *The Caretaker* in which the old caretaker moans continually about his inability to get down to Sidcup. If he were capable of this minor bit of mobility he believes that all would turn out all right for him. The question of action may be problematical for modern writers, but there seems little evidence to support the claim that they are devoted to inaction.

If we consider Hemingway, we can see clear lines of continuity with the Romantic tradition. The Byronic hero is obviously a prototype for the Hemingway hero. It is also obvious that the abstention from direct attempts to alter social order is part of the ethic of *A Farewell to Arms*; but it is certainly not part of the ethic of *For Whom the Bell Tolls*. Hemingway's characters, and Hemingway himself, are 'lonely, haunted, victimized' perhaps; but are they also 'devoted to suffering'? Robert Cohn of *The Sun Also Rises* (*Fiesta*) is devoted to suffering, his own, and it is for this reason that he is unacceptable to Jake Barnes and the other *aficionados*. Brett Ashley throws him over, in part, because he enjoys his suffering and is not capable of the action of Romero the bullfighter.

Action is of central importance to Hemingway because it is

the way to the 'moment of truth', to a clear revelation of the precarious condition of man. The commitment to action necessitates a confrontation with death. This *memento mori* increases the sense of being alive: by confrontation with an external denial of the self, one's sense of interiority is immeasurably heightened. Francis Macomber's happy life is short because it begins so late and because *life* is defined by the acceptance of the risk of loss. Shortness (or mere quantity) of life is irrelevant; quality counts. Action leads to an increased feeling of being oneself, but it does so by means of forcing a recognition of the not-self. Action then, mediates between *self* and *other* and because action is only possible when the reality of the external world is unquestioned, action offers a way out of subjective idealism without sacrificing personal individuality.

Kermode draws our attention to Yeats's devotion to action:

> Poets and artists, says Yeats in *Per Amica Silentia Lunae*, 'must go from desire to weariness and so to desire again, and live for the moment when vision comes like terrible lightning, in the humility of the brutes'. Tormented by the necessary failure of his life, appalled in conscience or in vanity, he can say, 'I suffered continual remorse, and only became content when my abstractions had composed themselves into picture and dramatisation'. This content is impermanent; the poet is thus perpetually divided against himself. Hence the distinction Yeats makes 'between the perfection that is from a man's combat with himself and that which is from a combat with circumstance'. Behind it lies the hopeless anger of an artist in love with action, with life.[34]

Kermode passes rather hastily over an important matter when he dismisses Yeats's comment about 'dramatisation' because the 'content' is impermanent. 'Picture and dramatisation' seem to be the key to Unity of Being, and even if such unity passes, it is deserving of attention. Kermode though, insists that Unity of Being is an impossible goal in the modern world, as his comments on 'In Memory of Major Robert Gregory' indicate:

> In the great poem itself the dead man's soldiership and horsemanship, qualities which might seem to associate him with the life of action, are vestigial; they serve only as hints, to

show how, in the teeth of the fate that was visibly overtaking him, he was able to achieve, in the life of action, that Unity of Being which is the ideal of the personal life, and which the present age denies.[35]

Yeats can be devoted to action as a man it seems, but Unity of Being is denied him because as a poet in pursuit of the 'romantic image' he must be devoted to consciousness and inaction. Poetry in itself, so conceived, can never be a form of action.

It would seem, however, that one of the images that is so important to Kermode, and to Yeats, that of the dancer, is inherently an active one. It is very difficult to be confident in any interpretation of those impressive lines:

> O body swayed to music, O brightening glance,
> How can we know the dancer from the dance?

but I would like to suggest that they could mean simply: we know the dancer, or the artist, by what he *does*, by his activity in the world and not by the state of his soul. Such a reading does at least draw attention to the fact that implicit in the metaphor of the dancer is a devotion to action. More important, the poem itself in so far as it is a 'dancer', is also active. The action of the dance (or the poem) overcomes the limitation of an inchoate subjectivity by formulating a ritual appropriate to that subjectivity. The artist's subjective impulse is combined with the objective, public revelation of the impulse; in fact, the two cannot be separated, the dancer is *actualised* only *in* the dance. The dance is the type of the perfect symbol, since the symbolisation is identical with the thing symbolised.

Denis Donoghue is much more explicit about the importance of action in Yeats's poetry. He takes issue with Kermode about the nature of the dance and the dancer. Kermode argues that it was the dancing of Loie Fuller that was most suggestive for Yeats: 'She is abstract, clear of the human mess, dead, and yet perfect being, as on some Byzantine floor: entirely independent of normal action, out of time.'[36] Donoghue disagrees:

> It would seem very strange if Yeats, after *The Green Helmet*, were to present fullness of being in an image itself timeless and bodiless. Indeed, the dance was a powerful image precisely because it was committed to body; an apt equivalent in our own time is the dance-drama of Merce Cunningham or

Martha Graham, which glories in the physicality of the body, in its muscular and nervous experience, in the resistance of the ground itself. Yeats's dancer is never allowed to circumvent the body or to grow wings.[37]

Yeats's insistence on the bodiliness of the dancer, Donoghue argues, reveals that he was not, as Kermode implies, restricted to the idealistic mentalism of 'vision' or of the romantic image. To recognise the body is to admit the necessity and the reality of action. Donoghue shows that action and vision need not be mutually exclusive: 'In the "Double Vision of Michael Robartes" the girl who dances between the Sphinx and the Buddha dreams of dancing and has outdanced thought; which I take to mean that in her Action is not distinct from Vision but is Vision itself formulated.'* Unlike Kermode, Donoghue does not believe that for Yeats action was possible only outside the poetry, in the world. He finds the poetry itself suffused with action:

> *The Wild Swans at Coole* is committed to action; not to thought or concept or feeling, except that these are essential to the full definition of action. We are to register action as the most scrupulous notation of human existence. . . . Action is silent articulation of experience.[38]

Whether or not one sides with Kermode or Donoghue in this most interesting debate about the role of action in Yeats's poetry, one thing at least seems clear: a central modern poet was not content with the passive 'vision'. If Yeats was imbued with a Romantic-Symbolist aura, with Celtic twilight and occult speculation, he was not content merely to accept this poetical inheritance, this Body of Fate, but must create an *antithetical* mask for himself in the pursuit of Unity of Being. It matters not if this Unity of Being was only attainable briefly; that it was impermanent does not detract from its importance as a goal for Yeats. If Kermode does not give enough attention to the element of Drama as a means to Unity of Being, Donoghue recognises that an understanding of drama is central to an interpretation of Yeats. He quotes Yeats: 'In Ireland, where the

* Donoghue, p. 119. This is an important idea which will recur in the philosophical discussion of 'action' below, particularly the notion that a 'form' can be an 'act'.

tide of life is rising, we turn, not to picture-making, but to the imagination of personality – to drama, gesture.'[39] And Donoghue draws the important conclusion: 'But he was always certain that drama is true because it is dynamic; it is the dynamic element which bridges the gap between consciousness and experience.'[40]

It is this question of drama which I believe to be of central importance. Drama is a form of action, indeed, it is formal action, which overcomes the tendency for 'vision' to deny the reality of the external world. There is no question of substituting 'blind action', in the romantic sense which Lewis condemns, for the paralysis of consciousness. The commitment to formal action does not deny the internal vision, or the mind and consciousness. Rather, formal action is the fulfilment, the realisation, the *actualisation* of vision. There is a passage in Yeats's *Autobiographies*, which neither Donoghue nor Kermode mentions, which indicates fully that for Yeats *drama* is a mode of *Action* and that it leads to Unity of Being:

> There is a relation between discipline and the theatrical sense. If we cannot imagine ourselves as different from what we are and assume that second self, we cannot impose a discipline upon ourselves, though we may accept one from others. *Active virtue as distinguished from the passive acceptance of a current code* is therefore theatrical, *consciously dramatic*, the wearing of a mask. It is the condition of arduous full life. One constantly notices *in very active natures*, a tendency to pose, or if the pose has become a second self a pre-occupation with the effect they are producing. One notices this in Plutarch's *Lives*, and every now and then in some modern who has tried to live by classical ideas, in Oscar Wilde, for instance, and less obviously in men like Walt Whitman. Wordsworth is often flat and heavy, partly because his moral sense has no theatrical element, it is an obedience to a discipline which he has not created.[41]

Self-dramatisation is a consciously and freely chosen activity – an act is by definition free, of course, otherwise it would not be an act, but merely reaction, or behaviour. The free choice of roles is essential for the full life, and yet the roles are different from the passive acceptance of a current code; that is to say they are different from strictly Social roles, or from institutionalised and accepted patterns of behaviour. To engage in self-dramatisation therefore is by means of action to recognise the reality of a world of other people, but it is not necessarily to give oneself up to Society. Here then is one clue to a way in which metaphors of drama might be being used in the post-Modern novel. Whereas the question of 'role-playing' in British fiction might lead one to conclude that the British novel is Social and conformist and orientated to the *status quo*, it need not necessarily do so. Metaphors of drama, and action itself, can lead into a very complex and commanding investigation of the nature of human life.

Aware of the dangers of a too long prolonged, or too intense introspection, and yet knowing of no other place to begin the search for poetry except in the 'foul rag-and-bone shop of the heart', Yeats searched after expressive forms. In this he is typical of the Modern period which declares that old and ready-made forms are anathema. The crisis of the Modern is precisely the absence of adequate cultural forms which would allow expression of individual subjectivity. The challenge is to find forms which are not necessarily to be judged only by their being new, or unusual, but by the degree to which they are appropriate formulations of an enriched sense of interiority, vision and imagination. The danger which faces the individual in the present century is that, in the absence of a widely accepted body of ritual, he risks collapse into narcissistic privacy. The spirit of the present age is to run as close as possible, for as long as possible, on the edge of the source of the danger. Some run too close for too long;* others, less venturous, never run at all.

It has become almost a commonplace to use the myth of Narcissus to epitomise the Modern. It is less commonly noted that the age also shows an awareness of what Prometheus, fire-bringer, source of light and civilisation, means to man. Nietzsche used two other gods to explain Greek tragedy, Dionysus and Apollo, and they might serve here as well. Dionysus represents an internal source of ecstatic energy, which is the energy of life operating at such intensity that it

---

* See for instance the story of the suicide of Harry Crosby as told by Malcolm Cowley in *Exiles Return*, or the more recent study of the prevalence of suicide amongst modern writers by A. A. Alvarez, *The Savage God*.

becomes destructive, and the celebration of the god ends with his dismemberment. Apollo is, again, light, clarity, comprehension: the source of form. For Nietzsche the emblem for the greatness of the early Greeks was an Apollo suffused with the essence of Dionysus. It is not a bad symbol for what the Moderns at their best could do. If post-Modern literature has tended to become more Apollonian, the best of it is still in touch with its roots.

We have seen that a 'Social' theory of Modernism (or an 'anti-social', 'vision'-oriented one) leaves out much of the essence of the period – an essence best caught by means of a consideration of idealism, solipsism, action and dramatic action. It is time to leave this discussion of the nature of Modernism to look briefly at some ideas about the Novel which are also weakened by relying too readily on a 'Social' terminology. Our consideration of these theories will serve to remind us of the importance of the individual in the novel and should reveal something of the way in which the novel encounters the problem of the relationship of the single man to a world of others. The discussion leads to some comments on a central Modern novel, Joyce's *Ulysses*, and once again the subject of action and agents arises, this time to be treated with reference to some recent philosophical considerations of the problems of action.

2 The Novel as a Social Fiction

Far too much criticism of the novel still depends on a reified concept of Society, arguing either that such a concept is essential to the traditional novel, or that it is death to the new and experimental novel. If an unqualified 'anti-Society' is inappropriate for the Modern period, so too is an unqualified 'Social' for the Novel. Sometimes the novelist's social responsibility can be spelled out in a grand fashion:

> It is sometimes said that this limited social commentary is the special field of the novel, and that when the shared social background disappears the novel is doomed. The novel deals with man in society, and it is most at home when it deals with an established society for readers who belong to the same world, or are near enough to it to give it an easy and intimate imaginative assent. And viewed in this light the moral function of the novel is the continual maintenance, repair and renovation of a cultural fabric. The critic's function is that of an inspector, to see if the job has been well done; and he works on behalf of the cultural fabric itself.[1]

This must be a reassuring assessment for the critic, even if it is a somewhat daunting thought to put in front of a young novelist about to take up his pen to pursue a tale of passion, intrigue, murder or whatever. Cold comfort to be told that one must work on behalf of that woolly generality the 'cultural fabric', when all one wants to do is to get down on paper the particulars of experience.

But there is a more urgent objection that must be raised to Hough's argument. Such an aloof and easy assumption that the Novel must serve culture is acceptable only so long as we can be sure that culture is serving mankind. Hough, of course, like most British critics, thinks of an ideal of English liberal society

63

when he speaks of the Novel in relation to Society. But if it is nineteenth century, Victorian liberalism to which he refers, we well know what it cost in human misery to build the empire, to build the factories and to run the mines. If we regard Hough as enunciating an idea which is meant to be generally applicable, we should perhaps look to Fascist Italy, where at least the trains ran on time, or to Nazi Germany which strove even harder for cultural and social stability, for a proliferation of good novels. Hough's conception of culture suggests an answer to the questions posed by George Steiner:

> Yet the barbarism which we have undergone reflects, at numerous and precise points, the culture which it sprang from and set out to desecrate. Art, intellectual pursuits, the development of the natural sciences, many branches of scholarship flourished in close spatial, temporal proximity to massacre and the death camps. It is the structure and meaning of that proximity which must be looked at. Why did humanistic traditions and models of conduct prove so fragile a barrier, or is it more realistic to perceive in humanistic culture express solicitations of authoritarian rule and cruelty?[2]

The response of course is to say that the novel must only serve 'good' society. But how is one to know, when the gradations between good and evil are often so minute and hard to comprehend? If the novel has a responsibility to society, that responsibility does not lie in a blind loyalty to existing forms. In order to work on behalf of life, it must be necessary at times to work against the prevailing order. If the novel is not capable of this, then it is really not worthy of attention.

How odd and how refreshing for the reader of modern novels to hear Lawrence on this (even allowing for a corresponding vagueness of terminology):

> And being a novelist, I consider myself superior to the saint, the scientist, the philosopher, and the poet, who are all great masters of different bits of man alive, but never get the whole hog.
> The novel is the one bright book of life. Books are not life. They are only tremulations on the ether. But the novel as a tremulation can make the whole man alive tremble. Which is

more than poetry, philosophy, science or any other book-tremulation can do.

The novel is the book of life. In this sense, the Bible is a great confused novel.[3]

If it can be said, in any sense, that Lawrence was working on behalf of the 'cultural fabric' – and one can imagine how Lawrence himself would have reacted to such an idea – then it must be that he does so only in a very (necessarily) roundabout way. His first concern is the integrity and freedom of the individual, admittedly often in open opposition to existing forms of society. Our understanding of the individual 'man alive' must be altered in a revolutionary way, Lawrence suggests, in order to admit into that understanding what modern society refuses to admit. Once separateness, isolateness of being has been achieved, then there is a possibility of marriage – and Lawrence is concerned with marriage as much as with individuality.

There is an obvious discrepancy in the definitions (or descriptions) of the novel offered by Hough and Lawrence. Lawrence's account we may be tempted to dismiss as wishful thinking (or worse). More likely it would be regarded as an idealistic prescription to which few novels can approximate. Most of us would hesitate at calling the Bible a novel or, vice versa, taking the Novel as our Bible – again we might imagine Lawrence's reaction to our hesitancy. The one particular merit of Lawrence's account, however, is the excitement it can arouse in the reader who has begun to be persuaded by various critics that the novel can be nothing more than social commentary. Lawrence clearly indicates that the novel seeks after fundamental truths of existence and so is worthy of our serious attention. Once again, as in Yeats, the modern artist's concern can be seen to be Unity of Being (what Lawrence calls 'the whole hog'). No matter what the relationship of the Novel to Society, there is a more fundamental subject for the novelist's – and the reader's – concentration. The Novel's subject is what it means to be, and how it might be possible to be, a whole individual; and the pursuit of this subject does not necessitate any idealised personifications of Society.

An overemphasis on the social side of the Novel leads to a counter-balancing claim that it is not Society at all to which the

Novel offers its support, but to the individual conceived as 'whole' or 'unified'. The individual who has achieved unity of being must be something other than that extreme narcissistic type of the individual we were considering earlier. If the individual is unified and complete, then he must be able to take a place in the world of other people; that is, he must have some relation to society – in Lawrence's novels, *Women in Love* for instance, a society of two is already enough. It is for this reason, because some relation to some society is necessary, that the 'social' theory of the novel can be very appealing. It is only when critics fail to deal with the subtleties of the Novel's way of viewing life that their terminology becomes inadequate. Here is Malcolm Bradbury, an interesting and perceptive writer, echoing Hough:

> The characteristic English novel is, I think, social, and assumes a relatively stable social order, a fairly high degree of social consensus both between the characters within the book and between author and reader outside it, and a more or less closed world.*

Here, by way of contrast is an attempt to get close to the nature of the novel's relationship to 'Society':

> The novel, according to a definition set by its particular origins and functions, is characterized by a powerful and demanding sense of contemporaneity, actual or imagined, or both. As a form, it mediates sociocultural immediacy. Life lived through in the novel consequently derives from a series of infinitely complicated transactions between the self and a society of other selves, all in a matrix of dense institutional structures; the reader's experience must also derive from a series of such transactions.[4]

To speak of an infinitely complicated set of transactions be-

---

* Malcolm Bradbury, 'Two Kinds of Novel', *The Novel Today*, Programme for the International Writer's Conference at the Edinburgh Festival, 1962, p. 19. One thing Hough and Bradbury overlook is the role of language in creating the consensus they seek. The novel can be meaningful or exciting only if it convinces us of the reality of a world which, initially, we do not know at all. Of course, for a language to be continuous, there must be some continuity of culture, but this tells us nothing particular about the novel, since with the disappearance of language and culture, all forms of literature, and not just the novel, disappear.

tween 'the self and a society of other selves' is to go a long way
toward setting the novel free and also avoid the pitfalls awaiting
the critic who insists on finding an Individual confronting – or
melting into – Society.

At times someone will don an odd sort of nationalistic spec-
tacles and divide the poles of being up among various contending countries: the English novel is then said to be primarily
'social' and 'closed', and the American novel is 'open' and 'individual'. The terms are obviously value-laden and it is difficult to
use them in a neutral way. J. Hillis Miller strives for a tone of
critical, descriptive objectivity:

> When the fiction is over the revelation is over, over in open-
> ended fiction in the silence after the last page of a failure of
> the protagonist to coincide wholly with the narrator, over in
> closed forms of fiction in the disappearance of the
> protagonist's detached self-consciousness when he *finds his
> true self and dissolves into the collective consciousness of the community*.
> American novelists have tended to feel that authenticity lies
> in maintaining one's separate individuality. In English fic-
> tion, even in the twentieth century, the attainment of a
> proper self has often seemed to coincide with the discovery of
> a place in the community. For such novelists the goal for the
> individual is the assimilation of his private mind into that
> public mind for which the omniscient narrator is a spokes-
> man.[5]

He betrays some of his real sympathies, however, in his remarks
on *Huckleberry Finn*:

> Free man or slave, he is still enslaved, like Tom, Aunt Sally,
> and the rest, by the linguistic and cultural patterns of his so-
> ciety. To negate these is still to remain within them, and so to
> affirm them indirectly. Whenever Huck speaks he is neces-
> sarily subject to this inexorable law. To speak at all he must
> speak lies, not only because his situation forces him to decep-
> tion, disguise, play-acting, but because the language of his
> community is inevitably the instrument of lies. The truth
> cannot be spoken directly in it, as Huck proves in the soli-
> loquy of his decision to rescue Jim. The choice Huck faces is
> therefore between false language and no language at all. And

this corresponds to the choice between participation in a false society and an isolation from other people which is like death. Society is always imaginary. Solitude is the way to the real.[6]

A curious type of logic in which a denial is an indirect affirmation (whatever that might be) and Truth or Falsity is not a function of propositions, but is a quality of language itself. If this is all *Huckleberry Finn* has to offer, the conviction that only Solitude and Death are real, then it is unfortunate it has not slipped into the obscurity which Miller (indirectly) indicates it deserves. If we ignore the unilluminating national division (what about Samuel Beckett and silence, or Saul Bellow on language and the community?), we have once again Spender's modern heroes pitted against Society and poor Huckleberry left struggling with a problem of Wittgensteinian proportions (can there be a private language?).

With a different assessment, Raymond Williams reveals (as does Pearce) that it is possible to discuss the value of society without opposing a pair of irreconcilable monads:

> We begin by identifying our actual situation, and the critical point, as I see it, is precisely that separation of the individual and society into absolutes, which we have seen reflected in form. The truly creative effort of our time is the struggle for relationships, of a whole kind, and it is possible to see this as both personal and social: the practical learning of *extending* relationships. Realism, as embodied in the great tradition, is a touchstone in this, for it shows, in detail, that vital interpenetration, idea into feeling, person into community, change into settlement, which we need, as growing points, in our own divided time. In the highest realism, society is seen in fundamentally personal terms, and persons, through relationships, in fundamentally social terms. The integration is controlling, yet of course it is not to be achieved by an act of will. If it comes at all, it is a creative discovery, and can perhaps only be recorded within the structure and substance of the realist novel.[7]

While Williams finds the 'separation of the individual and society into absolutes' first of all in the world and secondly reflected in the form of the novel, the argument of this chapter has been tending towards the view that this separation is most in evidence in the terminology of criticism of the novel. Williams's point of view is at least complex enough, adequate enough, to avoid being reductionist. He refuses to simplify his problem by opting for one monad or another: the result is that relationships become the centre of his discussion. There is no major disagreement with Williams in my suggestion that the novel is concerned primarily with the formulation and expression of personal, private experience. The attempt to find a form for the individual which would allow him simultaneously to be himself, and to be for others, is obviously a search, ultimately, for relationships. The latter way of putting it avoids the possibility that 'relationships' could mean nothing more than a sentimental 'getting on well with others'.

One might object to the somewhat confusing use of the word 'realism' by Williams. He offers a stipulative definition of 'realism' which would on occasion exclude a 'realistic' representation of a state of affairs; for instance, how could realism as defined by Williams reflect a situation which 'really' consisted of an impersonal society, or a relation-less person (a hermit, or a religious recluse)? We can overlook this however, and recognise that Williams's attention to the 'real' world gives rise to an interesting alternative to Spender's idea of creativity. Where Spender would say that 'vision' is all, Williams would ask of all visionaries – hermeticist, symbolist, subjective or whatever – a vision of what? Consciousness yes, but consciousness of what? As a result of his common-sense view of the world, Williams differentiates between a hypostatised Society (and the notion of a self-sufficient Individual) and a community of relationships.*

Although one would probably not call Lawrence a 'realist' in the technical sense of the term, one can see from the following passage that Williams's comprehension of the modern situ-

* In his discussion of Lawrence in *The English Novel: From Dickens to Lawrence*, (London, 1970), Williams indicates the primacy of personal identity over relationships: 'And in fact it's one of Lawrence's deepest emphases that we need to know . . . that we need to recognise other people in just this irreducible quality, quite before they are functions or influences or social or personal roles in our lives. I don't at all mean, by the way, that these are "pre-social" selves. I mean that they are there quite apart from though of course connected to our own observing existence.' (p. 176).

ation is not unlike Lawrence's:

> When the human being becomes too much divided be-
> tween his subjective and objective consciousness, at last
> something splits in him and he becomes a social being.
> When he becomes too much aware of objective reality, and
> of his own isolation in the face of a universe of objective re-
> ality, the core of his identity splits, his nucleus collapses,
> his innocence of his naivete perishes, and he becomes only
> a subjective—objective reality, a divided thing hinged to-
> gether, but not strictly individual.[8]

As with many of Lawrence's 'philosophical' pronouncements,
it is difficult to make coherent sense out of all of this passage. It
is clear at least, that Lawrence places the source of personal disaster in an over-developed 'objective consciousness'; that is, in
a rational, scientific cast of mind concerned only with the
impersonal facts of the outer world. Into the attack on positivist
consciousness, Lawrence would bring a renewed sense of 'inner
life'. It is also clear that while more 'subjective consciousness' is
needed, the whole individual is not one-sidedly subjective. The
last sentence of the passage indicates that a compromise solution is not to be looked for: a decision to be half inward-
looking and half outward-looking will not do.

What Lawrence seems to be suggesting is a creative merging
in which the subjective world is indistinguishable from the objective world, in which the subjective is, or becomes, objective.
The derogatory use of 'social being' need not be taken as an
unequivocal rejection of all society, or community. The 'social
being' is the man who no longer acts from a personal centre, but
behaves only according to what others expect of him; which is
to say that he is not after all a 'being'. Lawrence is not saying
that the individual is a 'different one'; he is saying much more
than that, he is a 'whole' one. For Lawrence, the first question is
not a social one, it is the question of how to make individuals.
Individuals, uniting subjectivity and objectivity will make their
own forms of association without necessary recourse to arbitrary or pre-fixed social roles.

It is Ian Watt who has spelled out the novel's role in expressing the historical emergence of the individual. He also, of
course, located the source of the novel in the historical emer-

gence of the middle class in the eighteenth century.* An interesting paradox can be seen to arise from these two 'sources' of the novel. As the novel continues to succeed in reflecting (and creating) more fully differentiated individuals, so we would expect it to become correspondingly incapable of rendering 'social reality'. Watt offers a convincing summary of the *way* in which the novel makes us look at society. We are made to see society (and the necessity of a society) through the eyes of an increasingly individual being, who begins to conceive of himself as existing apart from that society:

> Just as the modern study of society only began once individualism had focused attention on man's apparent disjunctions from his fellows, so the novel could only begin its study of personal relationships once *Robinson Crusoe* had revealed a solitude that cried aloud for them. Defoe's story is perhaps not a novel in the usual sense since it deals so little with personal relations. But it is appropriate that the tradition of the novel should begin with a work that annihilated the relationships of the traditional social order, and thus drew attention to the opportunity and the need of building up a network of personal relationships on a new and conscious pattern; the terms of the problem of the novel and of modern thought alike were established when the old order of moral and social relationships was shipwrecked, with Robinson Crusoe, by the rising tide of individualism.[9]

Here is a theory which indicates that the novel is by nature anti-Society, revolutionary, individualistic, visionary, *and* at the same time social in that the direction of its dynamic force is towards the uncovering of newer more adequate forms of being related. Although the 'new and conscious pattern' Watt is referring to is that of the emergent middle class, the usefulness of his paradigm is not limited by the strict application he puts it to.

Watt raises the discussion of the 'individual' to a philo-

* See Watt, *The Rise of the Novel*. It is not part of my purpose to consider the adequacy of such 'genetic' theories. Diana Spearman, in *The Novel and Society* (London, 1966) makes the cunning point that, properly speaking, there was no emergent middle class in the eighteenth century, because there were no 'classes' as such at that time, differences in 'status' not being equivalent to differences in 'class'.

sophical level by introducing the problem of the general versus the particular, and the dispute between 'nominalism' and 'realism'. So long as Truth was something which belonged only to the realm of the general, or the universal, the novel was not possible, he says. Realism once meant precisely the opposite of what it is now taken to mean: only universals were true since they were the only reality. Particulars, individuals, were mere imperfections (the older sense of realism is obviously related to the theory of Platonic forms). It was the change from 'realism' to 'nominalism', Watt says, which started the novel on its way. The nominalist position is that universals are merely the names we give to a host of coincident particular experiences. The particular, the individual experience became the touchstone of reality and it became not only possible, but interesting for an author to consider rendering the experience of a single human being.

Following Watt's lead we might drop the troublesome concept 'society' and say that the Modern novel is unremittingly nominalist, in its distrust of all generalities and its allegiance to particularities. Here is a well known passage from *A Farewell to Arms* for instance:

> I did not say anything. I was always embarrassed by the words sacred, glorious and sacrifice and the expression in vain. We had heard them, sometimes standing in the rain almost out of earshot, so that only the shouted words came through, and had read them, on proclamations, now for a long time, and I had seen nothing sacred, and the things that were glorious had no glory and the sacrifices were like the stockyards at Chicago if nothing was done with the meat except to bury it. There were many words that you could not stand to hear and finally only the names of places had dignity. Certain numbers were the same way and certain dates and these with the names of the places were all you could say and have them mean anything. Abstract words such as glory, honour, courage, or hallow were obscene beside the concrete names of villages, the numbers of roads, the names of rivers, the numbers of regiments and the dates.[10]

For Hemingway, generalities even in the language were to be avoided and the good writer dealt only in the physical, specific truth of the moment. Of course, Hemingway was not merely destructive in his attitude to old systems; he too was actively seeking new forms of personal order. His work contains the promise that the sun also rises on human relatedness. The more that the world of established Society is seen to be inadequate, the more Hemingway seems to be searching for replacement societies in small groups of *aficionados*. If there is no adequate external order, there is still no excuse for living a life bereft of internal order. If there is no satisfactory system of ritual and law in current Society, there is still a code of behaviour which must be learned (intuited) if a man is to live with dignity. So Watt's 'Robinson Crusoe principle' is useful in so far as it points out the *way* that the novel characteristically moves from isolation towards relatedness.

The terminology of 'universal' *v.* 'particular' is at least superior to 'society' *v.* 'anti-society' but still we do not have a full enough picture of the position of the individual in relation to the rest of men in modern literature. Perhaps the case can be put in a few sentences. The general characteristic shared by the set of 'all men' is not some abstract like 'human nature' equally shared out among all members. Instead, a member of the set is defined by his individuality, his uniqueness; he is like all the others in that he is not reproducible. An individual is recognised as a 'member' not by his body paint or by his conformity to a prescribed pattern of behaviour, but by the extent to which he is only himself. Individualisation then, creates the circumstance of alienation, but the way out of alienation is not to renounce individuality; it is rather to recognise that the common experience of humanity is to be oneself and alone. From that recognition then, it might be possible to discover, or create, rituals of order which make for community without violating individuality.

If anyone can be called a central figure of the Modern movement it is James Joyce, and one must ask: does such a central figure reflect or embody the general themes we have been considering? Stephen's phrase (which is too readily taken for Stephen's motto and Joyce's flag) 'silence, exile and cunning' outlines a life style for the artist and for any free, creative individual which has been seen as the characteristic legacy of Joyce. Taken at face value, the phrase could be treated as no more than another version of Hemingway's distrust of language and established Society. As Frederic Henry fled the nets of generalisation, so too Stephen tried to shuck off the nets of being. It is a commonplace to note that the more Joyce himself fled the nets proferred by Ireland, the more that country became his sole subject. It is also a commonplace to say that one is not to take Stephen Dedalus at face value.

A Portrait of the Artist as a Young Man might still (despite all the critical discussion of the matter) leave some doubt in the reader's mind as to how one should regard Stephen: as an autobiographical figure seriously endorsed by the author, or as a character who does not share all of his creator's thoughts and feelings, and who does not escape his irony. *Ulysses*, with its surprising (after the apparent Romantic solipsism of the close of the *Portrait*) creation of Leopold Bloom leaves little doubt that Stephen is not the only symbolic embodiment of Joyce's mind. Contrary to Stephen's impulse to alienation and isolation, Bloom wants very much to belong. The irony of his life is that he cannot belong; the society to which he aspires will not have him, and it is by this rejection that we come to judge the society portrayed in *Ulysses*. Stephen exhibits all the signs of being an artist, but he is not yet an artist. Bloom exhibits all the signs of a citizen, but he is not a citizen. What Bloom needs to make him complete is a society adequate to the signs of citizenship he displays. What Stephen needs in order to be an artist is to transform the privacy and possibility of his artistic 'vision' into the public actuality of a created work, into words on paper. What each needs, that is to say, is the other.

If the reader has been misled by the *Portrait* into the belief that Joyce's ethic can be summed up by 'silence, exile and cunning', then the following passage from *Ulysses* must be taken as a corrective. It comes from the 'Ithaca' section while Stephen and Bloom are strolling towards Bloom's home in deep discussion. Bloom has been running over in his mind the few previous occasions on which he had 'discussed similar subjects during nocturnal perambulations in the past':

What reflection concerning the irregular sequence of dates 1884, 1885, 1886, 1888, 1892, 1893, 1904 did Bloom make before their arrival at their destination?

He reflected that the progressive extension of the field of individual development and experience was regressively accompanied by a restriction of the converse domain of interindividual relations.[11]

If Stephen stands for the gain to be made by individual development, then Bloom reminds us of the loss, and we find that at the heart of *Ulysses* is the crippling paradox (it indicates what is crippling the artist in Stephen) of the modern world. What is lost is 'interindividual relations' (including love) and any society which might be based on interindividual relations. Stephen discovers the value of what lies inside the individual, and Bloom points to what lies beyond a single man: another man, and another.

Stephen, the artist, is individual, particular and isolated. Bloom has about him something of the universal: Man. And yet Bloom is no less of an individual than Stephen. He is perhaps more alone in Dublin than Stephen ever could be. It is in the 'Ithaca' section, when the two are together, that Joyce reveals more fully their significance:

What two temperaments did they individually represent? The scientific. The artistic.[12]

They are in fact complementary opposites, and the point of the story is that they meet. In a long passage which it is worth quoting in full, we see the differences of temperament revealed. The passage is a disquisition on Bloom's love of water and Stephen's abhorrence of it:

What in water did Bloom, waterlover, drawer of water, watercarrier returning to the range, admire?

Its *universality*: its democratic quality and constancy to its nature in seeking its own level: its vastness in the ocean of Mercator's projection: its unplumbed profundity in the Sundam trench of the Pacific exceeding 8,000 fathoms: the restlessness of its waves and the surface particles visiting in turn all points of its seaboard: *the independence of its units*: the variability of states of sea: its hydrostatic quiescence in calm: its hydrokinetic turgidity in neap and spring tides . . . the simplicity of its composition, two constituent parts of hydrogen with one constituent part of oxygen: its healing virtues: its buoyancy in the waters of the Dead Sea: its persevering penetrativeness in runnels, gullies, inadequate dams, leaks on shipboard: its properties for cleansing, quenching thirst and fire, nourishing vegetation: *its infallibility as paradigm and paragon*: its metamorphoses as vapour, mist, cloud, rain, sleet, snow, hail: its strength in rigid hydrants: its variety of forms in loughs and bays and gulfs and bights and guts and lagoons and atolls and archipelagos and sounds and fjords and minches and tidal estuaries and arms of sea: its solidity in glaciers, icebergs, icefloes: its docility in working hydraulic millwheels, turbines, dynamos, electric power stations, bleachworks, tanneries, scutchmills: its utility in canals, rivers if navigable, floating and graving docks: its potentiality derivable from harnessed tides or watercourses falling from level to level: its submarine fauna and flora (anacoustic, photophobe) numerically, if not literally, the inhabitants of the globe: its ubiquity as constituting 90% of the human body: the noxiousness of its effluvia in lacustrine marshes pestilential fens, faded flowerwater, stagnant pools in the waning moon.[13]

Immediately after this extravaganza, having set the kettle on the hob, Bloom performs his ablutions with the lemon flavoured soap purchased earlier and offers Stephen the chance to similarly wash-up:

> What reason did Stephen give for declining Bloom's offer?
> That he was hydrophobe, hating partial contact by immersion or total by submersion in cold water (his last bath having taken place in the month of October of the preceding year), disliking the aqueous substances of glass and crystal, distrusting aquacities of thought and language.

Bloom resists giving Stephen counsels on hygiene and prophylactic because of:

> The incompatibility of aquacity with the erratic originality of genius.[14]

This celebration of water is not a 'stream-of-consciousness' rendering of Bloom's mind. The words come (like a response in catechism) from the narrator who is somewhere above, perhaps paring his fingernails as he speaks. Bloom is drawn to water as if to an ideal which is infallible as 'paradigm and paragon', and yet he seems willing to admit that genius and water do not mix. Water becomes a symbol of the essential unity of all men, of their shared experience in the human community. If the human body is 90% water, how can individual men, sharing so much common substance, be so divided from one another? And yet, the 'universality' of water, its very commonness is demonstrated by a seemingly endless list of the 'erratic originality' of its manifestations. Its variety of forms and the independence of its units are not to be overlooked. Bloom's claim that genius and water do not mix must, then, be regarded as merely a diplomatic gesture to the unwashed Stephen.

As symbol, 'water' points to the overcoming of isolation and to the achievement of belonging – it points hopefully to the overcoming of the paradox of individuality and community expressed earlier by Bloom. It is interesting to note that it is possible to substitute throughout much of the passage the word 'language' for 'water'. A man's use of language is a major percentage of his humanity and the unwashed Stephen must give up his 'silence' if he is to be an artist in words. Joyce's use of language in *Ulysses* suggests very much its variety and 'unplumbed profundity': its quiescence and its kinetic turgidity; its persevering penetrativeness into runnels and gullies of thought and meaning: its variety of forms in different countries and yet its essential similarity for different human uses: its ubiquity and at times its noxiousness. Language is a set of signs which must be accepted generally before it can have any meaning, and yet the most important task of language is to give the private individual a sense of life and a means of expression. Erratic originality, or genius, will find in language both servant and master; it will express while it transforms the private impulse. It is universal and particular, public and private.

S. L. Goldberg has discussed similar subjects with reference to *Ulysses* and summarises the theme of the book this way:

> The central theme of *Ulysses* is consequently figured in its artistic theory: the spiritual kinship of citizen and artist, and their common need to accept, as the medium of their transforming activity, the present reality they share with all other human beings. . . .[15]

The use of the Homeric myths in *Ulysses* suggests that the reality that Stephen and Bloom share, is the same reality that has been shared by all other human beings since the beginning of history. Goldberg emphasises that it is the relationship, or potential relationship, between Stephen and Bloom that is of central interest in the novel. Bloom embodies much that Stephen has yet to learn:

> In *Ulysses*, it is Bloom, once a 'kinetic poet' himself, who now represents the 'scientific temperament' – a stability, a detachment, an engagement with the external world – that Stephen, for all his knowledge and potential imagination, has yet to achieve.

> In short, Stephen must learn to accept the world outside him, and in accepting, to love: the Holy Ghost proceeds from the Son. Without that, the impersonal wisdom of maturity is impossible. Stephen, the bitterly critical Antisthenes, must grow to the maturity figured in Bloom.

Goldberg also offers the following invaluable comment on Stephen's choice of 'silence, exile and cunning':

> The freedom he seeks is therefore not an unconditioned *self-expression*; his rejection of the 'nets' flung out to catch the young Irish imagination is not simply lawless and irresponsible. Even in the *Portrait*, where he is at his most immature, Stephen does not champion the limitless, undisciplined individual will against all the claims of society and accepted moral values. He never seeks mere nonconformity. Rather, it is *self-fulfilment* that he desires – the satisfaction of a moral necessity laid upon him and him alone. His conception of how to satisfy it is still vague and uncertain, but he recognizes from the beginning that it involves renunciations and a discipline of its own, and that there are ordered and impersonal standards for its fulfilment, even if he fails as yet to perceive that these are not merely aesthetic standards. In *Ulysses*, however, he has come to understand that his aesthetic objectives depend upon the artist fulfilling himself as a moral being, that aesthetic *stasis* and *kinesis* originate in, and reflect, states of soul. And it is here

that Joyce's conception of positive moral freedom, by animating the action of the novel, seems at once to continue and clarify the *Portrait*, and to cast a certain ironical light on Stephen's earlier immaturities.[16]

This makes it quite clear that it is inadequate as a commentary simply to say of Joyce (and of the Modern period, therefore) that he is anti-society. Both he, and Stephen, do in fact reject a present form or manifestation of society. They do not, however, reject all forms of ordering the self which could include the possibility, or lead to the founding of an adequate society. But the central concern of *Ulysses* is not primarily social at all. The central question is the one asked by Stein in *Lord Jim*: 'How to be?' What form of the self are we to choose, what model is the most adequate? We have seen that Joyce, characteristically of a writer in the Modern period – and perhaps characteristically also of a writer choosing the novel form – begins with the idea that the self is all interior, subjective, spontaneous and unbounded. He then moves on to a wider view, which includes the exterior world; that is, to a view which includes other people. The paradoxical truth attested to by the modern novelist is that each man *is* – and must be – an island, but to be fully himself he must also discover how to be a piece of the main (to put it in Bloomian language, each man is a unique drop which must recognise its position as part of an ocean).

For those wishing to maintain that Joyce espouses a more Romantic-subjectivist ideal of the self, there is always the evidence of the 'stream-of-consciousness' technique, which apparently renders the free-flowing, unordered impressions of the private self: impressions received *passively* both from the external world and from the subconscious. Goldberg offers a useful counter to this line of argument with a discussion that is based on a difficult and rewarding piece of philosophical investigation into Aristotle. The investigation leads to a statement of what 'epiphany' means in *Ulysses*:

Even its famous 'stream-of-consciousness' technique attempts not so much to record the characters' passive registrations of external reality or the laws of human psychology, as to render the very process in which meaning is apprehended in life. Subject and object are conjoined in continual *acts of perception or understanding*, both actualized in the one *act of epiphany*. It is among the very humblest, most *elemental acts of the moral being* that Joyce seeks to trace the significance of human life.[17]

The epiphany is not the subjective reaction to an object, and it is not the near-voluntary standing-forth of an object in itself. Epiphany is rather the act of knowing, in which the soul knows the form of the external object and so takes on the form of that object. The 'soul' in Stephen's and Aristotle's terminology is the 'form of forms'. The important point here is that the epiphany is the bridge between private and public, internal and external, subjective and objective, self and other. Also, 'knowing' is not passive reception: 'For Aristotle and his Scholastic followers, knowledge is the human soul in act, a realization of a potency, a perfecting.'[18]

Since it has already been asserted that the importance of *Ulysses* lies in its investigation into the adequacy of notions of the form of the self, it is worth following Goldberg further into the complexities of Aristotle as understood by Stephen and Joyce. The question at issue is, what does it mean to be a 'self', where does that self come from:

> Our complete biography would have to include acts of perception perhaps, and certainly acts of will, habits and the like, but since the soul is most fully actuated in knowledge of truth it is *acts of knowledge* that form the most important aspect of a man's life.
>
> On this view, *knowledge is an activity* that ends in a kind of possession. The mind reaches out and takes into its own life the form of the thing known, and in doing so it takes on that form itself. It *becomes* the form of the object, as it were. The subject and object are united in a single reality, a single form, which is at once *the actualization of the object-as-knowable and of the subject-as-knower*. The object cannot be known nor can the subject know except in relation to each other; the unity they achieve in the form of the object is the actual knowledge. Since the mind is capable of becoming all the forms in the material universe and in so doing actualizing its own potentialities, it may be said to be the form of forms.[19]

This line of argument is very appropriate to Stephen, but one must remember that Stephen's 'acts of knowledge' are complemented by Bloom's acts of kindness and love. Once again then, 'act' is a term of central importance in the understanding of a piece of Modern literature. Unlike Kermode in his analysis of Yeats, Goldberg has paid close attention to the necessity of defining a term which could too easily be taken as self-explanatory. An 'act' whether of knowledge or love, bridges the crucial gap between subject and object. The self-in-action is the more mature self and what Stephen will learn from Bloom is the way to become the 'artist as a mature man'. He will become the artist in fact, and in action, rather than merely in temperament, belief or potential.

Literature, of course, is not primarily a question of philosophy, although in Joyce's case it is very appropriate for the critic to resort to Aristotle since this is what Joyce invites. While we may be suspicious of literature which is too overtly philosophical or idea-ridden, it would seem to be justifiable for literary criticism to turn to philosophy for an understanding and clarification of terminology. The danger is likely to be that criticism of literary works which are in a profound way 'about life' will be too little informed by philosophy rather than too much. A brief look at modern philosophy will reveal its concern with two problems germane to the present discussion. Both of these problems can be seen to descend from Descartes's *cogito ergo sum*. One of them is usually called 'the problem of other minds'; the other is the very problem of action we have been skirting around.

The problem of other minds arises from Descartes's definition of the self, which he arrives at after a process of systematic doubt. I cannot doubt that I think (we shall leave aside criticisms of Descartes since we are not so much concerned with the truth of what he said as with the subsequent influence of what he said), therefore I cannot doubt that I exist. But, I can still doubt that anyone else exists or that there is any other thinking going on in the universe except my own. Descartes's formulation leads directly to the possibility that the 'external' world is only what I think it to be. This position is similar to that of Idealism, considered earlier, and it has affinities to Romantic thought with its emphasis on the transforming power of the imagination. We can see a version of this attitude in T. S. Eliot (and his debt to F. H. Bradley's idealism is well known) where the essence of being a self is in being conscious and ever more conscious. Once again one is forced to ask 'Consciousness of what?' The subjectivist, idealist position leaves doubt about the reality of the external world and is therefore ultimately solipsistic.

The second problem originating from Descartes arises because of the radical split between body and soul (or mind) which he found himself faced with. If the essence of the existing self lies in its 'mentality', in its consciousness of its thinking, then there is no clear way in which this mentality can be seen to be accommodated to the body. Descartes located the spirit in the pineal gland, but this bit of seventeenth century biologising solves nothing. How can the mind move the body? How can thought be translated into action? Rather than submit the reader to yet another summary of continental philosophy of this century which deals with action, I shall consider briefly the views of two contemporary British philosophers whose ideas contribute more directly to an understanding of the effects of the Cartesian split between thought and action. Stuart Hampshire tries to show the inadequacy of dualism:

> From the experience of action also arises that idea of the unity of mind and body, which has been disorted by philosophers when they think of persons only as passive observers and not as self-willed agents. An ordinary human action is a combination of *intention* and physical movement. But the combination of the two is not a simple additive one. The movement is guided by the intention, which may not be, and often is not, distinguishable as a separate event from the movement guided. I know that my action is performed at will, and I know what I am trying to do. But this does not necessarily imply that there has been some distinguishable mental event which was an act of will. I often cannot, in reflection or introspection, distinguish as separable episodes the thought of what is to be done from the actual doing of it. A philosophical dualism, which supposes that my history is analysable into two parallel sequences of mental and physical events, does not give a possible account of the concept of action.[20]

The philosopher seems at last to be finding the words to explain in detail and at length what the poet Yeats long ago intuited: that Unity of Being is a matter of overcoming the split between the inner and outer worlds, and the secret lies in 'action' in the world. It is important to notice that 'action' here is not the opposite of 'thought'. Hampshire is not advocating 'blind action' as a remedy for a paralysing academicism. Thought and action can be seen to be coincident when one starts from the point of view of 'action', rather than that of *cogito ergo sum*.

In *The Self as Agent*[21] (which appeared earlier than *Thought and Action* although Hampshire makes no reference to it), John Mac-Murray addresses himself to the same problem of dualism and his goal is a redefinition of what is to be the 'form of the personal', which he regards as the central philosophical subject for our time. By means of an analysis of the concepts of 'action' and 'agent' he demonstrates that it is only in relation to other selves that an individual can ever be fully himself. MacMurray offers a critique of Kant's dependence on the Cartesian principle:

> These two criticisms of Kant's philosophy – of its formal coherence and its formal adequacy – have a common root. It is that any philosophy which takes the 'Cogito' as its starting point and centre of reference institutes a formal dualism of theory and practice; and that this dualism makes it formally impossible to give any account, and indeed to conceive the possibility of persons in relation, whether the relation be theoretical – as knowledge, or practical – as co-operation. For thought is essentially private. Formally, it is the contrary of action; excluding any causal operation upon the object which is known through its activity, that is to say, upon the Real. If we make the 'I think' the primary postulate of philosophy, then not merely do we institute a dualism between theoretical and practical experience, but we make action logically inconceivable – a mystery, as Kant so rightly concludes, in which we necessarily believe, but which we can never comprehend. However far we carry the process of thought it can never *become* an action or spontaneously *generate* an action. We may formulate the dualism in different ways, as a dualism of mind and body, of mind and matter, of theory and practice, of appearance and reality, of subjective

and objective, of phenomenal and noumenal worlds, but we can never abolish it. Consequently I can never know another person, since thinking about another person can never amount to personal knowledge of him, nor even to personal acquaintance.[22]

Once the 'I think' is replaced by the 'I do', the reality of a world of the 'not-self' is necessitated as a field of action. Action is by definition conscious and intentional (or else it is mere reaction, or behaviour). The intentional, extroverted nature of action guarantees the reality of others and thus avoids solipsism. After considering various arguments about the nature of the other necessitated by the concept 'action', MacMurray says:

> We are left with one possible conclusion. The possibility of action depends upon the Other being also agent, and so a plurality of agents in one field of action. The resistance to the Self through which the Self can exist as agent must be the resistance of another self. The distinction between right and wrong depends upon a clash of wills.[23]

The dualism might also be formulated – and we have already seen that many critics of the novel tend so to formulate it – as a dualism of Individual and Society. It is clear that the split between self and society in the twentieth century is only a small part of a much larger, more fundamental philosophical issue. This fundamental dualism is the cultural and philosophical inheritance of the modern artist. He can choose one side or another of a split world (the alienated subjective, free, solipsist individual; or the Naturalist's world of the physically determined), or he can attempt to find a way out of the paralysing impasse. We can see that one of the struggles of some of the central Modern figures was towards Unity of Being by means of action, by means of actualising for a world of others what would otherwise be only private and potential. In the post-Modern period this struggle goes on.

The problem is not solved of course, and for the novelist the nature of reality is still problematical. What use then can any of this philosophical analysis have for literary criticism? How do we move from a philosophy of action to a hermeneutic of the novel? If we recognise that the novel is a *mimetic* genre then we shall have little difficulty moving from a discussion of a situation that pertains in life to ones that recur in fiction. Of course, we shall have little equipment with which to evaluate between individual novels which concern themselves with the problem that we have decided beforehand is the important one. The present discussion arises not out of a recognition of a need for an evaluative method. It arises instead in response to the charge that the novel is trivial in being merely 'social' and that it is no longer an interesting or vital form. The aim of this study is to try to show in what way the central problem of our time might be relevant to the fiction which is being written in our time. If we regard this problem and attempts to solve it (or to embody it in fiction) as important, then we shall correspondingly value those novels which show an awareness of it. It must be admitted that this position is as much a moral stance in face of the novel, as it is an aesthetic one.

With the concept of mimesis we are clearly in the realm of aesthetic, and we might judge an individual novel by its mimetic adequacy. Mimesis is, of course, a very troublesome word, too easily confused with 'realism', or representationalism. Realist or representational literature supposedly gives us a 'one-to-one' reproduction of the thing-in-itself, of the world as it can be experienced beyond the confines of the novel. Since it is generally accepted that the novel is a 'realistic' genre, it is also usually assumed that the duty of the language in a novel is to function as efficiently as possible in copying reality. The language in itself is not interesting and must strive for clarity, so the argument runs, so that one can see through it to the real world beyond.

In fact, it is not at all clear how any work of literature can be expected to produce such a one-to-one copy of the world, since to speak of something is to speak of it in a certain way; that is, any one description of the world focuses attention, selects details, emphasises and gives meaning. Language can 'say something about' the world, but it is doubtful if it can ever 'say the world'. It is to this problem that the French *nouveau roman* would seem to be addressing itself. The many different descriptions of an object point out to us the degree to which language is independent of the reality it describes.

David Lodge, in his book *Language of Fiction*[24] is forced to attack the realistic theory of fiction in order to redirect our attention to the primacy of language in the novel. His most telling point is one he gets from J. M. Cameron which says that literary description (fictional) is different from an everyday description of the world:

> The paradox – inherent in Cameron's argument – is that the imaginative writer creates what he describes. It follows from this that every imaginative utterance is an 'appropriate' symbolisation of the experience it conveys, since there is no possible alternative symbolisation of 'the same' experience.[25]

There is no 'experience' or 'thing' to be found beyond the words of a fiction, to which we might compare the fictional description to check its adequacy or appropriateness. Fictional description is unique in that the description of something is also simultaneously the creation of that thing. On this analysis then, mimesis does not serve as a concept which will bridge a gap between art and life. Having assumed that mimesis means *description*, Lodge establishes the independence of fictional language, but also comes close to making it a hermetic system, clean, perfect and useless. Despite Lodge's disparagement of inadequate novelists who appeal to life over art, one still wants to protest that life is more important than art and that the artist (and critic) who wants to serve art must first of all serve life. One is certainly justified in continuing to ask how experience does relate to fiction.

The dilemma is not so great in Cameron himself. Cameron makes it clear that art is concerned with the making of images (which is not the same thing as description), and by definition an image of a thing must be different from the thing itself. It is equally obvious, however, that there is a necessary relationship between a thing and its image. In the making of images there is great freedom for invention and distortion, whereas a 'description' must of necessity keep distortion to a minimum. So long as the fundamental relation of image to object remains clear to the observer, then the image is a meaningful distortion since the image can give us information about the 'thing', whereas the thing cannot comment on itself; like MacLeish's poem it must *be* but it cannot *mean*.*

To discuss fiction in terms of 'image-making' then, keeps

clear a possible distinction between 'realism' (or description) and 'mimesis'. Image-making is imitation, is mimesis. This can be put another way by saying that mimesis is an enactment of experience. There is an excellent example of mimesis in *Waiting for Godot* where Vladimir and Estragon decide to 'do the tree':

Vladimir: We're not in form. What about a little deep breathing?
Estragon: I'm tired breathing.
Vladimir: You're right. (*Pause*) Let's just do the tree, for the balance.
Estragon: The tree?
Vladimir does the tree, staggering about on one leg.
Vladimir: (*stopping*). Your turn.
Estragon: Do you think God sees me?[26]

Doing the tree involves holding up one's arms in a semblance of branches and lifting one leg to imitate the trunk; imitating is doing. For a moment one can see that there is a fleeting relationship between Estragon's 'doing' and the tree; the image of the tree is an enactment (or an attempt at enacting) of the essence of the tree. Beckett's point is, of course, that the imitative action does not really get to *be* that essence. For Estragon and Vladimir this means that they cannot escape the boredom of their 'waiting' by assuming the forms of Nature:

Estragon: We should turn resolutely towards Nature.
Vladimir: We've tried that.
Estragon: True.

Any consideration of mimesis must eventually have recourse to Aristotle. D. W. Lucas indicates that the wish to differentiate between mimesis and realism is not an unusual one: 'The stock translation of mimesis is "imitation". The first instinct of readers and commentators is to reassure themselves that imitation is not "mere copying".[27] Aristotle says that, 'Tragedy is an imitation, not of men, but of an action and of life, and life consists in action, and its end is a mode of action, not a quality.'[28] Now,

---

* Compare also Robbe-Grillet's emphasising that meaning is created: 'The world is neither significant nor absurd: it merely *is*. Things are "there" and they are only things.' *Snapshots and Towards a New Novel*, translated by Barbara Wright. (London, 1965), p. 92.

this remark is made with reference to tragedy, but in the *Poetics* Aristotle is concerned with imitation in all the arts, as the following commentary by S. H. Butcher makes clear:

> An act viewed merely as an external process or result, one of a series of outward phenomena, is not the true object of aesthetic imitation. The πρᾶξις that art seeks to reproduce is mainly *an inward process, a physical energy working outwards*; deeds, incidents, events, situations, being included under it so far as these spring from an inward act of will, or elicit some activity of thought or feeling.
>
> Here lies the explanation of the somewhat startling phrase used in the *Poetics*, ch. ii., that 'men in action' are the objects imitated by the fine arts: by all and not merely by dramatic or narrative poetry where action is more obviously represented. Everything that expresses the mental life, that reveals a rational personality, will fall within this larger sense of 'action'.[29]

Butcher corroborates and amplifies what we earlier saw S. L. Goldberg saying with reference to Joyce. Also, we find in Aristotle an interesting corroboration for the belief that a detailed consideration of 'action' in this larger sense belongs at the centre of a discussion of the novel. If action is the essence of life and of all the arts, then it is obviously not going to be a defining characteristic of the novel alone. But it is in the novel that there is sufficient scope – sufficient space and time – to study action in all its unfolding. The fact that the action imitated is not the completed act, or the act in the instant of physical performance but is instead the movement of the soul as it is becoming the visible movement of the body – or of the subjective becoming objective, the private becoming public – suggests strongly that a consideration of 'action' would be more than merely appropriate in an analysis of Modern and Contemporary literature which is so predominantly concerned with the interplay of inner and outer.

Butcher offers another valuable insight into mimesis:

> Aristotle saw in fine art a rational faculty which divines nature's unfulfilled intentions, and reveals her ideal to sense. The illusions which fine art employs do not cheat the mind,

they image forth the immanent idea which cannot find adequate expression under the forms of material existence.[30]

We can see the extent to which a theory of mimesis can keep free from the charge of 'mere copying', then. Art can imitate hypothetical or probable actions and this would seem to suggest that the role of the novel is not merely that of reflecting society. Its role is also to help societies, groups of men, discover ways of acting freely in the future. Literature does not merely give us knowledge about the past, or about former modes of society or 'manners'. The vicarious experience of fiction initiates us into the future (or is capable of doing so) by showing us alternative modes of action.

This is the attitude taken up by sociologists of literature who have been influenced by the literary theories of Kenneth Burke. Burke regards literature as 'symbolic action'. Whereas Aristotle would say that literature is an 'imitation of an action', Burke would say that it is symbolic action. He comes daringly close to committing the intentional fallacy in his account of the origin of art: 'The symbolic act is the *dancing of an attitude*' he says. The attitude, once danced, becomes 'equipment for living' in that it teaches us possible attitudes to situations. Poetry he says:

> *is* produced for purposes of comfort, as part of the consolatio philosophiae. It is undertaken as *equipment for living*, as a ritualistic way of arming us to confront perplexities and risks. It would *protect us*.[31]

The sociologist H. D. Duncan has taken up Burke's insights into the social use of literature and elaborated them into several books on the sociology of signs. He offers an analysis of the social meaning of 'great literature':

> It is the exploration through symbolic action of how men *can* act when they act freely in human society. Once this concern with free action is given up, literature (as we know it) must resign its claims to autonomy and return to fashioning sacred texts for church or state, go on developing more persuasive magical exhortations for buying goods and services, or resign itself to serving erotic desires in 'love stories'.[32]

The danger of a strictly sociological, or functional approach to literature is that it can easily be led into overlooking the ethical nature of 'great literature'. Literature not only creates possible actions for us to try out, it tends to evaluate those possibilities and to lead us towards an attitude to them. It is therefore very likely that a body of literature could create and endorse a set of attitudes and possible actions which are 'dysfunctional' for any particular society and are more disruptive of social order than otherwise. And this set of attitudes must be judged as good or evil according to whether or not the system of society referred to is judged to be good or evil.

It is probably wise to continue to be wary of the word 'society' in discussing literature, but those who do use it (and we have considered several in the course of this chapter) often have some of the most interesting and rewarding things to say about literature. It is always necessary to remind ourselves, however, that the creative imagination is, more often than not, running counter to the *status quo*. When literature offers us modes of symbolic action, it does so not to initiate us into a particular society, but to show us the way to act freely *and*, ideally, how to act freely in a way that entails the creation of a culture or a network of signs which ensures that we are not alone in the world with our freedom.

In another of Kenneth Burke's books, *A Grammar of Motives*, we find an exhaustive analysis of the way in which a key 'pentad' of terms interact to form a 'dramatistic' explication of motives. The pentad of terms is: Act, Scene, Agent, Agency, Purpose. In the chapter on the 'Act', Burke makes the following comments:

> In Aristotle 'things are more or less *energeia* (*actu*, from which our 'actuality' is derived)'. In scholastic realism 'form is the *actus*, the attainment, which realizes the matter.' 'As Saint Thomas says, and as the whole Peripatetic doctrine teaches, *forma per se ipsam facit rem esse in actu* (or, as it is often expressed, *a form is an act*).' And when discussing the characteristic distinction between existence and essence, the article on Aquinas defines existence as 'the act of essence'. Similarly in his comments on Aristotle's *Metaphysics*, Aquinas refers to the soul as the 'act of an organic physical body capable of

life'. Etienne Gilson's *God and Philosophy* states the matter succinctly in observing that for the scholastics existence is 'an act, not a thing'.[33]

Here we can recognise the coincidence of the Modern desire to 'make it new', to find a specific, unique form for every expression, and the almost inevitable interest of the Modern writer in the 'act'. Action need not be seen as the negation of consciousness and order; it need not be blind, passionate, romantic, or dionysiac and destructive. There is a sense in which an act is the essential fulfilment of an 'idea'; it realises potential by giving it form. Once again, the form that it gives to inchoate subjectivity is not necessarily a pre-existent form derived from institutions of Society. It does seem possible for us to recognise forms, or acts, *as* forms even if we have never seen them before. The new grammarians tell us that language is inherently 'creative' and that each speaker is capable of producing at any time a completely new sentence of which he has no previous experience and may never again repeat exactly. Similarly there seems to be a grammar of forms, acts and motives which allows us to recognise forms and acts in an 'outer world of other people'.

The consideration of Aristotle, Burke and Duncan has indicated that it is justifiable to carry over to literature a philosophical concern with the meaning of action in the day to day world. It is possible to see ways in which literature might be said to originate in action and have action as its goal, or end. It has been argued that literature is a public form which mediates between two forms of action: the author's and the reader's. But there is still the problem of confronting the specific works which must give justification to any theorising. How might action reveal itself in particular works? What might we expect to find in individual works of Modern and Contemporary fiction, if what has been said about action is valid? We should expect to find the question of the relative value of subjectivity (or personal freedom) as opposed to objectivity (obedience to a world of fact) being investigated as a question of taking or refraining from action. We might expect to find, as we did in Chapter 1, the highly subjective J. Alfred Prufrock, asking himself whether he dare walk upon a beach, or whether he dare eat a peach. Or we might expect to find Mathieu Delarue, the central figure of

Sartre's *Les Chemins de la Liberté*, choosing at last action and commitment even though it means certain death. We would expect to find that the literature of 'consciousness' of the Modern period carries with it a disturbing question (which may be faced or not faced by any particular author or any of his characters) about the meaning of consciousness in a world which demands action. In particular, and repeatedly, we should expect to find that the novel in the twentieth century concerns itself with the question of drama; that is to say that 'dramatic' is a central problematic term (and source of metaphor) for the novel. And it is this metaphor of drama, or ritual, which will be the key to the analyses of specific works in subsequent chapters.

'Dramatic' became for a long time a term of almost unqualified praise when used in discussions of the technique of fiction. Henry James and after him the impressionists like Conrad and Ford, paid allegiance to the method of 'showing' as opposed to 'telling'. The author's task was to dramatise experience, to render it, and not to tell us about it. This belief in the value of dramatising experience in the novel brought with it a growing resentment of the presence of the authorial voice, or the dreaded omniscient author. Wayne Booth* has successfully indicated that there is nothing in itself wrong with an authorial presence and nothing inherently good about a totally 'dramatic' method, if that is taken to mean that the work must appear to have had no author. The convention of fiction allows us to read a fiction as if it were true, and at the same time to be aware that we are immersed in fiction and not reality. That question of the technique of fiction can be regarded as settled and it will not be laboured again here. It has been brought up simply to point out how the Moderns, with their extreme emphasis on subjectivity and individuality seem to have developed a counterbalancing tendency to dramatise experience as if to remove from literature the taint of too much personality. The more important the individual becomes in a system of belief, the more necessary becomes some saving sense of the possibility of drama, of the possibility of acting with others.

Another way in which action and drama manifest themselves in the novel is in the matter of role-playing, and it is here that we

* See *The Rhetoric of Fiction* (Chicago, 1961).

come full circle back to the relation of the individual and literature to Society. Role-playing is of course of interest to the sociologist, but the present discussion will be restricted to the question of roles as it actually appears in literature, and the meaning roles take on there. In so far as the Modern period is characterised by a belief in the value of the subjective individual and the destructiveness of established society (and it has already been argued that this is a reductionist view), it can be seen that role-playing, or doing one's duty, will be regarded very suspiciously. The public man who takes a part, smiling or not, who takes his place on a corrupt stage with corrupt directors and producers in charge, cannot but sacrifice his integrity. If the real self is internal, then any particular external manifestation of the self, any projection of appearance, is to some extent a falsification of oneself. From this situation arises the use of the phrase 'play-acting' in a denigrating way. To play-act is to be inauthentic; it is to be living in 'bad faith'.

Sartre's Mathieu, in *The Age of Reason*, is in a muddle over appearance and reality. He discovers that he can 'perform' in a social situation and yet feel that his behaviour is unreal, a betrayal:

> 'What can be the matter with me?' he asked himself. It was like what had happened in the morning; all this was just a mere *performance*, Mathieu was somewhere else [34]

As he pursues the question of whether or not he exists, Mathieu reflects on the barman:

> Around him it was just the same: there were people who did not exist at all, mere puffs of smoke, and others who existed rather too much. The barman, for instance. A little while ago he had been smoking a cigarette, as vague and poetic as a flowering creeper: now he had awakened, he was rather *too much* the barman, manipulating his shaker, opening it, and tipping yellow froth into glasses with slightly superfluous precision: he was impersonating a barman. Mathieu thought of Brunet: 'Perhaps it's inevitable; perhaps one has to choose between being nothing at all, or impersonating what one is. That would be terrible,' he said to himself: 'it would mean that we were duped by nature.'

The dramatic role of the barman takes on such an emphatic reality that Mathieu begins to doubt that there is anything at all behind the mask. This doubt becomes a near horror at the suggestion that that is all one can hope to do, imperfectly impersonate oneself. If the self is conceived of subjectively, then all attempts to act one's life out for others become mere 'play-acting'. Mathieu eventually overcomes the dilemma by ignoring it. Faced with an invasion by the Nazis, in *Iron in the Soul*, he chooses to stay and fight rather than capitulate like the majority of his countrymen. Mathieu's philosophical doubts become, in retrospect, mere cocktail-lounge neurosis. In the extreme situation, facing sure death from an invading army, one must act and one becomes on the instant of choice, what one has chosen to be. The self becomes the history of one's choices and acts, which are public.

There is a curious discontinuity in Sartre, between the doubts Mathieu has about the reality of roles, which occur in the effete and decadent bar-room and the solution of the problem, which occurs on the battlefield. What if those extreme situations just never crop up? In the absence of an invasion of Nazis, how does one get over the problem? How does one act in everyday social situations in order both to be oneself, and to be there for others? If all social gatherings, all bar-rooms, and all bartenders doing their job are given over to falseness and play-acting, and one's *real* self can be found only *in extremis*, then there seems little hope for the daily ongoing life of the majority of men.* Sartre *solves* the problem posed by Mathieu, but he does so by denying that it is a real problem. One must not play-act, one must choose and act, and that's that.

Conrad's *Lord Jim*, like Mathieu, is plagued with too much imagination and as a result is incapable of action at a critical moment. Unlike Sartre, Conrad continues to take Jim's subjective dilemma seriously and the novel *Lord Jim* is extended beyond the trial scene, to give Jim a second chance. The second chance is given because of doubt that the extreme situation is a valid indicator of a man's worth and potential. It is in the ordinary social routine and in domesticity in Patusan that Jim is finally judged, and judges himself. In Conrad we find the faithful

---

* Denis Donoghue expresses a similar idea about the necessity of literature's locating itself in *The Ordinary Universe*. See below.

Malay steersmen who play their role by staying at their posts despite the fact that the Patna appears to be sinking. They represent an ideal of conduct to which Jim is not adequate. But Jim, because of the very excess of imagination which interferes with his ability to act, remains interesting. The book explores the further life of an individual who, like the artist, seems valuable in himself despite the fact that he has not fulfilled a role in Society. Jim creates his own role in Patusan and the excessive dreamlike quality of the second half of the book suggests strongly that Conrad's ultimate sympathy is with those who *do* work in the ranks, and that excessive subjectivity is of no interest unless it can be made to work in the world, unless there is a role for it to play.

It is with this question of 'acting', then, that one might expect to find the novel most fully occupied: acting in the double sense of choosing action as opposed to contemplation (or subjective imaginings) and in the sense of 'performance', as if on a stage. An author who is completely subjectivist and anti-society in his attitude will tend to value blind impulsive action and reject 'play-acting'. There has been a tendency to say that this is the essence of the Modern. Denis Donoghue puts it this way: 'It is enough to say here that from Schopenhauer to Valéry, Eliot, and Beckett modern literature has tended to yield up the terminology of action and to commit itself more and more desperately to the terminology of consciousness'* My argument is that the Modern period, while it can be said to have inherited and developed a stance that directs attention inward to the soul rather than outward to the world of drama, has not been content to relinquish the world and terminology of action. It has, rather, occupied itself with a prior and more important question, and once again it is Stein's in *Lord Jim*: 'How to be?'

This question is prior and primary in the sense that it insists that the first requirement is some incontrovertible feeling of subjective, personal validity and freedom. But the Moderns did

* Denis Donoghue, *The Ordinary Universe: Soundings in Modern Literature*, Faber (London, 1968), p. 178. Donoghue adds: 'Meanwhile the desperation that lies under the brightest images in modern literature is the result, I would suggest of two factors: the loss of the terminology of action; and the fear that the remaining idiom, the terminology of consciousness, is a blind alley, a delusion, a falsification, at best a fiddling accompaniment to the burning of Rome.'

not rest with the subjective self. As they increasingly discovered the geography of the individual existence, they developed a corresponding interest in the geography of the world at large. The problem they posed was posed in its most difficult form and gives rise to the paradox: the individual is absolutely free and independent if he is anything, but he cannot be thus unless he can find a way to be with others. The search is for rituals of transformation which will make the private public without destroying it. As Philip Reiff has put it:

> The guardians of any culture must constantly protect the difference between the public and private sectors – and encourage forms of translation between the two sectors: that is the meaning of ritual in all traditional cultures.[35]

The goal of the modern is thus a culture, it is a vision of the possibility of a city in which absolute individuality would not be incompatible with membership. It does concern itself with the terminology of drama, action, commitment. If it is 'anti-society', it is not opposed to the community of man – even though it would have welcomed the disappearance of a particular manifestation of society. Any desperation of the Modern writer originates because it seems increasingly impossible for *any* society to provide forms of order, rituals, which would encourage the development of all members into completely free human individuals.

The contemporary period is no easier to summarise, of course. This discussion began, some time ago, with Stephen Spender's strictures of the post-Modern period. There is now perhaps some reason for believing that while Spender tells some of the truth about the Modern period – its visionary quality – he leaves out some of the story: the struggle for a compensatory vision of public life. The contemporary period is not rich in exciting literature; it is not breaking new ground as the Moderns did. But it is not quite accurate to summarise the period as merely 'orthodox' and negligible. In some of the recent practitioners of the novel we shall discover not only a full awareness of the dilemma posed by the writers of the Modern period, but also a willingness to struggle with the dilemma and to attempt to work out some tentative furthering of the way that leads to the paradoxical, visionary solution.

We find around us a great proliferation of competent, average novelists and novels which are not at all concerned with the problems raised here. The 'traditional' novel will probably always have its place as a form of popular entertainment, unless this role is usurped by television.* Not all writers, nor all readers need be interested in life on the artistic frontier. It is sufficient for an age of literature that at least some of its best writers will interest themselves in the search for new forms and new methods of expressing the overarching problem of the time. The problem for our time is still that of the 'form of the personal' and we shall see that there are still some novelists who can express the problem, *and* express an attitude to it.

The tendency to look out on the world and away from the subjective world of the individual has been strengthened as the dangers of excessive introspection have become more manifest. It has become increasingly clear to many novelists that what is 'out there' must be seen clearly, before the 'in here' can be realised. There has been a growing interest in the possibilities and meanings of 'action' and in the validity of role-playing, both in the sense of dramatising the self and in the sense of simply doing a job. Spender's charge is only plausible because some novelists have insisted that it is only through 'outering' what is inner, that life is possible. Such an attitude has consequences for society, although it does not mean that the contemporary period is orthodox, or social. In fact, it may mean the overthrowing of any particular form of society; but in the long run it means that some form of society, of community, is not only possible, it is necessary. The contemporary period would seem to be rediscovering that man is a political animal, in the widest sense of that term. In doing this it continues in the direction indicated by the Modern period. It is on the same road, with some of the same equipment. But it has begun to express more and more of what was only implicit in earlier works.

The following chapters will be devoted to an analysis of some recent novels in which action and metaphors of drama are of

---

* Dorothy Sayers for instance has been successfully adapted for television. I think though that the private pleasure of reading is not yet (*pace* McLuhan) in danger of disappearing. It seems that television serials actually encourage viewers to read the original.

central importance. Some at least of the post-Modern novelists can be seen to be continuing the tendency of the Modern to seek transcendence in action, especially in ritual or dramatic action. The goal of these individual discussions is the one announced near the beginning of Chapter 1: to attempt to account for the recurrence of such dramatic metaphors without having to admit that the post-Modern novel is in 'bad faith' in that it counsels capitulation to established, external, social order.

3 Language, Mimesis and the Numinous in Joyce Cary's Second Trilogy

The problems entailed by first-person narration and the novel of the 'unreliable narrator' are well known. A first-person narration will give the reader a fuller experience of a particular subjective view of the world, which is a desirable end, while at the same time it will make it impossible for the reader to see how this subjective point of view is meant to square with the world as experienced by others. What value are we supposed, or ought we, to give to any one point of view in the search for truth? The first-person narration poses an implicit question of evaluation: how important is this evidence? If the subjective point of view is also untrustworthy, that is, if we cannot take everything reported as being made up of true or sincere reports, then we have a problem of validity as well as one of evaluation. In Joyce Cary's trilogy we find three first-person narrations which are apparently the tales of 'unreliable narrators'. It is perhaps not surprising then that Robert Bloom concludes his study of Cary's second trilogy with the belief that the reader's attempt to extract a coherent vision from the three novels is hopeless, frustrating, impossible:

> But his inclusiveness is a liability as well as a strength, for it impedes his ordering of his own energies and the energies of his characters. He fails to provide us with a reliable means of concluding from the novels themselves something more than that the world is senselessly divided and sustained by a compelling, frequently disastrous, vitality.[1]

There is a limit, however, to the unreliability of even the most perverse narrator. When he reports on his own feelings, for

---

* The trilogy comprises: *Prisoner of Grace* (London, 1952), *Except the Lord* (London, 1953), *Not Honour More* (London, 1955). All references are to the standard edition published by Michael Joseph.

instance, or his reaction to an event, we can regard his report on himself as reliably accurate – as being the only possible one in the circumstances – unless there is a cogent reason for believing that he might have a reason for lying about his own reaction. A murderer who describes his intense remorse at his deed may be thought to be fabricating this report in order to influence the jury. If, on the other hand, he says that at the time of the killing he felt nothing, that he killed with as little involvement as an executioner, or feels after the deed as little grief as Meursault shows over his mother's death, then there is no reason for disbelieving him since he has nothing to gain by lying – there is one extreme possibility, that he is seeking martyrdom. Also, if a subject reports on an event, we may distrust his interpretation of the event, the meaning he draws out of it or attributes to it, or the emphasis he places on his own role in the bringing about of the event; but from his account we can be reasonably sure that something did in fact happen, and that it is possible to work our way through testimonies to something which is an irreducible fact of experience.

At the end of *Not Honour More*, for example, we may find it very difficult to decide whether we should approve or disapprove of Jim; whether we should regard him as a poor distraught man driven to extremities in the defence of necessary principles in a 'rotten' world, or as simply a madman who has transformed a sense of personal injustice into an operative principle in the public world. Whatever attitude we take – and it is no casual decision, Cary is surely right to make it so hard for us to judge since our decision in this sort of affair is crucial to our conception of the way life ought to go on – there is little doubt that Jim Latter murders his wife (Chester's ex-wife at this point), Nina. Jim himself tells us that he has killed his wife, and offers his apology for so doing, and the authorities declare that he was not insane when he did so and is therefore fit to stand trial. About his sanity we perhaps cannot be sure, but that he kills is indubitable. This irreducible fact then offers us a base from which we might begin to evaluate Jim. If he happens to strike us as a character deserving of sympathy despite, or because of, his general left-handedness in life, then we must look closely at him to see just what it is in him that makes him a force opposed to life. If Cary's work is infused with vitality, with the force of life, then perhaps we should look for a clue to evaluation by asking what sort of people, what sort of actions, further life.

If to have an inclusive vision of life means to have no evaluative basis whatever, to see the evil in the world as equal in value and desirability to the 'good' (which is, in fact, to deny any difference between the two), then there is no justification in saying that Cary's vision is fully inclusive. It is selective, evaluative and critical. Which is to say that it is a moral vision, as well as a vital one. To accept that there is evil in the world, that forces of destruction are at work as well as forces of creation, and on top of that to say that it is unrealistic to deny life simply because it can never be ideal and pure (or that the individual cannot escape some degree of corruption), is not to confess oneself unable to differentiate between good and evil or to say that the world is 'senselessly divided'. Gulley Jimson[2] fights in himself, and more so against the similar tendency in his supporters like Nosey Barbon, the temptation to give way to an all-encompassing grievance against injustice in the world. There is no doubt about the evil in the world — the Nazi movement provides the background for the action of *The Horse's Mouth* — and Gulley several times refers to Hitler's contempt of 'modern art'. No matter how unjust one's circumstances may be, or how little suffering is merited, to allow oneself to become bitter is to nurture the worm in the bud, it is to do the devil's work and to destroy any pleasure in life. One must not indulge what may seem like a reasonable desire for justice in life. Cary is quite clear that 'justice' is not an operative principle in Nature, although it is a possibility in the creative sphere of human action.

It is very easy to distort Cary's position. To say that he believes that there is no justice in the world is to equate him with Jim Latter who has no love of life left: 'Because of the corruption. Because all loyalty was a laugh and there was no more trust. Because marriage was turned into a skin game out of a nice time by safety first. Because of the word made dirt by hypocrites and cowards. Because there was no truth or justice anywhere any more.'[3] Not only does Cary seem to be saying that there is no justice, but also, to return to our starting point, his profusion of first-person, unreliable narrators makes it impossible for the reader to judge just who is deserving and who not. Bloom calls Cary's world the 'indeterminate world' with the implication that there is nothing final which can be known about it. To say that the world is indeterminate is to say that human knowledge is incapable of stating what is the case. Which is to say that there is no knowledge, and one can say nothing both meaningful and true about the world. Except, of course, by means of 'point of view', and so Cary's vision is readily distorted into that of a multiplicity of subjectivities with no possible connections between them and no possibility of justice.

To that bleak and inaccurate picture of Cary's fictional world we might add that at least he escapes from the solipsist trap; if there is only subjectivity, at least he recognises that there is more than one subjectivity. It may or may not be that Cary says there is no truth; it cannot be denied however that he says that if there is a truth it is complex, since it involves many individual points of view. The human circumstance is hard to understand precisely because it comprises individuals who are different. We are perhaps too ready to assume that the 'point of view' novel, or here the multiple point of view work, implies an inescapable relativity. To speak of 'point of view' is already to begin to admit that reality is only in the eye of the beholder, that there is no 'objective' truth about the world, simply a multiplicity of attitudes, or visions, all of which if not interchangeable are at least 'equal' in that no one of them has any more validity, or claim to be 'true' than any other. By offering us three points of view in his trilogies, Cary would seem simply to be emphasising that the only truth is what we each say it is, and his only virtue over others who have said the same thing is that he reminds us that we are not alone; he is a solipsist who insists on being also a democrat.

But does a work made up of three points of view necessarily imply a cynical relativity? Does the absence of a guiding and authoritative author make it impossible for us to make any judgement about the characters in the novels? Bloom's response would be yes to all questions:

In the end, the world which the trilogy presents is not a coherent, explicit vision; it postulates only a plurality of beliefs and commitments. The three novels assert merely that there are people who see and judge like Chester, others who see and judge like Jim, some, like Nina, who, neither seeing nor judging decisively enough, are torn asunder by ambivalent inclinations. It is a spacious world, inasmuch as Cary is willing to suffer all fools gladly; but it is vitiated by a relativistic inclusiveness which makes it ultimately unsatisfying.[4]

It is scarcely praise to say that Cary's world is spacious because he has too little nerve to do other than suffer fools gladly. Are we to conclude then that the second trilogy is populated only by fools? Whatever we think of such a judgement, we must recognise that it is a *judgement* of the characters in the book. Does the absence of an overt judgement by the author in the book, give us licence to exercise our own judgement at whim? It is not necessary to believe that because there is no open commentary by the author, no intrusion to point the way, that what the author is saying is that it is impossible to judge at all so you had best rely on fancy or prejudice, since all is one. We get a clue to the working of the critic's mind when we notice that he believes that a work of art must, in some way, be seen to 'assert' something. If, contrary to what might seem to be the case, Cary believes that judgement is necessary, despite the fact that it is so difficult, so nearly impossible when one understands the case from several different points of view, and believes also that judgement must be *exercised* rather than accepted or merely registered by the passive mind of the reader, then the absence of an authorial judgement becomes a part of his method. The assertion of a judgement then, would frustrate his aim, which is to put the reader in the position of having to judge, even though judging is apparently impossible.

We may not all accept such a formulation of Cary's stance, and even if we do, we may not accept that it is a desirable formal method for a novelist to choose. But at least we would accept that the absence of an authorial judgement is not necessarily an infallible indicator of a negative cynicism. There are two possible implications to be drawn from such an absence. Either the author believes that judgement is impossible and should not be attempted; or he believes that it is necessary though apparently impossible and he has so structured his work as to demand of the reader a judgemental involvement – the reader must act rather than record. It is this second possibility which I would argue is the most appropriate for Cary.

The rhetorical mode of each of the three novels is that of evidence given to influence a coming judgement. *Prisoner of Grace* opens thus:

> I am writing this book because I understand that 'revelations' are soon to appear about that great man who was once my husband, attacking his character, and my own. And I am afraid that they will be believed simply because nowadays everyone believes the worst of a famous man.[5]

Except the Lord not only gives us evidence, it provides a verdict, Chester's judgement on himself: 'It is the story of a crime, of a soul, my own, plucked back from the very edge of frustration and despair.'[6] *Not Honour More* is Latter's statement to the police after his arrest: 'This is my statement, so help me God, as I hope to be hung.'[7] An author whose rhetoric invites us to judge while all the time he himself is working to frustrate our ability to judge by hiding the truth behind the vagaries of 'point of view' would be inconsistent if not perverse. How then can we account for the multiple first-person form? We can account for it, that is demonstrate its appropriateness, by noting that Cary wishes us to approach the act of judgement only after having understood as thoroughly as possible, from the inside, the minds of the protagonists. By living with three individuals for the length of three novels, we discover anew what it means to judge, what justice means. We discover again that evaluation concerns people.

It is perhaps appropriate to recall one of the sources of the 'point of view' novel, Browning's poem *The Ring and the Book*. We are not surprised to hear that Henry James was a great admirer of Browning's poem and its point of view technique.[8] Browning, like Cary, had an intense interest in character, and his elaboration of the story found in the old yellow book is interesting over its enormous length because he can show us the 'facts' through the eyes of first one character and then another and make us believe first one story then another, while he creates believable individual characters. It is the Pope's task to look closely at all the contending versions of the facts:

> Truth, nowhere, lies yet everywhere in these –

Not absolutely in a portion, yet
Evolvable from the whole: evolved at last
Painfully, held tenaciously by me.[9]

It is not surprising that Cary cannot have recourse to a Pope to make a judgement in his novels. Even if we did find some character in the novels offering a summing up, we would either distrust or resent him. And yet, even for Browning, the Pope's word is not the end of the matter. As Browning says in the opening chapter, when he outlines the sequence of events and speakers in the poem, the Pope's judgement is only a prelude:

Then comes the all but end, the ultimate
Judgement save yours.   (ll. 1220–1)

The multiple point of view makes judgement difficult in order to involve the reader actively in judging.

Although he gives the reader more direction in forming a judgement, Browning's poem does not 'assert' its meaning. He knows well enough the limitations of a single point of view, how little able any one man is to speak the Truth:

Our human speech is naught,
Our human testimony false, our fame
and human estimation words and wind
(Book XII, ll. 834–6)

Browning was in no doubt that there was a Truth beyond human attempts to speak it, that behind 'these filthy rags of speech' there was the Word. The filthy rags can, however, be transformed into cloth of gold by Art:

Why take the artistic way to prove so much?
Because, it is the glory and good of Art,
That Art remains the one way possible
Of speaking truth, to mouths like mine, at least.
(Book XII, ll. 837–40)

Art finds a way to Truth because it avoids assertion, which must rely on the words of one man; Art is more roundabout, and more reliable:

But Art, – wherein man nowise speaks to men,
Only to mankind, – Art may tell a truth

Obliquely, do the thing shall breed the thought,
Nor wrong the thought, missing the mediate word.
(Book XII, ll. 854–7)

The principle of the 'point of view' work does not necessarily eliminate truth then. It serves instead to remind us of the primacy of individual lives, of people; to show us that a life is after all a life, although no single life can hope to encompass all of truth. Art transcends fact and allows us to approach Truth.

Is such a summary of Browning really appropriate to Cary? Certainly Cary would be less overt even than Browning about Truth; perhaps he would even deny that there is any *absolute* Truth, but we need not bother to try to demonstrate that his works are based on a conception of absolute Truth. For the contemporary reader it is irrelevant that Browning's work falls back on such a belief; we can dismiss the Pope's authority while still admitting the necessity of his acting, after the most careful consideration, and so maintaining an institution of *human* justice. A meaning emerges from Browning's poem, and all that is necessary is to demonstrate that a coherent meaning can be found to emerge from Cary's trilogy, for that is what has been denied.

Before trying to show that the trilogy does 'mean' more than that the world is senselessly divided, let us follow the comparison with Browning a little further. There is no direct evidence to hand which would indicate that Cary knew or relied on Browning, but if he did not know the poem, he has uncannily produced his own version of a very Browning-like situation. The second trilogy is the story of two men and one woman, Jim Latter, Chester Nimmo, and Nina. Nina, the youthful lover of Jim, marries Nimmo and while married to him bears children begotten by Latter. Divorced from Nimmo she marries Latter; they find Nimmo has moved in on them at Palm Cottage where Nimmo, old and lecherous 'interferes' with Nina. Believing that his wife has doublecrossed him with Nimmo, Latter kills both of them out of an impulse of his 'honour': 'Because there was no truth or justice anywhere any more.'[10]

The Ring and the Book is also a story of two men and a woman, Guido Franceschini, Guiseppe Caponsacchi, and Pompilia. Caponsacchi helps Pompilia to escape from Guido and Guido believes that they have run off together. He pursues his wife and kills her and her parents. His plea is similar to Latter's:

> He, brought to trial, stood on this defence —
> Injury to his honour caused the act;
> That since his wife was false, (as manifest
> By flight from home in such companionship,)
> Death, punishment deserved of the false wife
> And faithless parents who abetted her. . . .
>
> (Book I, ll. 805–10)

Both stories are presented in a similar manner, in a technique known to readers of Browning as 'dramatic monologue'. Each is concerned with the way truth evades a single direct attempt to grasp it, and each author is concerned with, enamoured of, the development of his characters and the investigation of their minds and motives, and with the problem of judgement.

It is not necessary to try to establish a closer thematic or structural link between the two works. The similarity is enough to suggest that Cary was familiar with Browning and that he found himself dealing with a situation with similar complexities. It is clear also that Cary believed in the ability of art to tell a truth obliquely. One of our assumptions about the 'dramatic monologue' is that, although it is clearly a single 'point of view' and we have no authorial assertion about the value of the monologue, the speaker in his choice of words will give himself away. The Duke in 'My Last Duchess' has always provided enough clues in his speech to allow innumerable successions of readers to reach what nobody would call an unfair assessment of his character. What of Cary's characters, do they not provide in their monologues enough information to allow us to conclude that they stand revealed even though there may be disagreement and contradiction on matters of fact from one narrative to the other?

One can readily see that the quality of the language in the trilogy deteriorates as it nears its end. Nina's story is the fullest, covering the longest stretch of time in the most coherent way. Chester's story in *Except the Lord* deals with his own youth and not with the events which form the material of the other novels. The language is at times inspired beyond what Nina is capable of, but it is also at times full of the bombast of the professional politician who has for too long had easy recourse to the jargon of mob-swaying. The first paragraph of his story reveals the histrionic tone he is capable of: 'If I draw back now the curtain from my family life, sacred to memory, I do so only to honour the dead, and in the conviction that my story throws light upon the crisis that so fearfully shakes our whole civilization.'[11] He makes his motives sound so high that we are immediately on our guard for insincerity. We do not have to have read the other two volumes to understand that the man may be trying to whitewash something, trying by fine words to influence judgement of himself. The language of *Not Honour More* is at times nothing more than a debased, scribbled series of notes put down by the Captain who prides himself on his honour and his honesty, and has a corresponding distrust of language. His functional style often suppresses articles (both definite and indefinite), personal pronouns and connectives:

> Copy of this speech already in our files with note of Chief Constable's query and Frant's answer to lie low for moment in view Nimmo's local influence all parties.
> Conveyed magistrates' Chief Constable's warning to Nimmo and received personal note from Bootham requesting private meeting clear up difficulties. Offering assurances.
> Answered not aware of difficulties. Matter quite simple.[12]

At times its crudeness reveals the depth of his hysteria:

> That's the password for politicos – that's the pill for punks – that's the joy call to the love feast. Come on, boys and girls, we understand each other. We're a putrid lot. Let's get together and sing unto our putrefying lord the hymn of the putrid. Don't blame anyone for anything.[13]

Disgusting as his use of words can be at times, he is capable of a curious kind of inventiveness when he explodes. When his nerve is touched he gives up his military taciturnity and lets flow a stream of words that could be called poetic if it did not habitually run in a sewer. He calls Chester 'a poor old fester on a dying ramp. A shit-merchant who's so buried in filth he can't smell himself.'[14] It is crude, and no doubt offensive, but there is a germ of intelligence and wit perceptible, nevertheless. When someone praises Nimmo to him, Latter responds 'I didn't

doubt Nimmo was a first-class gas squirt and clack merchant.'
One thing Latter is not guilty of, at least not all the time, is
worn-out metaphors.

Despite its moments of exciting flash (and where would the
novel be without some vitality in the language?), Jim's language, freed only for the purposes of invective, uses any potentially creative energy for attack and destruction. No matter how
truthful he tries to be in his sparse reporting of the 'facts', we are
surely right in suspecting that because he debases the vehicle
for discovering and reporting truth, he will miss some essential
in the story. He relies on assertion and forswears Art, 'This is
my statement, so help me God, as I hope to be hung.' Artless-
ness and assertion may be honest, but truth is many-sided and
complex.

It is always difficult, of course, to know how much weight to
give to titles, particularly titles like the three of the second trilogy which are, two of them at least, ambiguous. *Except the Lord*
seems to me to be fully explained by the Biblical passage quoted
by Nimmo:

> Except the Lord build the house, their labour is but lost that
> build it. . . .[15]

and it serves simply to indicate what Nimmo says it does, that
religion is, and has been for him, prior to politics. The other two
however are more difficult. '*Prisoner of Grace*' is obviously Nina's
description of herself, but it is also Cary's choice as the most
appropriate title. We must suspect the 'absent author' of some
collusion here, since he assented to the title enough to let it
stand when he sent the book for publication. A prisoner of grace
is someone like Nina who is a prisoner, but who has 'grace' or
beauty despite the loss of freedom. Or else, she is a prisoner,
gracefully, having surrendered her will to the obviously over-
powering Chester. Or, she is a prisoner, and yet she has grace,
freedom, to come and go as she pleases. All possibilities are perhaps correct, and there may be other possibilities. The last one,
however, comes closest to the truth about Nina: she is Chester's
prisoner, a prisoner, that is, of his love for her, and yet she is
free; she has not surrendered her ability to choose, as is clearly
evidenced by her leaving Chester and marrying Jim.

The title of the last volume *Not Honour More* comes from that old soldier's lyric:

> I could not love thee, Dear, so much
> Loved I not honour more.

How are we meant to take this title though? Does Cary himself
endorse Lovelace's sentiment? Does he himself believe, and
does he expect us to believe after reading the trilogy, that one
must love honour before one is capable of loving a human
being? that without honour there can be no love? If he does,
then perhaps there is some validity in Harry T. Moore's claim
that Cary wrote nineteenth century novels in the twentieth
century[16], except that the nineteenth century is even too recent
a date. The phrase itself, though, taken out of context and put
at the head of a book suggests another possible interpretation.
As a phrase it is a truncated imperative utterance; it might for
instance be the kernel of the sentence 'Do not honour more thy
father than thy mother.' It might also be a response to the question, 'What should I do when a love of honour leads me to
murder the woman I love?' Answer: 'Not honour more.'
Another possibility is that it is an indication of the relationship
which should hold between love of honour and love of people.
The directive then is to love not honour more.

A tentative case can be made then that the trilogy expresses a
meaning which is accessible from 'internal' evidence. We do
not necessarily have to fall back on Cary's later comment:

> What I believe is what Nimmo believes, that wangle is in-
> evitable in the modern state, that is to say, there is no choice
> between persuading people and shooting them. But it was
> not my job to state a thesis in a novel, my business was to
> show individual minds in action and the kind of world they
> produce and the political and aesthetic and moral problems
> of such a world. In short (in the trilogy), the political situ-
> ation as I conceive it in *my* world of the creative free indi-
> dual.[17]

I see no reason why the reader should not have the benefit of an
author's comment on his own work, and if there has been a
misreading, or a doubtful reading, then the external directive
from the author is a welcome aid. It may be that the work itself

offers nothing which would allow the reader to conclude from 'internal' evidence that the novels do what the author says they do. If so, then this 'external' evidence is useless, because the books themselves will not be found to reveal the attitude that the author says he wanted them to reveal. It is possible though, that readers have missed the implication of the work all along, that the evidence was there but nobody looked hard enough at it, or worked to understand it. Then 'external' evidence such as Cary's preface is not a confession of the work's weakness but an aid to discovery.

Robert Bloom regards Cary's comment as a regrettable necessity. He regards it also as an inadequate commentary on the novel since it 'awards the palm to Chester over a false issue.'[18] Bloom's point is that 'In the novels Jim does not desire to shoot people as a means of running the state, but merely to proceed in all things truthfully, justly, and honorably, if a little inflexibly.' But Bloom is wrong; Jim himself says that he 'killed her for an example because it was necessary'.[19] Later he regrets his action because it has not taught the nation anything:

> It has been a bitter thought to me in these weeks I'm going through hell for nothing. That I killed my darling to no purpose; that this great country is so blinded and bound, so hocussed and gammoned by the bunkum boys, the smart ones, the power and money merchants, it doesn't know where it's going or what it's going there for and it's too bewildered to care.[20]

Clearly it is not out of order to suggest that Latter tries to run the state by murder. He has inextricably fouled up the personal and the public. Practical, functional man that he is, he kills for a purpose, to provide an example, and he is furious when the press humanise him to the extent of suggesting that he had a human motive in passion. Bloom is incorrect also when he suggests that it is *Cary* who says, in the passage from the preface, that Jim desires to 'shoot people as a means of running the state'. It is an inspired insight into Latter, but it is Bloom's own, though he disowns it. What Cary says is that 'there is no choice between persuading people and shooting them.' What Jim fails to do, is to persuade Nina, to persuade Chester, to persuade the nation. Honour is destructive if it will not submit itself to language.

And it is perhaps just there, with the idea that untempered honour, unmitigated honesty, innocence and idealism are destructive, that we come close to a one sentence statement of the meaning of the trilogy.* There is an Ibsenesque undercurrent running through the novels and it is possible to see a coherent meaning emerge at the end, but it is not a simple assertion of truth. Cary is not a 'realist' opposed to *all* ideals as fictions which blind us. The implication of the last novel of the three is not: 'There is no honour left in the world', nor is it 'Let there be no more honour since it is destructive.' Rather the title points to the balance which must be kept – or to the way the scales should be imbalanced, in favour of love. The directive in the title is: not honour *more*; let there be honour and honesty and integrity of course, but not more than love. And love, as the trilogy shows, is flexibility, it is accommodation, it is being a prisoner of grace, it is the art of politics – in the family and in the state.

The trilogy, however, cannot be reduced to a statement of its theme, and the richness of its meaning can only be revealed by means of a detailed discussion of each volume. In considering the novels individually I shall attempt to treat them in their published order: *Prisoner of Grace, Except the Lord, Not Honour More*, but there will of course be inevitable cross-referencing. The major part of the analysis will be devoted to the first novel and the themes revealed there will be further developed with reference to the other two books.

Prisoner of Grace is Nina's story of her life with Chester Nimmo and Jim Latter, and is the fullest presentation of the triangle of relationships which is the subject of the trilogy. Nina is balanced between two attractions: that of the private 'romantic' love that she has for Jim, and the exciting public life that Chester offers her. Her oscillation between these two men is reflected in the way the action of the novel shifts between the town and the country, and also in the way in which the dream of romance is in conflict with the political 'reality'. Nina's nature is originally formed by the easy and pastoral countryside, but she moves into closer and closer contact with 'city life' after she meets Chester. The novel, and the trilogy, reveal that the dream of absolute subjective freedom which the country, and

* There is a similar message in Graham Greene's *The Quiet American*.

romance, allows, is potentially dangerous. Similarly, a life lived totally according to the dictates of 'policy' is ultimately dehumanising precisely because it takes no account of the subjective individual. If subjectivity, romance, dreams, fairy tales are not to be dangerous, then they must be made to work in the public world. On the other hand, actions in the public world must be reflections, or realisations, of inner states of subjective awareness (what Chester learns to call a sense of the 'numinousness' of existence). The self is fulfilled when it acts as a mediator between a rich state of inner being, and an outer world of public doing. It is this state of self-fulfilment that Nina is seeking in her position as 'mediator' between her two men, neither of whom can give her all she needs for a full life. Jim is too private and romantic and yet she loves him; Chester is too public and although she does not seem to love him, she needs him too.

Robert Bloom insists that Nina is morally reprehensible in not choosing her lover and rejecting Chester:

> To have become an emotional and ideological prisoner to a man who embodies the untrammelled ethic of politics, to insist repeatedly on the insurmountable complexity of every important issue, we discover in Nina, is to become morally inept, to be disposed to an indiscriminate, self-destructive emotional charity, to be a danger to oneself and to those whom one insists one loves.[21]

There is no denying that Bloom has some justification for what he says; indeed, Nina herself offers some powerful supporting evidence for his attitude:

> And I knew then that I should never get rid of Chester, that I dared not do so. And I saw that it was no good pretending that I merely tolerated an old man's whims because he was pitiful – I did not love Chester and I had never loved him, but now, more than ever, at the end of his life, I was in his power.[22]

It must be noted, however, that Nina is overpowered by Chester's weakness, as it were, by his need of her at the end of his life. She is powerless because of her choice not to harm a man, whom she may not love, but for whom she has some consideration, and with whom she has some kind of *human* bond. It is worth asking more closely what is the nature of this bond, and more importantly, one must ask just what is the nature of the 'love' she has for Jim? Bloom seems to believe that there is no possibility for her but to choose the romantic love she could have with Jim. Nina, herself a romantic by nature seems to agree. And yet it may be that there is another sort of love, not romantic and so little like what one normally calls 'love' that it looks, superficially at least, like bondage.

First though, what of her relationship with Jim Latter? Nina's description of what Jim's love-making means to her is so full of a sense of lush yet invigorating and regenerating sensuality that one might well wonder why she stays with Chester at all:

> And afterwards I was so moved not only in my body (which felt as if it was *changed* – into another kind of material, lighter and quicker, and, as it were, more living and more eager) but in my mind, as by the sense of a grand event, a dedication and a solemn pledge (all the more *serious* because it had come with such an unexpected sensation). . . .[23]

Nina more than once has recourse to Jim for this unexpected sensation which makes her feel 'more living and more eager' and he fathers all of her children. Sexuality for Nina is not a mere physical relief but an event which involves her completely. It does not, however, involve Jim in quite the same way. Her account of the 'grand event', the 'solemn pledge', continues in this way:

> a dedication and a solemn pledge (all the more *serious* because it had come with such an unexpected sensation) that I was a little shocked to hear Jim say in a tone of calm satisfaction, as if he had completed a deal by signing a contract (but Jim had a strong sense of contract), 'That's all right then. Now you belong to me, and you can never have anything to do with that poop-stick again – not if you have a grain of honourable feeling.'

One of the many minor comic touches of the novel is to be found in Nina's naive and yet revealing parenthetical aside. Plainly Jim is not so much a romantic sexual hero as he is a real-estate hustler anxious to sign a contract, or an explorer planting a flag on conquered territory. The full experience of sexuality which

Nina has is not something that Jim gives to her; rather it is an experience which he facilitates. He contributes nothing but an occasion and an atmosphere which frees Nina's own possibilities for sexuality. She may not quite be capable of 'honourable', feeling, but in 'feelings' themselves she is rich. Her experience transcends that of the man who thinks he is 'possessing' her.

Chester himself is more than a mere 'poop-stick' as Jim wishes to believe. Jim's knowledge of sexual technique was something that he had 'picked up' in India 'where young people actually learn it out of textbooks'. It is little wonder that the textbook technique of Jim's is not enough to keep Nina faithful to what she thought was a 'solemn pledge'. There is something in her relationship with Chester that leads her to introduce him to the new delights which cannot be exhausted by sharing:

> I was suddenly inspired to show him (with him it needed only the slightest indication which would seem almost accidental) something of what Jim had revealed to me.[24]

From this time on Chester cannot get enough of her and the gift of Jim's is partly the cause of his later jealousy of Chester when Chester is pursuing Nina at Palm Cottage. Jim can spark off a passion in Nina, but he cannot sustain it. Chester, who seems capable only of 'political' acts, shows that he has a fully alert sense of life's possibilities and once he is given a hint, quickly learns the nature of other acts.

The reason that Jim can provide a romantic atmosphere which awakens Nina's sensuality is perhaps to be found in their long and close relationship as children. Cary presents a very convincing picture of the tensions which inform such a childhood romance. They are bound together not so much by an idyllic and innocent companionship, as by a frustrating battle of wills which neither likes but which neither has the power to break off. When they are having a picnic at Rockpit, Jim and Nina foolishly dare each other to swim in the stormy sea. At the slightest suggestion from Nina that there is any danger, Jim plunges into the deepest breakers, as Nina had immediately undressed to swim on Jim's saying that she was sure to 'funk it'. Although they suffer torments: 'Now both of us had turned green, in blotches, the horrible colour of very white skins in an

East wind', neither will relent in the 'spite game'. Nina tells us that Jim 'would have thrown away his life to get a single cry of fright out of me.' Nina too prefers death to accommodation at this early stage of her life:

> I was so enraged against Jim (thinking how happy I could have been alone with a book in front of the nursery fire) that I should have been quite glad if I had fallen off the cliff on the way up and killed myself.[25]

Although Jim will later try to recapture this exclusive relationship with Nina (his nostalgia for the past is in part a desire to remain always a child), their early relationship is far from ideal. As Nina says: 'We were, in fact always carrying on a kind of war to dominate each other or to stop being dominated.'

The internecine passions are Laurentian in their intensity, but this battle ends characteristically in silence, in the refusal to communicate: 'And when at last he came out I would not speak to him. We dressed in silence, sat down shivering in our wet clothes, on separate rocks to eat our sandwiches, and went home ten yards apart.' At this early stage, neither Nina nor Jim has learned what Nina is later to discover from Chester, that 'relations need managing'. If management is an offence by the artificial against the honest spontaneity of love, it is also the way to freedom of choice which guarantees love. Although Nina fights bitterly with Jim as a child, she does not do so as the result of a decision freely taken:

> For it was not spite that kept me silent; it was a kind of heavy mass of tangled feelings which surrounded me and tied me in on all sides, so that even if I could have spoken I should not have known where to begin.[26]

Although she is later to become Chester's prisoner of grace (which is paradoxically to be a prisoner of freedom, since grace is freedom), here she is a prisoner of the too intense, too emotional and romantic attachment she has to Jim.

There is even a suggestion of Romantic incestuousness about their relationship: 'We were like brother and sister, and yet we were not so; and this situation is always dangerous for a girl, because she is drawn into very particular – I mean very confidential – relations with a young man.'[27] Here is the source, possibly, of the romantic atmosphere which stirs up in Nina such moving passions in her later life. Even though there may technically be no incest (Jim does take Nina into his bed but it is only for comfort and warmth), the demanding and exclusive intimacy threatens to eliminate all outside contact, all other love. It is necessary for Nina to marry exogamously if her life is not to be dominated by her feeling of being 'inside'. Chester will come to offer her a 'political' (as close as Chester can come to a 'classical' mode) release from her romantic, inchoate passions. Chester is the master orator (what Jim ingeniously if cynically calls a 'talky boy' or 'first-class gas squirt and clack merchant'), and having committed himself to the power of the spoken word, he has willy-nilly committed himself to lying and insincerity, to offences against love by 'policy'; in short, to 'wangling'. As Cary says though, wangling is inevitable in the modern state. The 'human' way, of speech and action, is the only possible way even if it is not a romantic and ideal way. Nina and Jim, in their early over-abundance of feeling, cannot formulate or report these feelings and, deprived of expression and therefore of choice also, both are slaves to destructive impulses:

> Then he [Jim] would rage again and tear at me as if he wanted to kill me (and I really think he did – I mean, it was the same rage that makes people do murder, and in the most cruel ways); but however he beat me and whatever he did, I would stay limp and not say a word. This, of course (because he realized that he could do nothing to me except batter me or kill me and that even then I should not care), made him still more furious, especially as he thought I was doing it on purpose; though, in fact, I could not help it. All I could do was try to ignore the whole horrible situation, and I was quite ready to be killed if only it would stop. And it would go on sometimes till I wished I were dead.[28]

This foreshadowing by Nina of her murder by Jim, and also of her suicide attempt, points up an important theme of the trilogy: language is power, freedom and the ability to act, and the only alternative to the free exercise of human power is inhuman violence and destruction. Nina is, of course, equally responsible with Jim for this early brutality. Although Nina will learn from Chester a respect for language and an ability to use it as well as a willingness to 'manage' relations, Jim will not. Jim believes that Chester's and Nina's addiction to speech ('But I knew it was no good talking to her.') makes them incapable of perceiving the Truth: 'She couldn't understand she was up against something bigger than either of us or anyone's happiness.'[29] Jim calls this bigger something Truth, or Honour, but it is clearly Death that is bigger than human power and freedom, and his reflections on the murder – Jim is moved to extended articulation only to try to keep his honour sound after he has killed two people – reveal that Jim has acted out of the same imprisoning passion that motivated him as a child:

> I did it because I, myself, had to do it. There was no other choice for a man who wasn't prepared to live like a rat.[30]

Jim, of course, has chosen. He has chosen to relinquish freedom of choice in the name of an abstract principle. In trying to escape what he believes to be a verminous existence, Jim himself renounces human status.

Cary shows quite fully, then, why Nina is both attracted again and again to the romantic aura of her youthful lover, and why she must continually be moving beyond the limits he would impose on her. Under Chester's influence, transcending Jim's boundary lines becomes a habit and she even carries to him the sexual delights that Jim was sure would bind Nina to him for ever. Whereas Jim would like always to be regressively 'inside', Nina learns how to live in a world beyond herself. Jim does get his chance, though, at an exclusive relationship with the adult Nina, after she leaves Chester and runs off with Jim to Palm Cottage. There their childhood relationship takes on a slightly different form, but it is still a battle of wills. Only now, Nina is willing to let Jim have the illusion that he is winning.

At the cottage, Nina is again pregnant, and finds that Jim is marshalling her life. He keeps a close watch on all her activities (as perhaps he has need to later on when Chester arrives), limits her reading and regulates her bed-time and diet. All this is natural for the expectant father. However, he does occasionally allow his desire to control Nina to run to extremes and according to his whim he would take her 'sailing beyond the heads, in the roughest weather'.[31] This is certainly not the sort of activity that a solicitous father-to-be would encourage, and Jim takes Nina on such dangerous trips simply to exercise his control over her. Nina's conclusion is that Jim is a frustrated politician: 'Perhaps Jim has always needed to govern something or somebody and now that he has neither horses nor Lugas he can only rule over me.'[32]

Although she is Chester's 'prisoner of grace' in the trilogy, she does come close also to being Jim's possession or 'slave'. She finds herself wondering how she could endure 'such a "life of slavery"'. Cary explains in his preface about Nina's 'brackety mind'. Her mind is fond also of qualification by means of 'inverted commas'; so that she speaks of a 'life of slavery' and the implicit qualification indicates that although Jim might be trying to make her his prisoner, and although she does find her life being run by him, she has an unassailable independence: 'For I saw that so far from being Jim's slave, I belonged to myself more intensely than ever in my life before.'[33] It is because she has a secret unannounced ground of inner freedom, that she can submit lovingly to Jim's demands: 'It was from this secret place, the independent calm as of a private fort, that I found it so easy to submit to his whims. . . .' When Jim finds her tractable, he is pleased and goes so far as to offer a compliment, saying that she 'seemed to have learnt at last that even a pretty girl can't have it all her own way.' Nina, however, has yet another secret from Jim: 'I did not dare to tell him that if this was true he owed a great deal of the new woman to Chester's skilful discipline.' As Chester's 'prisoner' she seems to have learned from him the way to inner freedom and also enough of the politics of marriage to know that she must 'manage' such a difficult husband by not telling him everything that may happen to be true.

Such a split between her private self and her public appearance spells disaster for this marriage though. Nina does her best to manage a life with Jim, but the lie that his honour forces her into dooms the marriage. The attempt to make love a bond necessitates escape. Lawrence makes a similar point about the bondage of 'love':

The bond of love! What worse bondage can we conceive than the bond of love? It is an attempt to wall in the high tide. . . . This has been our idea of immortality, this infinite of love,

love universal and triumphant. And what is this but a prison and a bondage?

Lawrence insists that love must be balanced by a counter-force; since love is a movement inwards towards the centre, there must be another centrifugal force:

> And love is a travelling, a motion, a speed of coming together. Love is the force of creation. But all force, spiritual or physical, has its polarity, its positive and its negative. All things that fall, fall by gravitation to the earth. But has not the earth, in the opposite of gravitation, cast off the moon and held her at bay in our heavens during all the aeons of time?[34]

On the basis of such a principle we can understand Nina's movement between the two men in her life: with Jim there is a coming together, a pastoral privacy of love in Palm Cottage with the danger implicit in such privacy; with Chester there is the exhilaration of an active life in the public world. The situation that Lawrence is describing refers to two people, who come together in love and then separate into isolate individuality. Cary's version involves two types of men, each representing one necessary attribute for the full life, and one woman who comes closest to self-sufficiency when she tries to balance the two sources which nourish her. Her tragedy is that the two men are not one.

Only when we have looked closely at the last two novels can we see just what are Chester's virtues (his vices are easy to spot), but Nina's narrative in *Prisoner of Grace* does give a substantial clue:

> He was, in fact, far wiser and deeper in his 'political' idea of human ties than I had been in my romantic one. For where I had said, 'It is just what they say of so many important public men, that all they want in a woman is a competent mistress and someone to look pretty at the head of their tables', I found myself bound to him in a relation which was still 'spiritual'. For I knew a Chester unknown and unimagined by anyone else in the world, a man full of whims and nerves and feelings, who needed from me something that I only could give, not because I was a woman but because I was myself, because I knew him through and through, because our ways

had grown to fit each other, because he could trust me. . . .[35]

Nina is bound to Chester not by anything he does, nor any direct force he can exert on her (he can exert a powerful indirect force at times, by means of a threat to Jim's career), but by their knowledge of each other and by their years and years of shared experience. She is bound to Chester not because he needs something from her, but because he needs her as a person, in herself. By submitting to this 'bondage' Nina gains a renewed sense of *self*, because Chester sees her clearly as an individual being and not as someone who is merely an adjunct to his career, or his physical needs. Of course, Chester is astute enough not to let pass any extra advantages he might get out of their relationship.

Nina indicates more precisely just what quality of Chester's makes him so satisfactory a husband and politician (for Chester the two roles are not dissimilar):

> For men of imagination (and imagination was Chester's great strength; it enabled him to enter into other people's feelings) are very easily entered by imaginary anxieties, and even wild fancies. Their strength is their 'weakness'.[36]

Elsewhere she makes the same point:

> The truth is that a man like Chester, just because he had such a lot of imagination, such power of putting himself in other people's places and minds, was *nearly always sincere*.[37]

The primary use of imagination is to see other people, to put a limit to oneself by something like 'negative capability' and affirm the reality of others. As Shelley suggests in his *A Defence of Poetry*, this use of imagination is the foundation of civilisation as well as love. Because Chester has this ability of identifying himself with other people's circumstances, he is a good politician. It can be seen also that it is *necessary* for such a man to be a politician, to live by a complex set of rituals and laws in order to avoid the misuse of this power. The unbridled imagination, once freed from a context of human expectation and law, can become susceptible not only to wild fancies, but also to destructive myths. Cary suggests that it is necessary for the Artist to be also a Politician. Chester is not only a good politician, however.

His quality of imagining the lives of others amounts in fact to a
kind of love, and although Nina can say that she has never loved
Chester – which is true if one sticks to only the romantic sense of
the word – there is a sense in which she has been loving him all
along, by knowing him and by being known.

The position that Nina ultimately finds herself in, drawn by
'love' to one man, and 'prisoner of grace' as a result of thirty
years marriage to another, is not a comfortable one and its tensions suggest disaster. Nina is not courting death by the end of
her life, however. She can recognise that death comes to all
whether risks are run or not, and she is willing to be sacrificed if
necessary so that love and happiness may at least have a
chance. Her willingness to be sacrificed is another indication of
the degree to which the ability for self-transcendence develops
in her during her life. The willingness to die for something
beyond herself is not at all like her earlier suicidal frame of
mind, and it puts her well beyond any charge that she is
'morally inept'. At the end of her narrative she shows herself
fully conscious of the dangers of her situation, and she reveals
exactly what Chester has given her in the struggle for a full life:
a sense of 'politics' and much more important, a respect for language. Jim and Nina are now married, but into the middle of
their ménage at Palm Cottage, Chester has managed to insert
himself, and Nina does not wish to send him away:

> So that the life which was going to be so simple and restful,
> my 'retirement from politics', is more difficult and compli-
> cated than ever, and also, of course, more 'political'. I have to
> consider every word I say and everything I do. The tension is
> like a perpetual crisis. I notice that my hair is turning white
> and I am so thin that my frocks hang on me. But what is so
> strange is that I have never before been so much in love. You
> would say that neither of us has known till now what is meant
> by a grand passion – I suppose Jim, like me, feels that every
> day may be the last.
>
> But how could I make him understand that it is because
> that happiness is so precious to me I dare not turn Chester
> out. For I should know that I was committing a mean crime
> against something bigger than love.
>
> I should despise myself, which is, I suppose, what Chester

means when he says that such and such a 'poor devil' is 'damned'. And I am terrified of 'damnation', for it would destroy my happiness and all the joy of my life, and Jim can only shoot me dead.[38]

Nina is in the middle of a personal relationship requiring all the best 'political' abilities and she is now willing to be fully conscious, and responsible for all her words and deeds. The necessity for 'politics' arises with the clear perception of the needs of other selves. Her attitude to 'love' seems finally to be moving closer to that of Lawrence, who says, 'Love is the happiness of the world. But happiness is not the whole of fulfilment.'[39] In trying to balance between her two men, Nina is striving for fullness of life and for self-realisation; and this can only be achieved by perceiving and admitting fully the reality of other people. It is because Jim has not sufficient imagination to overcome the limits of his egocentricity that he is far more culpable than either Nina or Chester for the disaster which ends their lives.

Before going on to consider Chester more fully, let us look briefly at how Nina's romantic fancifulness indicates the potential evil of a mind which is only romantic and is used only for self-satisfaction. I have already suggested that the trilogy is built around an alternation of scene between town and country. This alternation of scene reflects Nina's oscillation between her two men. Chester moves from the moor, 'real Lorna Doone country', to London and then to a prestigious position in the government, and finally back into the country setting of Palm Cottage from where he tries to get back into power during the 1926 strike. Nina has her strongest roots in the pastoral setting of Palm Cottage which exists between two 'special moods': that of the moor and the over-civilised beach.[40] Chester learns how to transcend the romantic limits of his 'Lorna Doone' origin on the moor and becomes 'political'. Jim belongs to the 'overcivilized beach' (one remembers his fondness for yacht-racing) and yet is capable of the savagery of the most uncivilised inhabitant of the moor. Nina is capable of both extremes, at least in her mind, at times lapsing into a romantic identification with Nature, and at other times responding to what she calls the 'machinery of society'.

While Chester is a member of the government, having just

survived the Contract Case by selling his Banks Rams shares, Nina is visited by Goold who proclaims that Chester has been corrupted by his career and in particular, 'it is London that has destroyed him, London society'. Nina adds a humorous corrective to this by noting that, in fact they did not move in 'society' although there were a 'lot of society people who had taken us up':

> Indeed, I had often thought it was a blessing that we were outside society, because being in society means that you have to be 'social' and tremendously friendly with people, even if they are bores; and goodness knows we had enough bores already in our political assortment.[41]

This is the unsocialised Nina speaking, the one who has not yet found a reason not only to put up with social duty, but to enjoy it. She finds this reason in her son Tom, when he takes her to a number of parties:

> It is true that there were plenty of parties, but I doubt if people nowadays would think them at all gay. There were too many rules and formalities. Tom would complain when he went to a ball that he had to dance so many 'duty dances' with plain stupid girls who danced so badly that he would much rather have been in bed. And he had to pay so many formal calls, and send out so many flowers to hostesses, that he would prefer not to have any parties at all. But, in fact, he never refused a party or a ball, and he was extremely particular about the shape of the tall hat in which he paid his calls.
>
> For if the parties were sometimes dull and social duties often a bore, there was somehow a great pleasure in feeling that the 'social machinery' was at work and that we were playing our part in it.[42]

Tom has the dramatic impulse and so enjoys dressing up in the proper social costume and taking part in the elaborate social ritual, which is his introduction to theatre (many of the parties are frequented, or held by, his theatrical friends the Tribes). Nina has learned enough of the dramatic art from Chester and her son to be capable also of enjoying the social drama.

Nina reverts though to her pastoral self, and when she runs away from Chester the first time (with no intention of marrying

Jim yet), she goes to the family farm of Buckfield, and she is clearly shucking off the residue of London society:

> But I thought that the relaxation of Buckfield was not so much in the climate as the 'atmosphere' of the place itself. It was quite true that after only one night at Buckfield I felt relaxed, but it was not so much in my flesh (though I slept there so deeply that it was like passing out of the world altogether for hours on end) as in my whole self. Something tense in me seemed to dissolve away in that sleep, so that my mind, when I waked up, was not, as in London, at once concentrated to meet some 'crisis'; it seemed to have spread itself abroad all through the house and yards, even the gardens and fields, the lake (full of weeds and mud) and the local sky. For one thought of Buckfield as having its own sky. . . .[43]

There is a life-renewing vitality in the countryside which speaks to the essential innerness of the individual. Jim at times seems to embody this secret power; when he wins the yacht race by means of a tricky shortcut, Nina tells us that it was 'as if there were a private sun inside him throwing out its secret rays and making that kind of special energy inside one which obliges southern people to dance in the streets.'[44] Freed from the artificial constraints of the man-made forms and conventions of 'society' the soul expands and is refreshed; Buckfield, the pastoral countryside, is another Eden. Although Nature is an obvious source of restorative energy, it also encourages a dangerous relaxation and expansiveness of the ego. The mood requires the absence of other active wills, and although Nina is vaguely aware of Bob who has to work 'twelve hours a day to keep the place "going" ', she is willing to see others reduced to service so that her romantic expansiveness will be uninterrupted. Ultimately the reality of the external world fades:

> all seemed to be going on inside my feeling as if my lazy mind, in relaxing, had become much larger and aware of quite a different kind of life, a life, too, in which it was much more delightful and much 'easier' to live.[45]

Chester's doctor, Connell, comes on the scene to reveal just how illusory this escape is and Nina must return lest Chester initiate some retaliation against Jim through his department. Cary suggests that while the secret world, the romantic world in which the self knows no bounds, is essential for a full sense of interiority to develop, there must be also a recognition of the demands of other wills for a similar free expansion, and this means that politics is the art of survival and the art of life. Politics, however, as we shall see, is effectively human only when it is a realised symbol of an intuition of the natural energy that Nina knows so well how to tap.

Buckfield, like Palm Cottage has the magic of life, and the insubstantiality of a fairy tale. Palm Cottage, as we have seen, is a sort of half-way house between moor and civilisation, but it is more exotic than a mere compromise between the two extremes, 'it was like something from a thousand miles away, from the south of France or Italy in Spring.'[46] Nina remembers it 'as sparkling in all its walls and windows', and the mists of rain were like 'a liquid light poured out of the sky and blowing about as it fell'. The sense of brightness, expansiveness and distance is called up again when Jim and Nina meet early on, after Nina's marriage to Chester, and recall their childhood:

> And such was the effect of our surroundings, of the glittering atmosphere through which we slipped like dream royalties in Hans Andersen, among a noise like fountains, of the immense calm sky all round us, the fields brought down to the size and brightness of velvet rags heaped in a workbasket, and the villages, even the town of Ferryport, reduced to quaint models such as one might see in some millionaire's nursery, that such alarming remarks came to me without the least shock. It was as if they had been rendered harmless, on the way through this beautiful transparent air full of contemplation as lucid as itself (though, of course, it was my contemplation), so that Jim and I and our private passions seemed also far off, comprehensible, and therefore easily dealt with.[47]

Behind the beauty of the fairy tale lies a desire for magical power, the ability to reduce all the rest of the world to one's power. The impulse to see life as a romantic fairy tale which politics and publicity can only destroy or vilify, has in it its own source of dehumanisation, even more dangerous ultimately than the power of politics to corrupt the pure soul. For Nina in her princess mood, the villages and towns filled with real other personalities become nothing more than 'velvet rags heaped in a workbasket'. There is no danger, perhaps, in a merely aesthetic response to life, but the materialisation of people, and the reduction of them to quaint models, is acceptable, if ever, only so long as one has an ethical use for the 'workbasket'.

When Nina, for her purposes of private fiction, indulges her wish to roll the world up into a ball, she does so only to enjoy its beauty the more, even though she trivialises it in the process. It becomes a toy for her pleasure. As a child she was fond of a toy kept by her aunt Slapton in a small drawer with darning things. It was one of the 'glass balls in which, if you turned the thing upside down and back again, a little snowstorm, marvellously real with slow drifting silent flakes, fell upon three minute persons coming away from a grey church, extremely perpendicular, with a castellated tower. . . .'[48] Nina is fascinated by 'the realness and the smallness of this world which I could hold in one hand'. What Nina is doing, as a child, is indulging in a fiction, and it would seem that the point of the passage is that to impose one's private fiction on the world is to turn it upside down. If Nina were to hold the world in one hand, we may feel that she would treasure it. If it were Jim Latter, however, who was holding it, we might fear that if the snow did not fall quite correctly, or if the figures in the scene did not hop on order, then he would close his fist on the fragile ball or else dash it to the floor. Jim's crime is that he ultimately yields, under considerable pressure admittedly, to the temptation to punish the contemptible world – at least, some of the creatures in it – because it does not live up to some private fiction of it that he has but cannot convincingly or persuasively articulate.

Characteristically, Chester takes the romance out of even a fairy tale. He makes of his son Tom's, aged six, bedtime story an occasion for education (or propaganda):

> And it seemed to me now that Chester used his cleverness with Tom to give the child political ideas. The giant in Jack the Giant Killer was always a wicked Tory and the wolf in Red Riding Hood had a face just like Joe Chamberlain. Of course, Chester seemed to do this as a joke.[49]

Nina says that her greatest fear over Chester's manipulation of

the fairy stories was that her son would become a 'party man':
'I knew, of course, that there must be parties and fighting between parties, and I suppose propaganda is better than
murder, but I was horrified by the idea of turning a child into a
partisan.'[50] Her fears prove to be unfounded and Tom turns out
to be nothing more than a fairly talented nightclub revue artist.
Chester's corruption of the fairy tale would offend those who
find in such tales a mysterious and ineffable beauty, or those
others who find there psychological complexities and arche-
typal symbols. At least Chester knows the difference between
fiction and reality. He would sooner debase the fiction into
propaganda, than try to run the state by murder because
life is not adequate to his fiction.

Of course, Chester is capable of making his own fictions
('lies' is what Nina and Jim call them) in the political field. He
knows how to keep secrets when it is 'politic' to do so, and he
knows how to throw up a smokescreen of confusion and misre-
presentation. Nina is highly ironic at Chester's equivocation
about his shares in Banks Rams, agreeing that for him to have
told the whole truth might have produced 'a *great injustice*, that
is, the ruin of Chester's career'. Her emphasis makes it clear
that she *is* being ironic here and is not stupidly praising everything that Chester does. But she cannot escape admitting that,
although she does not like what he has done, he does have an
acceptable motive, politically speaking. For, 'anyone knows
that the noblest men have thought it right to be careful of how
much they tell. Nobody, for instance, would say to a country at
a critical moment, "You have no army and no proper
defences", because it might stop it trying to defend itself.'[51]
The example she uses is a more convincing one than Cary's in
the preface. He is speaking of Cripps and the proposal to
devalue:

> Technically speaking he did not tell a lie, but this is not the
> point, the point is that he had to deceive. Of course any
> mother will lie to a nervous child about the doctor or the
> dentist. She will say that a dangerous painful operation will
> prove a trifle, that the dentist won't hurt. She has to do so for
> the child's good.[52]

There is a suggestion here that politicians have the same relationship to and rights over the populace, as parents over children, and the implicit patronisation is not in the best spirit of democracy. The principle of lying as a sometime necessity is nevertheless clearly made. What makes Chester's fictions, his lies, ultimately harmless and non-violent, is his public accountability. Chester has already committed himself to the workings of a democratic political system. The system is not ideal since it permits, even on occasion encourages lying and deceit. Democratic politics protects against the great lie, the destructive megalomaniacal lie of the despot, because its acts are all finally public and open to rejection by the people. Some lies are permitted in the system, because they grease the wheels, but the whole machine is a necessity working for a desirable end, and government itself cannot become the hallucination or private fantasy of any one man.

This question of how much one can or need tell, is a central and recurring one in *Prisoner of Grace*, and it complements the pastoral-city, romantic-classic themes we have already considered. The pastoral and the romantic are also secret and private; they are destroyed by publicity and civilisation. Secret retreats, like the telling of less than all the truth, are life-reinforcing so long as they do not become all-engrossing. Fictions are acceptable so long as they retain a clear and useful relationship to life. Secrecy becomes dangerous when it becomes uncommunicativeness, or incommunicability. In politics secrecy is permissible because there is a real and pragmatic limitation to the effect of 'lies'. It is a different matter in interpersonal relations. There is a politics of the family, Nina discovers, and although it includes 'managing' people, it does not permit secret arrangements between factions. Her son Tom persuades Nina not to tell Chester that they have been frequenting the Tribe's 'circle':

> And this private enjoyment of ours, each visit to the Tribes and their "artistic" circle, was like a conspiracy.[53]

This promise is followed by the necessity of keeping another secret, that Tom is engaged to one of the Tribe girls. This strange deceit within the family leads to a scene when Chester discovers the truth. Chester had been thought incapable of affection for his family, but Nina had 'forgotten again that under all his performances and maxims Chester's love for me was real. It was a true thing that he could not help. So my "deceit" had made a deep wound – he never forgot it.'⁵⁴

Since Nina is, in a sense, a mediator, it is appropriate that her novel should offer a balance of two possibilities; that it should have a theme which is apparently inconclusive in its duality. If secrecy, or the meaning of secrecy and privacy is one of the central subjects of the first novel, then it might seem that all one can conclude is that secrecy can be either a creative resource, or a destructive one. Nina exists at the centre, between her own deep need for introspection and privacy (which she seems to share with Jim) and Chester's public-official personality. The secret, the private, the pastoral and the romantic are a source of renewal, as we see when Nina runs to Buckfield. Equally, though, this secret world encourages a narcissistic ego-centricity, or even more an ego-expansiveness which envelops all of the natural world to the exclusion of the reality of other human beings. The penchant to secrecy can lead to crime as the minor incident of Nina's stealing of the glass-ball indicates. The refreshing of the ego leads to the trivialising of the world full of people. To the extent that this source of refreshment depends on being 'out of the world' it is a little like death, and when Nina visits Buckfield a part of her does seem to die through her deep and prolonged sleep. In Jim, as we see in the final novel, the private vision, even though it is perhaps based on ideals, becomes incommunicable and ultimately murderous.

Rather than being simply 'about' politics, or about the impossibility of judging, the trilogy is also about the effects on life of various personality orientations. Jim's is ideal but destructive. Chester's is corrupting, perhaps, but does it contribute to life in anyway other than by refraining from physical violence? Obviously Chester makes some public contribution in his life but the question that Cary insists that we ask of Chester is, does his personality type offer a richer life to the individual, does his pragmatic, public self in any way enrich the inner man? Nina says that by opposing her romantic sense of life Chester has helped her to mature, even though life with him is full of crises, struggles and battles. It is on Aunt Latter though, that we can see the most apparent effect of Chester's presence.

At first dead-set against him, she eventually comes around, having sensed with her keen nose for political talent an exciting possibility in Chester. Chester uses her to his advantage, particularly as an overseer for Nina. Aunt Latter is then dismissed, apparently at Chester's whim. She becomes, again 'apparently', an implacable enemy of his, until he makes an obviously artificial attempt at reconciliation (to enlist her political help), and she surprises Nina with her immediate volte-face. She aids Chester in his attempt to move in on Jim and Nina at Palm Cottage, near the end of the novel.

> Aunt Latter, too, would never have agreed to putting Chester out. Indeed, his arrival had had an extraordinary effect on her. She had stopped drinking and spent all day with her files. And though no one paid any attention to her notes (which were hopelessly beside the point), composing them (what she called her dispatches) made her forget her grievances against us all.[55]

Chester brings Aunt Latter out of her private bitterness against the world, expressed in part in her incipient alcoholism, and (even though the result may not be impressive) she begins once again to work in the world. She is composing a book about Chester which, Nina says, will perhaps be the most damaging of all, so that the effect of Chester's personality is not limited to making people work for his own gain; he seems to offer a stimulus to life in general.

This stimulus results from the fact that he is a person who can *do things*, he knows how to make changes and use power, and power is something people will live and work for. The effect on Aunt Latter is an 'unexpected refreshment':

> She was able to feel that she was once more among the people of 'character' who did things – the 'strong souls' who take upon themselves the responsibility (and the guilt) of managing the world.[56]

There are times, even with an untrustworthy first-person narrative, that one feels – and there is certainly no more evidence in this case than one's intuition or sense of the way the language of the text rings in the mind – that the author speaks through his narrator, and surely this is one of those places in which Cary makes his attitude to Chester abundantly clear: he takes upon himself the responsibility and the guilt of the necessary job of managing the world. If there is a loss of personal integrity or honour, or more precisely a loss of 'good report' since reputation counts as much as fact in the world of politics, then Cary indicates that such a loss is a desirable sacrificial offering that the individual should be willing to make in order to take his place in the ranks. The balance between privacy and public life that *Prisoner of Grace* offers is after all only apparent, there is a slight weighting of the scales in Chester's favour.

Nina herself feels the same sense of refreshment that she describes Aunt Latter as experiencing. Chester makes a speech, in his thin and cracking old voice and in a mimicry of his former platform manner, that in its rhetoric is an example of the type of political oratory common in North America (for instance, John Kennedy's inaugural address, or Martin Luther King's 'I have a dream' speech), mixing convincing idealism with slightly overblown language:

> I cannot breathe that stifling air of the prison-house; I must see sky even if it be but a rag between the storm-clouds; I must follow that gleam. Let it be a phantom as they say – a dream – I must pursue. I can no other; for me there is no life but in freedom.[57]

Although she feels that this speech is as ridiculous as 'Jim's notions of honour', Nina is stirred:

> it brought back to me a confused feeling of excitement, wave on wave; not perhaps that which I felt years before at that meeting, but a quite new one. I was recalling not only the old thrill of Chester's voice . . . but something that belonged to the time, to my life with Chester; that started up in me like a spring in dry ground.[58]

Chester's civic stance, his political personality, can still reach to and draw on more primitive roots which the natural imagery, 'wave on wave', 'like a spring in dry ground' suggests. Chester's public self is not made out of a denial of a rich and free inner life. The public role which seems to deny the mystery and secrecy of individuality, is in fact the most economical, and most conserving and life-enriching mode of expressing that inner life. The mask of the man of the *polis* is the only effective mimesis, the only way of enacting with the minimum betrayal through transformation, of that vital sense of wild and free interiority.

If life in society looks like imprisonment, that is mere illusion which will disappear with a closer and more demanding look, which Cary offers us. The ego, if it satisfies only itself, will expand without limits and, tyrannically, transfigure the rest of the world. It also risks the fate of Narcissus. If the ego is put into action, however, if one trusts in public life to represent and 'mime' the inner self, then paradoxically it is as if one discovers a new inner 'spring in dry ground'. The apparent prison is the only way to a freer life for all. Chester, like Nina, is also a prisoner of grace; that is, a prisoner of freedom.

The recurrent metaphor associated with Chester throughout the trilogy is that of the drama. On the hustings, and in private life, he is an 'actor', he plays a part, plays a role, is artificial. In conversation with him Nina wonders 'Is he going to strike some attitude: Is this going to be another Lilmouth drama?'[59] Nina notices that after the shares scandal 'Chester had become a little more dramatic, more excitable; even in private life he seemed sometimes to be "acting himself".'[60] When Chester tries to impress someone he is 'putting on one of his special performances'.[61] Shortly after his marriage to Nina, Chester goes out of his way to overcome the awkward situation of welcoming Jim to his house:

> The two men, I thought, might have been long-lost brothers in some melodrama. But if I was inclined to see something comic in this dramatic meeting, it was only, I think, for the same reason that I had once been inclined to laugh at Chester's dramatic prayers; because I did not want to be carried away and reformed.[62]

True to Chester's nature, his son Tom takes up the theatre, particularly of the Ibsen and Strindberg type: 'Tom began a long speech about realism and honesty and getting down to earth and technique and originality. ...'[63] Eventually he becomes a moderately successful revue comedian, his hit act being a take-off of a blustering politician which everyone, except Tom, recognises as Chester. Nina sees it at once:

But even before he began to speak I saw that he was mimicking Chester – his first gesture, raising his hand to stop the
applause was purely Chester's – and when he began to speak
it was one of Chester's speeches.[64]

The imitation is so close that 'he seemed not just to be imitating
Chester but to *be* Chester'.[65] Of course, Tom cannot admit that
his originality and genius owe anything to anyone other than
himself. He believes that by taking up 'art' he is moving as far
away from his father's sphere of activity as possible, but instead
he simply reveals that the basis of Chester's success and influence is his artistry. Although his motive is understandable, in
refusing to see his father behind his imitation Tom is deluding
himself with the belief that artistic creation is creation *ex nihilo*.
Also, of course, he has a latent respect for his father and would
regard any mimicry of the great man as 'a piece of dirt'.[66]

Tom is compromised in a raid on his London club and after a
period in clubs in Germany where he 'began to drug as well as
to drink', and where 'he was a failure as a mimic', Tom commits suicide. What he has failed to see, and it is one of the more
important points made in the first book, is that successful imitation must of necessity have a solid relation to its 'ground', that a
convincing image is an image *of* something, it is based on experience. The implication of this is that Chester, although he is
apparently the master deceiver because of his dramatic artistry
in politics, must have some solid ground of 'true' experience
and conviction which makes his *mimesis* so effective. As Nina
remembers, 'under all his performances and maxims Chester's
love for me was real.'[67] So under the apparent deceit and betrayal of the drama of public life, lies the irrevocable truth of
vital individual, inner life and conviction.

The metaphor of drama which is established to characterise
Chester in *Prisoner of Grace* is continued and further explored in
Chester's own novel *Except the Lord*. The relation of politics to
private life is explored with reference to another family, that of
Chester's father and his brothers and sisters. In this context,
and in the context of Chester's early labour union agitations,
the theme of privacy and secrecy is also carried on. Chester is
confronted for the first time with 'a fundamental question in
politics': 'when and where is one justified in telling a flat lie?'

This concern is echoed in the private world by Georgina's (Chester's sister) decision to lie to her father about the suggestion that the grocer 'G' has been molesting her. Her lie changes her relationship with her father and he 'became to her a person who, like ourselves, sometimes needed to be handled, managed, who could not be trusted to know his own advantage.'[68] In this very close community of the family, Chester begins to learn about politics. What it takes him longer to learn, is that Georgina's subterfuge is undertaken out of a sense of duty to the family. If she admits that 'G' has been pressing his attentions on her, her father will take her out of the shop and the family will lose the candles necessary for Richard's studies, as well as the salary she can earn. So, out of a sense of duty she can lie. Chester undertakes to use some of the same techniques of secrecy and plotting in his first political activity and it ends disastrously partly because he has not yet discovered the fullness of commitment to duty exemplified by Georgina, which puts a necessary limit to equivocation. His novel is the story of how he came to realise the role played in his life by his sister: 'I had come at last and my heart was beating again strongly to a heart that could not know despair because it forgot itself in the duty of its love.'[69]

Chester's narrative does not deal with the same period of time covered by either Nina's or Jim's stories, and so it can offer no clarification of specific issues raised in either of the other two novels. This apparent failure to have Chester refer to relevant events discussed by Nina is not Cary's love of mystification indulging itself. What Cary seems willing to allow himself is a little of 'that blindness to common justice between man and man which is not unusual among saints, who see all men as sunk so deep in obligation to God that their various merits are as corn to the height of the sky.'[70] What matters ultimately is the fullness and continuity of life, and not the sorting out of minor grievances among individuals. So the second novel does not try, advisedly, to add further evidence to that given by Nina. Instead it independently develops its themes which contribute to the mosaic of coherent meaning which emerges from the trilogy as a whole.

From the very complex 'tissue of interests' that is his early life in Shagbrook, Chester learns as a child that politics properly understood is the art of human relationships. Only as it moves further away from its ground in the family and the organic community does politics become bureaucracy. While it takes Nina much of her life to discover that she must be conscious and responsible for her words and deeds, Chester discovers it as a child:

> The rare visitor driving through towards the high tors might think Shagbrook a mean collection of cottages scattered on a hillside, but he would be very wrong – it was, a highly complex and delicate balance of personal relations between families and persons, who were obliged to live so close together that the whole of everyone's actions, and almost his thoughts, was open to inspection by all the rest. There was no such thing as privacy, for though a general discretion caused every prudent person to be careful of what he said, in public, each had intimates to which all was disclosed. Thus everything was known, all scandals circulated continually beneath the smooth surface of mutual caution.[71]

The last two sentences indicate that even one's intimates feel it a public duty to reveal confidential disclosures. What is commendable about such a community is the interest that individuals take in each other. There is a genuine wish to know, and to admit the reality of other people, with the result that there is no room for lazy expansive subjectivity such as Nina's. Which is, of course, the community's deficiency: it does not allow for privacy, or creative isolation and individuality. And yet Chester offers such a community as an ideal, as at least a viable and realistic social system operating on a 'reciprocity of obligation and reprisal, a balance of powers in which true charity and fellow-feeling . . . mingled with what I must call real politics, a system established over years of trial and error.' Whereas Nina discovers with a measure of horror that politics invades family life, Chester reveals that it is in the family that *realpolitik* finds both its origin and apotheosis.

The political system of a society cannot, however, be nothing more than the family of the small community writ large. A fully civilised body politic needs complete individuals who choose membership freely. Chester goes through a necessary, even if painful and unpleasant, period of subjective development, a period of separation and isolation. This period of fascination with his own inner self leads ultimately to the wronging of his sister Georgina. At about the age of twelve he had not yet learned the inward look: 'Children of that age are not used to introspection, indeed, not capable of it. All their energies and senses are turned outwards.'[72] This naive unselfconsciousness must be relinquished, however, so that he can become aware of 'the disease at the true centre of my being'. In the innocence of childhood he learns that one must be careful in one's choice of words; this innocent truth must be tried in the full experience of love and life, however, before it can take on the significant meaning that Nina gives it at the end of her narrative. So too the innocent unselfconsciousness of the child must be refined in the fires of experience. Self-knowledge entails a time of inward-looking, to be followed by a newer 'organiz'd innocence' in which the senses are once again turned outwards, but from a known centre.*

Led by Dolling and Lanza the orator, and by his experience of the power of drama at the Lilmouth fair, Chester becomes enamoured of the power of words. At the same time he becomes deeply introspective and secretive, not telling his family that he pays regular visits to Dolling. In part at least, this new secrecy is the result of the growth of an 'inner life':

> When and why does the love of solitude and secrecy come upon the child – the need to be alone? I was much alone at this time – I had lost Richard and my private agonies were not for Georgina. Alone I brooded and tortured myself. Yet I sought loneliness and secrecy not only to practise my oratory, but simply to brood. It seemed that some instinct drove me to be alone with my thoughts even though they were unhappy ones.[73]

Chester later describes this attitude as being 'not so much self-centred as astonished by the drama of my own soul.'[74] The result of this astonishment at inner richness is that he fails to

---

* The terms 'innocence', 'experience' and 'organiz'd innocence' are used with reference to Blake, whose influence on Cary is obvious in *The Horse's Mouth*. Chester traces the 'journey from innocence through the necessary anguish caused by experience, to that "re-organized innocence" which is liberty and freedom.' See Margaret Rudd, *Organiz'd Innocence* (London, 1956), p. 19.

understand 'the crisis of another's life, a crisis without comparison, more tragic, more peremptory, than my own, it was because my mind was so wholly preoccupied with its own
extraordinary adventures that all else seemed commonplace
and ordinary.'[75] The other life he refers to is Georgina's. Georgina has asked Chester for advice on Fred Coyte's proposal to
her. She does not love the man and does not wish to marry him,
but she is being swayed by her sense of her family's need of the
security he can offer. In retrospect Chester is able to show guilt
at his complicity in her decision. His complicity is the result of
omission rather than commission. The failure to act, the failure
to take conscious responsibility is once again signalled by the
refusal (or inability) to speak. Chester questions his younger
self:

> Did he perceive the enormous advantage to himself, to his
> own secret ambition, of a settled income, of leisure to read, to
> think, to study, even to go to university?
>   All I know is that I did not speak. I remained, as it were, in
> a dream, pretending even to myself that the girl was uttering
> merely a fantasy which was not worthy of my serious
> attention.[76]

A period of secrecy is necessary to the growth of the soul, but
Cary, and Chester, make it clear what the cost is in human
injustice of this individual growth. The inner dream makes responsible action impossible.

Equally necessary, and equally costly, is Chester's secret organisation of a union of farm labourers. Secrecy is necessary because of the obvious threat of retaliation by landlords against
the men. Chester's idea is one that many would approve of;
trying to better the lot of the oppressed is commendable. Where
he errs is not perhaps in the secrecy of his undertaking so much
as in its privacy; he is not equipped to handle the job alone. He
suffers the 'anxiety of those pledged to some secret enterprise'
when it is discovered that there is a traitor at work 'selling me
and the rest of his comrades'.[77] The men who have joined the
union are turned out of their jobs and under the pressure of
their crushing poverty, three of them seek vengeance on Chester, who narrowly escapes their rage with only a cut head.

The private committee-room plotting he engages in with

Pring has a slightly wider base of public accountability, but the secret manoeuvres during the strike lead to even more violence, with professional thugs being brought in to beat up a few of the uncertain strikers as examples. Chester's secret letter to the committee reveals the coarseness of his sensibility at the time:

> The women were obviously much alarmed in case I should recognise them – there is no doubt that the new policy has had all the success we anticipated in bringing the scabs into line, B and L and party deserve high praise for the efficient manner in which the assignment was carried out. The whole operation took less than six minutes and the police had no chance of interference. The last of our men had been withdrawn from the action five minutes before the first copper arrived. And it is noticeable that he received no information except from one young girl, daughter of the man dealt with.[78]

This passage is a perfect example of the effect of corrupt politics on language that Orwell drew attention to in 'Politics and the English Language'. That Chester himself chooses to reveal this document is evidence of the maturity he later achieves, and of his growth in moral perception. As a budding political activist Chester has not learned how to act responsibly. He acts from mere 'policy' without realising that political actions and concepts must be related to a ground, an intuition: 'What is the purpose of all this – that he who founds argument and policy upon our intuition of human goodness will not be disappointed.'[79] Chester's narrative demonstrates the extent to which he strayed from this intuition of human goodness by straying from the family. One example of the human goodness and self-sacrifice with which he re-establishes contact is offered by his sister Georgina who rescues him from the street when he has been thrown out by Pring.

Chester uses the image of a building and its foundation to express what went wrong with his first attempt at political activism. He recalls how a bawdy house once fell down and its 'dirty squalor' was exposed to the afternoon sun: 'So I myself was now a ruin with all my secret places laid open, and I was astonished at their mean appearance.'[80] This echoes the phrase from one of his father's favourite psalms which provides the title of the novel: Except the Lord build the house, their labour is but lost that build it. For Chester this means 'that unless he aim at the life of the soul then all his achievement will be a gaol or a mad-house, self-hatred, corruption and despair.'[81] This realisation heralds his return to religion and his ten years as an evangelical preacher, during which time he rediscovers the meaning of the religious experiences induced by his father. So he moves from involvement in an organic community, to subjective individuality, to a concern with radical politics, to the nurturing of the life of the soul and ultimately returns again to the political scene where he will spend his life. For Chester, the relation between politics and self must finally be a mimetic one. The political system, and individual political actions, must be symbols, or images, of the soul. As Aristotle says, mimesis is the imitation of an *action*; so politics at its best is the *enactment* of the potentialities of the soul, and it is no surprise to find Chester referring to the 'conscience of a nation, the active soul of a people'.[82] It is only when the self is conceived of as an agent – or more specifically, as a dramatic agent – rather than as a 'patient' or passive, subjective consciousness, that Unity of Being can be achieved and solipsism overcome.

It is at Lilmouth Fair that Chester is overwhelmed by a cheap melodramatic production; with the art of the drama, the art of life. This scene is probably the most important one in the whole trilogy for an understanding of the work, and deserves some emphasis. The play is 'Maria Marten' a melodrama based on the infamous murder in the Red Barn. For Chester this drama has a meaning that pervades life. He describes it in terms that are usually reserved for the first experience of love, or sex: 'a man's first experience in the theatre opens a new world to him'.[83] The art of the theatre comes to stand for the art necessary for civilised life:

> Is there not an element of drama still not only in our churches, but in the ritual of government? You may be sure that what has survived for centuries in spite of criticism has powerful motives for existence. Believe me, art, and especially the drama, above all the popular drama, has a fearful power and responsibility in the world – it acts directly upon the very centres of feeling and passion.[84]

The acting, the action, in itself and apart from the moral

import of the play – its theme of the 'cruellest kind of wrong inflicted by the rich upon the poor' has an obvious effect on his social beliefs – is of fundamental importance to Chester. Even before entering the tent he mistakenly thinks he has had his first glimpse of actors, 'my first wild notion, those are actors, gave me a sense as if the blood had run out of my heart.' The barker himself is a powerful figure:

> The man's face was crimson and dripping with sweat. His shirt was grey with moisture, his voice was that hoarse grating screech which makes one wonder how long a throat can survive, but every inch of his body was in action. Sometimes he banged on a great drum, then he would blow a post-horn, and with great sweeps of both arms he would introduce to us the actors.[85]

When he finally sees the real 'actors', the 'mysterious passion which had seized upon me ten days before, to see an actor, was not disappointed. . . .' The mature man speculates on what it could be that so moved him:

> What is it in the actor, the stage, that casts so powerful a spell on the young imagination? I still feel in my old nerves the vehement tremor of that night. Is it that impersonation by itself has some secret and immemorial power over the growing spirit – some primitive urge older perhaps than humanity itself?[86]

It is not the play itself, so much as the technique: the actor, the stage, that is important. It is acting, being in action, and 'impersonation' that are important. There is more than an echo here of Aristotle on 'imitation'. There is also perhaps a subdued metaphysical speculation on the idea that man is made in God's image; the urge is older than humanity since God himself was the original of mimetic artists.

This impulse to imitation explains Chester's adopting of the ideas and attitudes of Lanza, Dolling and Pring. However, mere mimicking is not mimesis. One is not meant to copy others, but to enact or dramatise oneself: by means of public action to enact, mime or present an image of one's deepest soul. Since the image of a thing is not the same as the thing itself, and yet there must be a necessary relationship between image and object, this mimetic relationship between the private self and the public self guarantees both personal integrity and public responsibility. It also reminds us of the creative possibilities of 'role-playing' in society. Chester is overwhelmed by the 'astonishing power' of the actor, and yet it is quite plain that this power can exist only in the 'role' that defines it. Similarly, Chester – who does not himself aspire to be a stage actor, although his son Tom does – surrenders himself to a 'vision of glory, of power, by means of the spoken word'.[87] The subjective self attains its power, and its completion, by means of choosing a system of signs which must have public currency before they have any power or significance. It is in language, in speech, and in mimesis that subjective impulse becomes a public and creative actuality.

The power of language, although it offers transcendence, does not guarantee truthfulness and Chester is aware of the possibility of evil in the art, as his reflections on the villain Corder in 'Maria Marten' indicate. It is from his father that he learns his first lesson about the necessary relation of the 'filthy rags of speech' to an underlying ground to all human experience. He waits on the mountain top with his father's faithful for the coming of the end (in a scene that would gladden Frank Kermode)* and realises in the repeated failure of human calculation, the inadequacy of formulated religious beliefs; and yet, the event does prove to be a revelation, the meaning of which Chester will gradually realise during the course of his life:

> It is not for nothing that the psalmist has said, 'I will lift up mine eyes unto the hills from whence cometh my help.' No doubt God is in all things. It is His life which maintains the physical world, as the soul of man carries his body for a vesture. But those who choose the mountain tops for that intuition of the numinous in us, in which it seems that we break through the boundaries of the word into the very centre of the Divine Mind, are not deceived. For the word and the works of man, however necessary to his worldly life, hide from his daily imagination the primitive grandeur of creation.[88]

Chester later repeats the image of 'vesture' when he laments: 'It

---

* See *The Sense of An Ending* (New York, 1967), in which similar apocalyptic scenes are discussed as the basis of fictions.

might have been said of me with awful truth that my webs had not become garments, nor did my works cover me.'[89] On the mountain top was planted the germ of his later realisation that his father's calculations are after all only man-made illusions, mere 'fictions of the end', but that the justification of the illusion is its power to evoke the numinous reality of experience.

The skilful use of the power of words is the resource of the father of lies in Milton's *Paradise Lost*. Father Nimmo tried to draw out the moral for his children:

> When he would read Milton to us he would warn us against the charm of that devil, pointing out that the conflict in that great poem is between a real good and an evil so terrible that it could scarcely be conceived – the absolute government of cruel and lustful egotism – the utter destruction of the very idea of liberty, of love and truth. How, he asked, should we like such a world? I agreed with my father – but Satan still carried an irresistible appeal.[90]

In Cary's world it is found to be better to give oneself over to the artistic power, to the attraction of mimesis and language, than to withdraw into secret incommunicativeness and wait for, or force, the world to become the shape of one's egotistic fantasy. Art may entail lies, but it is *for* life, while the renunciation of art is a capitulation to Death: that is perhaps the central meaning embodied in Cary's trilogy. Although Chester responds to rhetorical skill, he does learn the other lesson from his father (discussed above) which counteracts any major evil that might arise from speech.

In fact, it is Jim Latter who is most likely to be associated with the lustful desire for tyrannical government that comes from the devil. Chester's response to the villain of 'Maria Marten' is:

> Is it fanciful in me to discover in Corder, the cut-throat of a booth drama, some tincture of the Lucifer who took upon himself all guilt and defied the very lightnings of Heaven?[91]

It is the defiance and courage of Lucifer-Satan that attract Chester, but the epithet 'cut-throat' directs our attention to Jim Latter who does not shoot to run the state, but he does cut his wife's throat. Jim's own account of events, given in *Not Honour*

More, is pervaded with dramatic irony; that is, an irony of which he is not aware. Rather than being supported by an underlying reality, Jim is constantly undermined. There is even an ironical ambiguity, referred to earlier, in the title, which is ostensibly only a reference to the martial ideal expressed in Lovelace's lyric, but which could also be Cary's imperative response to the implicit question: What should one do when Honour leads to the necessity of killing one's beloved? Not Honour more.

Ironically, Jim is forced at last to resort to language to make his position clear. He must, that is to say, put himself in the position of the 'talky boys' in the 'talky-house' (parliament) whom he so much despises. Although he hopes to defend himself, instead, as in a monologue by Browning, he incriminates himself all the more. His use of the language reveals the brutishness of his perceptions, as we saw earlier. It is Chester's skill in language that he most wants to destroy: 'I said, there's only one way out with that kind of crook, to shoot him. He may be as clever and tricky as you like but cleverness won't stop bullets.'[92] His fanatical belief in his own righteousness puts him at odds with the use of language by other men: 'They'll call it murder, but what I'm out for is truth and justice.' He sees himself as 'a bit of truth [with] a gun in its hand'. At times the perversity of his vision of public life can be given forceful expression. Chester has accused him of not understanding the situation:

> 'God damn it,' I said, 'I think of nothing else. Fifty years of it. Since you and your gang set out to pimp for every gimme in the game. And bought your first ponce's pants with Nina's money – and Nina's soul. The situation. A whoreshop for syphilites – everything goes because you'll all get it. And how smart we are at the dirt. You've poisoned everything you touched and it's still working. A living shanker. And you think no one'll notice if you talk big enough. You think you can talk it away. Like a bill in your talky house. Good or bad – talk it out – talk out the loyalty and the truth. Talk out the man who dares to have some faith – some principles.'[93]

Jim is not completely bereft of a curious kind of inventiveness, but since his enemy is 'talk', language, he is the enemy of creativity.* Like Satan he has a lot of energy, and this energy can be attractive; but, like Satan, Jim uses his energy for perverse ends. Jim is a bad artist, as he is a bad actor. As he says to Chester, 'Damn it all . . . we all know the facts. There is no need for play-acting.'⁹⁴ On this occasion as it happens Jim is right about the facts, since the issue is Jim's fathering of Chester's 'son' Tom. In general, though, Cary demonstrates in the trilogy that 'facts' are often so hard to know, and of so little use when they are known (Jim's siring of Tom does not make him any the less Chester's son), that precisely what we all do need is 'play-acting'. Jim, however, turns what should be a living and tense drama with a multiplicity of agents in a unified field of action, into mere melodrama when, like Corder, he resorts to the razor.

There is another point to be noticed about Jim's language: he tends to use animal imagery to describe people. The people who gather around when Jim has attempted to shoot Nimmo in Palm Cottage (the first murder attempt which is abortive) make 'a kind of hissing like a lot of snakes tangled up together and working up to a bite.'⁹⁵ Of Nimmo he says, 'Yes, he's as clever as a monkey.'⁹⁶ When Nina gives up on an attempt to persuade Jim, 'She looked as calm and cool as a waxwork – and I knew she had gone mule as I called it.'⁹⁷ A taxi pulls up and Jim notes, 'Young man like a snake driving.'⁹⁸ Of Chester's secretary Bootham he says, perhaps with some justification, 'I knew him then for just another rat in the sewer and I daresay he felt it.'⁹⁹ The same image is repeated when Jim briefly explains why he had to execute Nina and Chester, because 'I couldn't live like a rat.'¹⁰⁰ Chester and Nina learn how to admit the reality of other human beings, but Jim removes the adjective from Aristotle's 'political animal' and would reduce all mankind to vermin in order to maintain his integrity and his honour.

Occasionally the pettiness of the man will show glaringly through his apology for murder. Chapter 26 begins: 'I'm accused of being suspicious and cranky. Look at the facts as now revealed.' Who but the meanest of 'politicos' would worry

---

* Jack Wolkenfeld, *Joyce Cary: The Developing Style* (N.Y., London, 1968), believes that Jim's language is characterised by an 'absence of metaphor and meaningful rhythm' while displaying an agressive quality of 'force and full commitment'. I would insist, however, that Jim's language is at times highly metaphorical and his metaphors reveal the corruption of his artistic possibilities.

about defending himself against a charge of crankiness when he has been charged with murder? In fact, Jim begins to behave exactly as he accuses Chester of behaving, as a cranky politico trying to keep his public image clean. As Nina suggests in her narrative, Jim is not only an artist manqué, he is a frustrated politician as well:

> Perhaps Jim has always needed to govern something or somebody and now that he has neither horses nor Lugas he can only rule over me.[101]

She is allowed to repeat the charge in *Not Honour More*:

> 'Do you really hate me so terribly? I'm not really a politico, you know. I'm really nothing. Poor Aunt Latter is turning in her grave to hear me say that, but the Latter half of me never grew up. It's you who are the politico – you take it all so seriously.'[102]

Towards the end of his story, Jim demonstrates the truth of this claim when he starts to reveal the 'melting' of ideas which he has earlier condemned. Having managed to persuade Nina to run away with him (they return to the scene of their childhood picnic, Rockpit), he leaves her alone – she is still recovering from her attempted suicide – to go to defend Maufe. He shows that he can be loyal to his comrades, but in doing so he loses the wife he claims to prize so highly:

> But I daren't leave my wife more than the inside of a day. When the case was coming on and it turned out I'd have to spend a day in London with my lawyer, to see the counsel for the defence, that is, two nights away, she had a weeping fit that frightened me. I'd never seen her cry before. I told her if I had to go away again she must come too. And to hell with the cameramen and the papers. We'd have to get tough to them. We'd have to learn to use them, for if the Maufe case went wrong, we must go for an appeal. And that would mean all the publicity we could find. For in this swindler's world, publicity is king.[103]

The truth about Jim is that he is split in two by his inconsistencies. When he wants something done, he willingly turns to the press for publicity and in the same breath condemns the press despite the fact that the papers may have a role to play in saving his colleague. Similarly, when he is about to kill Chester he says to him, 'You run your show on publicity for the mob and that's what I've got to do. To hit the headlines in a big way. To make an example.'[104] The man of honour sounds like any would-be starlet trying to break into showbiz. By the end of the trilogy Jim has discovered the necessity of being political and public, but it is too late and he has not the necessary human impulse – he has denied it for too long – to be anything other than a bloody despot.

The silence after the final paragraph of Jim's narrative is perhaps the only eloquent and meaningful silence of the second trilogy:

> She knelt down but said she could not pray, she did not think it would help. But would I forgive her, because she had truly loved me.
>
> I said it was for her to forgive me and I finished the thing in one stroke. She fell at once and did not struggle at all.

Many readers must have turned the page to see what the murderer felt after the deed, but those are the last abrupt words of the novel and the absence of any further comment reveals Jim Latter fully. The echoing silence after Nina's fall, after the 'thing' is 'finished', is an expression of what Jim has done, of what he has deprived the world. To satisfy secret and lustful egotism, eloquence itself must die.

What makes Chester's use of speech justifiable is its relation to an underlying numinous reality. What makes Jim incapable of human communicativeness is his denial of God:

> And Nimmo tells you God is love. Nimmo's god. A god that doesn't need to keep his word. A god in the love racket, turning out hot stuff for the papers.[105]

This is the bitterness of a spoiled child who cannot have everything his own way and sounds near to tears because God does not keep his word. Jim's blindness to realities seems at last not so much an active principle of evil as a pathetic immaturity. But the second trilogy reveals that political immaturity, in personal relationships, in the family or in society at large, is as close to evil as one needs to get.

The surprising thing about *Not Honour More* is not that Jim's character is indeterminate and cannot be known by the reader, but that Cary could provide so many obvious indications of just where Jim fails to be human and yet not make him into a cardboard villain. For the novel to be readable and interesting, Jim must not be boring, and so Cary gave him an energy which can charm, just as Milton's Satan has charmed so many readers. Cary's attitude to this charm however, is as clearly expressed as is Milton's. Chester finds a way past the murderous solipsism of Jim in the exercise of the power of language and in a mimetic presentation of self. Human creativity, Cary suggests, can offer us some release from the prison of self, and 'politics' is still a viable sphere of activity for the political animal.*

The vision of the world presented in the trilogy is not a simple nor a comfortable one. Cary does not offer us any way to find the undiluted Good Life. He is too realistic for that. To live is to be in a constant state of tension and crisis, and our only choice is between destructive egoism or creative, limited egoism. The human state is an imperfect imitation of the ideal state. Although Cary offers no guarantee that anything we do will work towards the achievement of a better world, he does suggest that of evils, we are free to choose the lesser. The trilogy, then, does express a coherent and moral meaning. Cary, like Browning and Milton, relied on Art rather than Assertion to make his meaning clear.

It is by means of a consideration of Art, in particular of the dramatic art, that the value of the trilogy is fully revealed. The severest criticism made of Jim Latter is that he is a bad artist (in words) and a bad actor. Cary believes in the artistic act; that is, he believes in the effectiveness of fictions. There is an interesting consistency between the form of his novels and the theme they express. The trilogy is a 'dramatic' presentation of points of

* It should be noted that Nimmo's infamous turnabout, when he goes back on his pacifist principles in order to become Minister of Defense, is not an indication of corruption, or power-hungry lack of character. It is an affirmation that the creative spirit must be willing and able to shuck off institutionalised roles in order to continue to play a vital part in the world. Nimmo's moving from pacifism to direction of the War effort is in the same category as Gulley Jimson's turning from one painting, whether The Fall or The Raising of Lazarus, whether successful or not, completed or not, or destroyed by a town council, in order to pursue a new inspiration and source of creative energy.

view with no apparent interference from the author; there are no authorial assertions. Just as Cary himself trusts the art of making fictions to carry his meaning, so too in the novels the characters who are best able to live as dramatic agents – and create fictions when necessary are most on the side of life. To conceive of the self-as-agent* is the best way to guarantee that the creative energy of the Romantic imagination does not become destructive fantasy. Muriel Spark has a similar theme but she gives it another turn of the screw. Since the dramatic fictions indulged in by some of her characters are at times the source of evil, she logically distrusts her own fictions and takes steps to counteract any dangerous effect they may have by consciously drawing attention to the novelist's art. From this one step, an endless, witty, circle develops: If Muriel Spark's fictions are not to be trusted, then can one trust the criticism in them of the role of fictions in the lives of her characters, and . . .

---

* It is perhaps no accident that the concept of the 'self-as-agent', which comes from Professor MacMurray's book of that name, is appropriate in a discussion of Cary. Professor MacMurray knew Cary in Oxford and he has told me that he used often to take tea with Cary. It may well be that Cary's conversations with MacMurray had an important effect on the development of his own ideas.

4 Cannibals, Okapis and Self-Slaughter in the Novels of Muriel Spark

Hugh MacDiarmid has said that Scotland's contribution to culture can be summed up by the phrase he borrows from Professor G. Gregory Smith, 'Caledonian antisyzygy', and that the individual Scottish character is at its best when it partakes of, and manifests, this antisyzygy. MacDiarmid refers with approval to some of the 'profoundly penetrating phrases' used by Smith to describe Scottish literature and character: 'Almost a zigzag of contradictions; a reflection of the contrasts which the Scot shows at every turn, in his political and ecclesiastical history, in his polemical restlessness, in his adaptability' – 'Varied with a clean contrair spirit' – 'Oxymoron was ever the bravest figure, and we must not forget that disorderly order is order after all.' – 'There is more in the Scottish antithesis of the real and the fantastic than is to be explained by the familiar rules of rhetoric. The sudden jostling of contraries seems to preclude any relationship by literary suggestion. The one invades the other without warning. They are the "polar twins" of the Scottish Muse.'[1] On this account, as we shall see, Muriel Spark is clearly a Scottish and not an English novelist, despite, or because of, the fact that she lives permanently in Rome and has said (perhaps a little too readily adopting a fashionable idiom) that 'It was Edinburgh that bred within me the conditions of exiledom; and what have I been doing since then but moving from exile into exile? It has ceased to be a fate, it has become a calling.' She has also said of Edinburgh that, 'It is a place where I could not hope to be understood.'[2] Such a statement might tempt the critic dwelling in Edinburgh to take up temporary lodgings in Penicuik, or Musselburgh, or even Glasgow, but what is obviously called for is some of that clean and

151

Caledonian 'contrair spirit'.

An antisyzygy is a union of opposites. It is not to be conceived of as a fusion of contraries in which the two lose their identities and become one, but as an existing together of mutual exclusives. The 'new' critics made antisyzygy, in the form of paradox and irony, the centre of their dogma and saw it as the essence of the creative use of language. Muriel Spark's work can be seen to be constantly striving to realise an antisyzygy. When the union of warring opposites is achieved, the work is suffused with wit and comedy. When the union is incomplete, or frustrated for some reason, as in *The Driver's Seat*, the work becomes sombre, bleak, horrifying, tragic.* The nature of the unity after which Mrs Spark is striving will be the subject of this chapter and will be investigated with extensive reference to several of her novels. It might be useful, before such an investigation, to suggest how her preoccupation appears in some of the fiction.

Barbara Vaughan of *The Mandelbaum Gate* struggles to overcome the contradictions of her past, having one parent who is Jewish and one who is Church of England. Herself a convert to Catholicism, she has come on a pilgrimage to the divided city of Jerusalem, and long before the 'Six Day War' crosses from the Israeli to the Jordanian side through the Mandelbaum Gate, which becomes 'hardly a gate at all, but a piece of street between Jerusalem and Jerusalem.' On her spiritual pilgrimage she, and briefly also the diplomat Freddy Hamilton, overcome the limits of mere reason:

> For the first time since her arrival in the Middle East she felt all of a piece; Gentile and Jewess, Vaughan and Aaronson; she had caught some of Freddy's madness, having recognized by his manner in the car, as they careered across Jerusalem, that he had regained some lost or forgotten element in his nature and was now, at last, for some reason, flowering in the full irrational norm of the stock she also derived from: unselfquestioning hierarchists, anarchistic imperialists, bloodsporting zoophiles, sceptical believers – the whole paradoxical lark that had secured, among their bones, the sane life for the dead generations of British Islanders. She had caught a

* Compare her own comments on the book: 'I frightened myself by writing it, but I just had to go on. I gave myself a terrible fright with it. I had to go into hospital to finish it.' 'Keeping It Short,' *The Listener* (27 Sept. 1970), 413.

bit of Freddy's madness and for the first time in this Holy
Land, felt all of a piece, a Gentile Jewess, a private-judging
Catholic, a shy adventuress.[3]

In accepting the contradictions of her life, Barbara Vaughan
achieves a release from 'an unidentified confinement of the soul'
and becomes, as a result, capable of action and adventure. Obviously the pairs of opposites which characterise Barbara
Vaughan have some autobiographical significance for Muriel
Spark, but some readers may feel that the potential interest of
the difficulties of a 'Gentile Jewess' or the worries of a private-judging Catholic is cripplingly slight. The general subject,
however, which these examples suggest, is a comprehensive
and important one. It is, once again, Unity of Being. The theme
of the Unity of Being which can arise from the union of
mutually exclusive opposites, freedom and authority, may be a
Catholic one, but it is also a catholic one.

Interestingly enough, Barbara Vaughan responds to Catholicism not because of her own sacramental nature, or out of fear
of death, or out of a mere need to conform, but for a much less
likely motive, respect for its 'moral philosophy':

> To Barbara, one of the first attractions of her religion's moral
> philosophy had been its recognition of the helpless complex-
> ity of motives that prompted an action, and its consequent
> emphasis on actual words, thoughts and deeds; there was
> seldom one motive only in the grown person; the main thing
> was that motives should harmonize.[4]

There is perhaps a frustrating confusion here between the
'helpless complexity of motives' and the necessity that these
motives harmonise; and there is certainly a self-satisfied smug-
ness to the mind which will gloss over the difficulties of such a
'philosophy'. Despite the inadequacy of Barbara's philosophical stance, however, one can see in this passage Muriel
Spark's characteristic preference for the visible, the actual and
active surface as opposed to the unseen internal about which
one can only speculate, as Eliot does in 'Burnt Norton':

> What might have been is an abstraction
> Remaining a perpetual possibility
> Only in a world of speculation.

What might have been and what has been
Point to one end, which is always present.
Footfalls echo in the memory
Down the passage which we did not take
Towards the door we never opened
Into the rose-garden.

What matters for Barbara Vaughan is what is actualised, what is done, and the possibilities of rose-gardens are just not interesting. She refuses to believe that 'people should tear themselves to bits about their motives'[5] and in this sentiment echoes January Marlow from the earlier novel *Robinson*: 'I see no call to tear myself to bits over motives. They are never simple.'[6] This turning from the internal to the external is characteristic of much post-Modern literature; and the turn is made in the attempt to recreate a balance lost as a result of the Romantic over-valuing of subjective 'feeling' and interiority.

One other brief passage, this time from a short story 'Bang, Bang, You're Dead', illustrates in another way the union of opposites that Muriel Spark envisions, and takes us closer to the general subject of her best work. The story itself is too complicated to summarise briefly, but it concerns a case of murder arising out of confusion of identity and an inability to face the Truth. Sybil, the central character, is quite able to face reality, about herself as well as about others, and she proves ultimately capable of mastering the arts of life. In her youth she pursued obsessively the delights and resources of 'a room of one's own'. With maturity she learns to overcome this isolation (which is more like a 'retreat' than 'alienation') and to move into a world of others:

> She rented a house, sharing it with a girl whose husband was fighting in the north. She was twenty-two. To safeguard her privacy absolutely, she had a plywood partition put up in the sitting-room, for it was another ten years before she had *learnt those arts of leading a double life* and listening to people ambiguously, which enabled her to mix without losing identity, and to listen without boredom.[7]

The two aspects of the 'double life' are, on the one hand,

absolute privacy – and absolute freedom in so far as this is
conceivable for the isolated individual – and, on the other
hand, the ability to be a member of a social group without sacrificing one's individuality. The leading of a double life then, is
not a compromise nor a passive acceptance of conformity, or
schizophrenia. Rather, it is an artistic achievement. The 'artificial' life, and all the abilities of the artificer, are seen to be
necessary for self-fulfilment. With this ability both to be for herself and for others, Sybil attains the capacity for objective self-
evaluation: 'Am I a woman, she thought calmly, or an intellectual monster?' The degree to which she has come to terms
with herself is indicated by her response to her doubts: 'She was
so accustomed to this question within herself that it needed no
answer.'

The antisyzygy that Muriel Spark aims at then is the union of
the private and the public, and in this she is in conscious reaction against the Romantic rejection of Society and the City in
favour of Nature.[8] It may be that the Scots as a nation were
never given over to the uniformity of Romantic nature-worship,
but it is the argument of this study that it is a 'post-Modern' –
and to a lesser degree a Modern – and not only a Scottish characteristic to envision the personal and social completion of the
individual. Before going on to consider this subject fully with
reference to Mrs Spark's novels, I would like to consider her
theory of fiction, since she is one of the few British novelists,
as Frank Kermode has several times indicated, who make a
theory of fiction a central part of the novels themselves. This
theory of fiction might be seen to be based on another traditional Scottish trait: thrift, or, to use the word that Muriel
Spark herself uses again and again, economy.

One might be tempted to say that, given the Scot's penchant for thriftiness, then Christianity is the only possible
religion for the nation since it offers the extra value of three-
in-one. Similarly, and less blasphemously, the antisyzygy
might be particularly Scottish in its offering two-in-one; and
Muriel Spark's attempt to unite the private and the public is
one important manifestation of this economy. There is no
doubt that Mrs Spark is fond of somewhat stereotyped jokes
about her homeland. For instance, in *The Ballad of Peckham Rye*
(and one of its central themes is 'economy'), one of the charac-

ters notices a newspaper article announcing that a new anti-sex drug has been developed at the University of Edinburgh. She may well have a similar private joke about her prose style, which has become increasingly economical; at times her prose approximates the compactness of poetry. But there is a much more informative pun which Muriel Spark finds in the word. Economy is in fact synonymous with fiction.

To understand this use of the word, we must go to Cardinal Newman. Mrs Spark herself has said that Newman was a formative influence on her prose style (she mentions also Proust and Louis MacNeice). There is a passage in *The Prime of Miss Jean Brodie* which indicates that one section in particular of Newman's *Apologia* took Mrs Spark's attention. Sandy Stranger, who puts a stop to the expansive and potentially tyrannous Miss Brodie, studies Teddy Lloyd's technique of painting and when she discovers that every one of the figures in his pictures has Miss Brodie's face, she reaches a general philosophical conclusion:

> Teddy Lloyd's method of presentation was similar, it was economical, and it always seemed afterwards to Sandy that where there was a choice of various courses, the most economical was the best, and that the course to be taken was the most expedient and most suitable at the time for all the objects in hand.[9]

The passage suggests that Sandy is developing an objectivity – as yet coarse and fumbling – with which to respond to the over-subjective and over-personal ideal embodied in Miss Brodie. Her objectivity is not yet humanised, but in adhering to 'economy' Sandy is striving for objective truth rather than subjective imagining. Here is the source of much of the wording of the passage, if not of its specific meaning:

> The principle of the Economy is this; that out of various courses, all and each allowable antecedently and in themselves, that ought to be taken which is most expedient and most suitable at the time for the object in hand.[10]

This close echoing of Newman must indicate that Mrs Spark spent some time herself in considering this particular section of the *Apologia* and that not only the wording but the subject matter was of interest to her (this does not mean of course, that the subject matter in the Newman passage is necessarily the subject of the echoing passage from the novel).

Now, Newman's subject is equivocation; Economy means equivocation. He emphasises the necessity for telling the truth: 'the truest expedience is to answer right out, when you are asked . . . and that the first of the virtues is to tell the truth, and shame the devil.' The question is, however, are there situations in which Truth may be served better, and in the long run, by an expedient, economical, or equivocal response? Newman's answer is yes, a highly careful and qualified yes, which nevertheless earned him a great deal of bitter criticism. An equivocal response is not justified simply because it might save the speaker from difficulty, but because it can in fact be, in certain circumstances, the most efficient way of speaking the Truth. As Newman says, 'as to the Economy itself, it is founded upon the words of our Lord, "Cast not your pearls before swine" '. Such a doctrine, with its implications of aristocratic and esoteric knowledge which must be sugar-coated for the masses, would be a dangerous one for a novelist. For Newman, however, the central meaning seems to be that as long as Truth is the goal, then one is bound only to speak that form of words which will most serve the cause of Truth.

Implicit in all this discussion of economy is one justification, if not a theory, of fiction. As Frank Kermode has pointed out, Muriel Spark takes very seriously Plato's objection to poets: 'What seems to concern Muriel Spark more than the myth-fact antithesis is a much purer and more ancient issue, which lies behind all these conversations, and is, simply, are novelists liars? If not, what kind of truth are they telling?'[11] In the interview with Kermode, Spark herself refers to the medieval four levels of truth (which, in fact, underlie Newman's 'economy'):

There is metaphorical truth and moral truth, and what they call anagogical, you know, the different sorts of truth; and there is absolute truth, in which I believe things which are difficult to believe, but I believe them because they are absolute.[11]

Both 'fictions' and 'economies' are different sorts of truth, and fiction itself is an economical way of telling the truth. As Conrad well knew, the truth itself can be tedious and readers will prefer any sort of diversion to yet more reality:

> My task which I am trying to achieve is, by the power of the written word to make you hear, to make you feel – it is, before all, to make you *see*. That – and no more, and it is everything. If I succeed, you shall find there according to your deserts: encouragement, consolation, fear, charm – all you demand – and, perhaps, also that glimpse of truth for which you have forgotten to ask.[12]

The writer of fiction, or of 'impressions', may seem to have one goal, an overt one of telling a good story, or of making us 'see', but he has also another goal in truth. Fictions, then, are economical because they offer us diversion, and this very diversion, this apparent indirection, serves to find direction out. For Muriel Spark this close connection of fiction and truth is an important one:

> I don't claim that my novels are truth – I claim that they are fiction out of which a kind of truth emerges. And I keep in mind specifically that what I am writing is fiction because I am interested in truth – absolute truth – and I don't pretend that what I'm writing is more than an imaginative extension of the truth – something inventive.[13]

It is perhaps worth noting that such an attitude to fiction is neither an obvious one nor one that is universally accepted. The Romantic heritage of lyrical self-expression, coupled with a prevalence in our culture of confessional literature, make fiction seem less and less defensible since it substitutes, at best artificiality, or, much worse, bad faith, for open-hearted sincerity. One finds a very different attitude to fiction, for instance, in this passage from B. S. Johnson's novel *Albert Angelo*, which is discussed by David Lodge in the title essay of his *The Novelist at the Crossroads*. As Lodge points out, the book reads 'like realistic fiction', apart from the use of a few contrivances such as holes in the pages, until the beginning of the fourth section entitled 'Disintegration':

> – fuck all this lying look what im really trying to write about

is writing not all this stuff about architecture trying to say something about writing about my writing im my hero though what a useless appellation, my first character then im trying to say something about me through him albert an architect when whats the point in covering up covering up covering over pretending i can say anything through him that is anything i would be interested in saying. . . .[14]

Although Lodge admits that this passage is 'an extreme strategy for achieving an effect of sincerity and authenticity' and that it comes 'so late in the work it is more of a gesture than an achievement', he seems content to accept the dismissal of fiction and applaud the author who, in his subsequent works, stands 'defiant and vulnerable on the bare ground of fact' and who takes the 'fundamentalist Platonic position that 'telling stories is telling lies', but at the same time experimenting with form to bring writing into closer proximity with living'.[15]

What is perhaps curious about Lodge's attitude is that despite the title of his earlier book, *Language of Fiction*, in this essay he pays no attention whatever to the language. The passage from Johnson is not necessarily sincere, but merely a technical 'strategy' or 'gesture' meant to achieve an effect of sincerity; it is an experiment with form. But does such writing in itself bring writing into closer proximity with living'? Is such a proximity possible? Perhaps an impossible question to answer. One can merely note the lack of persuasiveness in Johnson's language. Some subterranean objection to the word 'hero' is covered over rather than expressed by the comment that the word is a 'useless appellation'. If useless, why put it down in the first place? If sincerity in language is achieved merely by beginning a paragraph with 'fuck' and then dropping punctuation and capitals, then sincerity itself must be an insignificant commodity. It is worse though, it represents the writer's abdication of responsibility and a surrender to cliché and inexactitude. In fact, the passage struggles to tell us that the author wants to tell us something; it 'shows' us nothing, and all that it 'tells' is that fictions are lies.

One might have expected Lodge, with his interest in language, to refer to a theory of fiction such as the one suggested by the philosopher Max Black: that fictions involve violation of grammatical rules. Black bases his idea on a passage from Bentham:

> A fictitious entity is an entity to which, though by the grammatical form of the discourse employed in speaking of it, existence be ascribed, yet in truth and reality existence is not meant to be ascribed.[16]

Although he does not use it, a perfect example of Black's theory is E. E. Cumming's line, 'anyone lived in a pretty how town', which violates the grammatical use of 'anyone' and 'how', to produce a pleasing, and, in the poem, meaningful, fiction. If fiction is freedom from grammar, it is also to some extent freedom over fact. As Black says:

> Language must conform to the discovered regularities and irregularities of experience. But in order to do so, it is enough that it should be apt for the expression of everything that is or might be the case. To be content with less would be to be satisfied to be inarticulate; to ask for more is to desire the impossible.[17]

To renounce fiction, then, is to renounce the power of saying what might be the case, and it is to risk inarticulacy; a risk that B. S. Johnson runs in his attack on the overt form of language.

Theories of fiction have, of course, important effects on the type of novels an author produces. The topic is however important not merely because of formal or aesthetic niceties. Form does affect content, and an author's theory of fiction is part of what he has to communicate about life. Johnson says, 'Im trying to say something not tell a story telling stories is telling lies and I want to tell the truth. . . .' He rejects 'invention' which is 'pure lying'. He claims to want to tell the truth, but one begins to suspect that he believes that there is no truth to tell. His attitude to language seems to corroborate this suspicion: 'since each reader brings to each word his own however slightly different idiosyncratic meaning, how can I be expected to make my own ––'. The passage, characteristically, breaks off, frustratedly unable to complete itself. The picture which emerges is that of a man holding tenaciously to an inchoate and inexpressible 'truth', unwilling or unable to submit to language, let alone fiction. It comes as no surprise to find the following paragraph in the conclusion to one of Johnson's subsequent works *The Unfortunates*:

> The difficulty is to understand without generalization, to see each piece of received truth, or generalization, as true only if it is true for me, *solipsism again*. I come back to it again, and for no other reason.   In general, generalization is to lie, to tell lies.[18]

The dilemma is that of a man who believes that sincerity or self-expression is equivalent to telling the 'truth'. Sincerity which is so delicate that even language violates it must inevitably bog down into tedious insistence that I have something to say, but I cannot say what it is. Johnson quite rightly characterises his own work, both the form and the subject matter, when he says in *Albert Angelo*, 'so an almighty aposiopesis'. Because the beliefs are solipsistic, and the attitude to language is that silence is better than speech, aposiopesis, the inability or unwillingness to go on, is the only 'rhetorical device' left.

   This brief and perhaps over-emphatically negative consideration of Johnson's work, serves to illuminate what is entailed when Muriel Spark says that she believes in absolute Truth and yet believes in fictions, in inventions and economies. Her subject matter and her technique will show that for her mere sincerity is not enough. The belief in Truth here entails the belief that, since sincerity can be wrong or susceptible to error, then, art, artifice and artificiality are not inhibitors of man's individuality and his freedom. The invention of plots and the employment of 'style' may mask sincerity, but they facilitate truth-telling. Muriel Spark at times displays an almost Chaucerian sense of the gamesmanship of narration, reminding us again and again that this is but a game. Her drawing attention to the deployment of technical devices and of style serves to keep us conscious of the fact that we are exposed to 'fiction' and not 'reality'. At the same time, she uses style and technique for a serious end. Conscious of devices, she nevertheless goes on to tell a story and then to let the story have its way with us. She takes all the necessary precautions to defuse the lying potential of fiction, and then trusts it as an economical way of getting at the truth. Because she believes in Truth, and maintains a qualified belief in consciously recognised fictions and in the power of language, we might expect to find that her central thematic concern is with the dangers of solipsism.

From the very start, Muriel Spark fought with the novel; refusing to accommodate herself to its existing forms, she has continued to produce novels which are interesting in themselves as stories, and also interesting as forms. In an interview with Philip Toynbee she was aked, 'Did you perhaps regard fiction as an inferior form? Do you still?' She replied, 'I'm sure I did, and in some ways still do. I think of verse as the best way of saying things; the short story as the next best, and the novel as a rather lazy and third-rate form.'[19] The history of her attitude to fiction, from instinctive distrust to qualified and carefully understood acceptance, directly mirrors her central subject. With Newman she would agree that 'to speak the truth straight out' is always best. Accompanying this attitude is the rejection of conventional Society and the 'wisdom' of conformity. The heroine of her early work tends to be a figure who is alone, if not isolated or alienated, a complete individual unwilling to let personal relationships compromise freedom of choice: in short the romantic, asocial, individual. But, also from the very beginning, there is a doubt that the figure of the rebellious individual, imaginative and free, is a sufficient paradigm. From a belief in sincerity and a distrust of masks, she has begun to explore further and further the nature of role-playing. Once she had settled her reservations about fiction, she was able to turn to a subject which one would expect to be central for any novelist: the fictions which we make of ourselves in social situations. Having concluded that fictions are not lies, she seems similarly to be trying to express her conviction that the free playing of roles, the free choice of self-dramatisation is a creative achievement and a step towards real self-realisation. The culture she envisages is a combination of the two described by Yeats. Primary is Pater's ideal which creates 'feminine souls', a culture which 'is self-knowledge in so far as the self is a calm, deliberating, discriminating thing'. To this base she adds the 'Renaissance' ideal which, says Yeats, is 'founded not on self-knowledge but on knowledge of some other self, Christ or Caesar, not on delicate sincerity but on imitative energy.'[20] The final economy then, is the union of these opposites, the union of the private self with the energetic public self, of Truth with Fiction.

In order to arrive at such a picture of Muriel Spark's work, one must read her novels as if they were part of one emerging novel. This is not to say that they are continuous in the way that Faulkner's Yoknapatawpha stories are. Rather, they form a mosaic, each novel concerning itself with a central subject which is considered in succeeding novels from a variety of points of view. Although the interpretation I have offered thus far might suggest that Muriel Spark is a major talent, many readers would probably agree that her novels are in some way minor, even the most popular of them, *The Prime of Miss Jean Brodie*. The reason for this may be that, like Jane Austen she has chosen a small square of ivory on which to work, but she lacks Jane Austen's skill within such confines. There is certainly something in this, both as a summary of Spark's virtues and as a critical comment on her shortcomings. There is another way to consider the question, however. My own view is that because she continues to consider herself as primarily a poet, her distrust, at times almost her contempt, for the novel form persists; and this distrust is directly related to her theory of fiction. Because a fiction is only partial, only an economical way to present the truth and not the truth itself, then no one novel can ever present a satisfactory 'vision' of existence. A 'vision' of the world, once it pretends to completeness, begins to violate experience, to replace a living contact with reality. Once one novel is written, then, one is committed to writing another which will correct the imbalance suggested by the first.

Many of Muriel Spark's individual novels employ the device of repetition; this repetition seems to be also a feature of the novels taken as a whole. *The Girls of Slender Means*, not one of her best works, suffers precisely because it repeats too exactly themes, characters and incidents from earlier novels, especially *The Prime of Miss Jean Brodie* and *The Ballad of Peckham Rye*. When this system of writing novels works at its best, however, each novel appears to be a necessary part of one whole picture. For example, *The Public Image* presents one point of view, which is continued and to some extent modified or corrected by the following novel, *The Driver's Seat*. Further, a theme which is only latent in *The Driver's Seat* is picked up and becomes a major theme of *Not to Disturb*. One might regret that Muriel Spark's attitude to the novel has forced her to treat it slightingly and so refrain from embarking upon a 'major' work of fiction. The irony of the situation, though, is that all of her 'partial' fictions do add up to one picture. Her vision of life is a coherent one, but since she is very aware of the offence implicit in imposing a private imaginative vision on the public world, it is not fully presented in any one novel. Her novels are not meant to record a theory of the universe she has worked out and settled on; rather they are tentative explorations towards such an understanding. The qualifications, the care, with which she presents her own point of view, necessarily involve the reader in his own process of trying to make sense of his own life. It may be, as the 'myth-critics' tell us, that all books are part of one story, whether it be the search for a white goddess, or for a lost Garden of Eden. If so, then the rewards to be had from an overall look at Muriel Spark's novels justify our engaging on an eclectic and synthetic approach to understanding.

In her first novel, *The Comforters*,[21] the central character Caroline Rose gradually becomes conscious of the fact that she is being written into a novel. She does her best to thwart this deterministic presence in her life, by trying to refuse to travel by car, for instance, after she has overheard the narrator say that that is what she will do. She asserts her freedom of will against an apparently deterministic pattern of fiction:

> Her sense of being written into the novel was painful. Of her constant influence on its course she remained unaware, and now she was impatient for the story to come to an end, knowing that the narrative could never become coherent to her until she was at last outside it, and at the same time consummately inside it.[22]

The novel very neatly raises two matters at once here, the philosophical question of free will versus determinism, and the question of the nature of fiction and the degree of freedom that 'characters' are allowed (the ideological ramifications of the omniscient narrator).[23] When Caroline first begins to hear voices, she believes that she is perhaps suffering from neurotic delusions. She tried confiding in the Baron, and in her priest, but soon learns that she alone must learn how to live with her private fantasies. She goes along half-heartedly with Laurence Mander's attempts to record the voices and so prove scientifically that the voices exist outside Caroline's imagination. She knows that she is not overhearing the word of God – unlike Mrs Hogg who claims to have heard God speak in a vision, but is unwilling to say how she can possibly be sure that it was God – and she matter-of-factly, and correctly, concludes that she is overhearing the writing of a novel. The joke is, of course, that for characters in a novel – if they could have any consciousness apart from that given them by narrator – the narrator is like God: all-knowing, but not all-determining and therefore only a lesser god. Caroline's particular virtue is in not trusting the voices she hears; in not accepting them without objection. Since the narrator she overhears is in the novel as much as Caroline is, then the narrator is not to be trusted as a speaker of the truth since novels are fiction. Caroline is contemptuous of the idea that her life can be formed from outside by the dictates of Art. She accepts the presence of the voices, and by writing down what they say, by becoming increasingly conscious of the way in which they operate, she overcomes any threat they might pose and by the end of the novel we discover that she herself is writing the novel which is the record of her overhearings. Character and narrator merge and Mrs Spark has played a very witty joke with the fictional form and with the old saw that novelists do not create characters so much as follow their tracks through the story, taking down what they say.

Caroline learns to trust herself and to trust in what she hears inside herself even though it does not seem to coincide with Truth or Reality, because without this belief in one's own inner promptings, in one's inexplicable private imaginings, there can be no individuation. One must not confuse this inner activity either with lies or with Truth. It is the stuff that novels are made of, it is fiction, and it is valid and valuable in its proper sphere. Caroline's choice then, of making her private fantasies into a novel, is not a random one; it is a meaningful one which suggests that the proper place for fantasy is either inside oneself, or in Art, where fantasy is permitted. The role of Art is to make public and universal what must otherwise remain private and obsessive.

Caroline, like her author, recognises that life cannot be lived

entirely inside a novel, inside fiction, fable or myth. There must
be a ground in Truth and there must be freedom of will. There
is one character in the novel, however, who has no private life at
all, Georgina Hogg. She has made what should be private,
directly public without the mediation of Art. When she is not
fulfilling her public role, Mrs Hogg disappears:

> However, as soon as Mrs. Hogg stepped into her room she
> disappeared, she simply disappeared. She had no private life
> whatsoever.[24]

The reason for this disappearance is once again a joke. Mrs
Hogg is not a 'central' character, she is a mere device, a necessity or foil. As a result, when her role in the fiction is over she
can be dispensed with. She is a public figure in that everything
she is is contained in the words on the page, and when the
words do not present her, she does not exist. Caroline Rose, we
must imagine, exists independently of the words on the page,
since she can overhear them as they are being written. She is
never fully captured by the fiction, as Mrs Hogg is. We can put
this another way by saying that Caroline keeps fiction in its
proper realm. Her private life is a full, creative, imaginative fiction which she learns, by a process of rebukes, not to foist onto
others, except in the form of a novel. Mrs Hogg has displaced
private fiction-making into the public realm. What is most
objectionable about her is that she demands public and universal validity for her private fictions (her role as a Catholic) and
is, to that extent, tyrannical.

Mrs Hogg is not completely meaningless, although her
prime function is that of foil to Caroline. She contributes her bit
to the total meaning and can then be drowned as the villain she
is. On stage though, she is the emblem of the personal devoured
by the mask (and the mask is a fiction of the self). She is the official Catholic who uses her role as Catholic to express her 'fanatical moral intrusiveness' which is near to an 'utterly primitive
mania'. She herself has been devoured by her role and she
wishes to devour others in a similar way. She tries at one point
to convert Mervyn Hogarth (his name had been Hogg and he
had once been married to Georgina):

> Georgina was speaking. 'Repent and be converted,

Mervyn.'

He shuddered, all hunched in the chair as he was, penetrated by the chill of danger. Georgina's lust for converts to the Faith was terrifying, for by the Faith she meant herself. He felt himself shrink to a sizable item of prey, hovering on the shores of her monstrous mouth to be masticated to a pulp and to slither unrecognisably down that abominable gully, that throat he could almost see as she smiled her smile of all forgetting. 'Repent, Mervyn. Be converted.' And in case he should be converted perhaps chemically into an intimate cell of her great nothingness he stood up quickly and shed a snigger.[25]

Mrs Hogg has become enslaved by a fiction, by the social fiction of herself in her role as a Catholic in personal touch with God. Caroline has recognised that fictions have an inescapable reality, they well up in the creative mind, and so she accords them their place of independent and free operation. The source of fictions is the private self and they are to be given sanctioned publicity in recognised forms. She does not confuse an essentially private matter, her Catholic faith in the Absolute, which we must assume she hears inside her, with the other voices which are also fiction. Mrs Hogg makes what should have been a private belief into a social fiction and this reversal of the orders of Fiction and Truth, of Private and Public, leads to her depersonalisation and lets loose in the world a potentially destructive egotism.

So the novel seems to split neatly into two, with on the one hand the 'good guys', Caroline Rose, somehow recognising that she is not crazy and that fictions are different from belief in God although both are personal and have appropriate rituals for making them public. Mrs Hogg, on the other hand, exhibits bad faith by giving herself not to God, but to a Social role. There is something self-indulgent about the use of such hackneyed forms of heroine and villain in the novel, and if it arose because of Mrs Spark's distrust of the novel discussed above, then we can attribute the weakness of *The Comforters*, the feeling that Caroline is just too 'nice' to be interesting, to this very belief that the novel is limited to stereotyped divisions. That she might have disposed of too many large problems too summarily seems to have occurred to the author. In the interview with Frank Kermode in *Partisan Review* mentioned earlier, she said of *The Comforters*: 'Because I observed a kind of wantonness, as you call it, I decided the best thing to do was to stick to a plot, and stick to a formal outline and say what I wanted to say in that limit.' The 'wantonness' of *The Comforters* is well demonstrated by the easy way in which Mrs Hogg, who is after all one of the most interesting figures in the book, is simply dismissed as evil. The too ready judgement, the too sure sense of value and the easy recognition of evil and the easy victory over it, leave a feeling of having been cheated, or of having been exposed to Mrs Spark's state of mind, her calm of mind, after the process of suffering and expending of passion is over.

There is, however, a suggestion in the novel of this very uneasiness which the reader may himself feel. It comes in the figure of Eleanor Hogarth, who had once been a Cambridge friend of Caroline's and has recently been the mistress of the Baron Willi Stock, reputedly a Satanist. Caroline believes that Eleanor's 'real talent was for mimicry'[26] and this means that she must forever lack a personal creative centre, being condemned by her talent 'to mimic the best that had already been done in any particular line'.[27] There is a similarity between Eleanor and Georgina Hogg then, in that both are limited in personality and freedom because of their 'roles'. Eleanor is less demonic than Georgina and her presence in the book suggests that the question of 'role-playing' and of social fictions is more complicated than at first glance it seems. Although Caroline does not like Eleanor, she is nevertheless fascinated by her, 'fascinated and appalled':

Caroline was fascinated by Eleanor's performance. Indeed it was only an act; the fascination of Eleanor was her entire submersion in whatever role she had to play. There did not seem to be any question of Eleanor's choosing her part, it was forced on her, she was enslaved by it. Just now, she appeared to be under the control of liquor; but she was also and more completely under the control of her stagey act: that of a scatty female who'd been drinking: wholeheartedly, her personality was involved, so that it was impossible to distinguish between Eleanor and the personality which possessed her during those hours; as well try to distinguish between the sea and the water in it.[28]

It is difficult to make complete sense of this passage, especially of the last image. Despite the fascination, Caroline is clearly attempting to account for her own negative judgement of Eleanor and finds it easy to do so by noting that this dramatisation of the self has entailed a loss of freedom to choose. If Eleanor is an important character (or meant to be) then surely we should expect that this loss of freedom be explained; otherwise Caroline's superiority will be superiority only to 'straw men'. Is this loss of freedom the inevitable fate awaiting those who mimic? Does it overtake one by degrees? Or was there something in Eleanor's background which might explain her enslavement? As with Mrs Hogg, Eleanor is not meant to be taken 'seriously', even though they may raise serious questions. Caroline decides role-playing might be acceptable as long as there is a distance kept, so long as there is no complete submersion in the part. Caroline begins to show, that is to say, the dual attitude to fictions characteristic of her creator. One must retain the ability to distinguish between fiction and Truth (how?) and between 'Eleanor and the personality which possessed her' (how?). The passage concludes then, with the implied question, how distinguish between the sea and the water in it? and the question calls into doubt Caroline's whole process of thought and judgment.

Eleanor though, is no more than a device to facilitate Caroline's growing acceptance of fictions. Eleanor serves to point out to Caroline the danger:

> In former days, Eleanor's mimicry was recognizable. She would change her personality like dresses according to occasion, and it had been fun to watch, and an acknowledged joke of Eleanor's.[29]

Which is to say that the artistic, the mercurial, is to be encouraged so long as the very art draws attention to itself, advertises itself. Eleanor 'fell' when she no longer acknowledged the artistry, but became it; that is, allowed her private self to merge with the fiction:

> But she had lost her small portion of detachment; now, to

watch her was like watching doom. As a child Caroline, pulling a face, had been warned, 'If you keep doing that it will
stick one day.' She felt, looking at Eleanor, that this was actually happening to the woman. Her assumed personalities
were beginning to cling; soon one of them would stick, grotesque and ineradicable.[30]

Another implicit question must be faced here, and it is whether
or not Caroline Rose herself, a recent convert to Roman Catholicism, is about to find herself stuck in her role of true believer.
The danger though is clear; it is 'submersion' in a fiction, and
one must, like Georgina Hogg, 'fear death by water'. As in
Eliot, the traditional symbol of creativity, water, is also symbol
of potential destruction. If art is a powerful positive force, we
are being reminded that it must also have in that very force a
great potential for destruction.

Muriel Spark has described her own art as obsessional, and if
one of the meanings of grotesque is 'characterised by obsessions', then her own art is after all grotesque. Her grotesques,
her obsessions, include bachelors, the elderly, private-school
girls, and adherents of the occult. All of the characters in *The
Comforters* are grotesques; that is each has one quirk of behaviour which identifies him. Caroline hears voices, the Baron is a
Satanist, Georgina and Eleanor are trapped in dramatic roles,
Laurence Manders cannot abide the secrets of others and so
always opens letters and peers in drawers. Even the most
lively character of all, Louisa Jepp is a bit gnomish in her liveliness, and she carries on an activity that could be considered
grotesque for a grandmother, she runs a band of international
jewel thieves. Because Mrs Jepp has preserved an inner spring
of secret freedom, which even Laurence cannot ferret out nor
understand, she can play whatever grotesque role she likes
and not get caught, or stuck, in the mask. In fact, she indirectly brings about an event which begins to suggest that there
is a positive good to be achieved by the 'sticking' of an
assumed role. Andrew Hogarth, one of her band of thieves,
'poses' with his father as a Catholic pilgrim seeking a cure at
various European shrines. On their return to England, they
smuggle the diamonds in hollow plaster saints. Andrew himself, is really paralysed from the waist down and in genuine

need of a miraculous cure. And although there is no suggestion that he undertakes his 'pilgrimages' because he is pious as well as a thief, he does receive a miraculous cure and recovers the use of his legs, just as the smuggling racket is forced to cease. The incident is primarily a comic one, but once again Spark's humour has an idea behind it. The suggestion is that appropriate actions, even for the wrong reasons, can have beneficial results. Role-playing, if one happens to be playing the appropriate role, can be positive. The mask or role which sticks may limit the freedom of the face it hides, but it also gives it form and the freedom to act.

Muriel Spark's second novel *Robinson*[31] suggests by its title that it is a modern version of Defoe's tale of one man's attempt to live alone. Mrs Spark's concern is unlike Defoe's, however, in that she is not interested in the principles of middle-class economics and, as Carol B. Ohmann has pointed out, Robinson practises none of the husbandry of Robinson Crusoe, preferring to eat out of tins.[32] Instead, it is the spiritual which has driven Robinson to his island, where he fights a single-handed battle against Marianism, which he sees as a pagan survival in the Church (the fact that his middle name is Mary indicates that he is fighting against the feminine in himself as well). There is another suggestion in the title, however, which comes closer to the meaning of the book. Robinson is the name of the man and of the island he inhabits. The phrase lying behind the novel is therefore Donne's 'No man is an island', and one of its themes is the meaning of human relationships. The coincidence of the names of man and island indicates that a man can be an island, can be self-sufficient, at least to an extent. In this context, Derek Stanford says he recalls a poem of Muriel Spark's which begins:

'No man is an island.'
Oh no?[33]

This is the question around which the novel circles.

Living alone on his island, where he can make his own personal beliefs into a social system, Robinson is something of a special case. He demonstrates to January that the idea of being an 'island' is an ideal that should not be too easily discarded in favour of some comfortable belief in the value of being a piece of the 'main', or in 'human relations'. Robinson engages in a bit of pagan stage-play, by killing a goat and spreading the blood about so that it appears as if Robinson himself has been killed violently. Immediately, the familiarity between the three survivors of the plane crash is destroyed by mutual suspicion. Each discovers himself alone, suspecting the others and suspected by them. Faced with the fact of death, each man is an island, and must rely on his own devices in order to see clearly.

Robinson has advised January to 'stick to the facts' in her journal. None of the three (January Marlow, Wells, Waterford), however, is able to stick to the facts, which are that Robinson is not to be found and that there is blood on the ground leading to the Furnace, the chaotic, groaning, burning crater. Each goes beyond the facts to conclude that Robinson has been murdered and this fiction leads to more near murders (of January by Wells, and of Wells by Waterford). It is Robinson himself, of course, who initiates the fiction with the killing of the goat (which is diseased and must be killed anyway). So long as he was alone on his island, his private antinomian system was permissible since it affected only himself. Once personal fictions begin to affect the lives of others however, violence begins to well up as if inevitably. January reacts against the overextension of Robinson's individuality by disobeying his command that young Miguel should not be taught the Rosary. Although the absolute freedom that Robinson seeks on his island is not a possible paradigm for a system of Society which admits the reality of other individuals, the novel closes by re-emphasising the value of the belief in the ideal, in the fiction of such a possibility. One day, after the three survivors of the plane crash have been rescued and long since returned home, the island sinks into the Atlantic, and like Atlantis it takes on the proportions of legend and myth:

> And now, perhaps it is because the island is passing out of sight that it rises so high in my thoughts. Even while the journal brings before me the events of which I have written, they are transformed, there is undoubtedly a sea-change, so that the island resembles a locality of childhood, both dangerous and lyrical. I have impressions of the island of which I have not told you, and could not entirely if I had a hundred tongues – the mustard field staring at me with its yellow eye,

the blue and green lake seeing in me a hard turquoise stone, the goat's blood observing me red, guilty, all red. And sometimes when I am walking down the King's Road or sipping my espresso in the morning – feeling, not old exactly, but fusty and adult – and chance to remember the island, immediately all things are possible.[34]

As a fictional place in the mind, the island (like all dreams of exotic islands) is a place of first permission, where all things are possible and complete individual freedom can reign. The belief that emerges from *Robinson* is similar to Thoreau's claim that the free man is free in his mind, in his thought and imagination, and therefore mere physical prisons are meaningless to him.

In *Memento Mori*,[35] Muriel Spark's next novel, once again the 'facts' appear in the form of Death, which is 'the first of the four last things to be ever remembered'. The novel charts the way in which various people face the possibility of death, which is announced to them in a series of mysterious phone calls. Charmian Colston, the ageing novelist who is one of the few characters who is able to accept the fact of death and who is as a result the most impressive figure in the book, sees immediately through the mysterious phone calls:

'In my belief,' she said, 'the author of the anonymous telephone calls is Death himself, as you might say. I don't see, Dame Lettie, what you can do about it. If you don't remember Death, Death reminds you to do so. And if you can't cope with the facts the next best thing is to go away for a holiday.'[36]

The novel traces the way in which most of the characters 'go away for a holiday' from the Fact. It also demonstrates an interest in the multifariousness of humanity, in the inescapable fact that people are different from one another. As Charmian says, 'It is surprising how variously people react to the same thing.'[37] It is obvious on one level that the world is full of individuals, but the felt experience of this fact still comes as a surprise. Charmian, able to face the fact of Death, can also overcome solipsism and recognise the reality of other individuals.

Alec Warner believes that he too can see others as individuals and can respond to their uniqueness. He keeps file-cards on each of his acquaintances, ostensibly as part of his research for a book he hopes to write about the old. But his pretended interest in the diseases of others, and the causes of their deaths, is merely his own fiction, for the book will never be written. Planning it is his way of going on a holiday from fact – by pretending to be scientifically factual. We discover that his scientific method does not reveal the full reality of the other person:

> He felt suddenly tired and stopped a taxi. As it drove him home he ruminated on the question why scientific observation differed from humane observation, and how the same people, observed in these respective senses, actually seemed to be different people.[38]

The scientific method is itself a distorting medium, and since people look different from different points of view, there is nothing any more real, or revealing, in scientific observation. Warner believes that 'the method he had evolved was, on the whole satisfactory'. What he fails to perceive is that this very method is a fiction, which while it gives him some information about other people, puts a filtering screen between himself and the people he is trying to see. It is only by looking at fact that fictions can be seen for what they are – not lies, but expressions of individual nature – and full humanity be attained.

As he lies about to die, Warner 'frequently searched through his mind, as through a card-index for the case-histories of his friends, both dead and dying'. He is on holiday from the fact and since he has forgotten, Death comes to remind him to think of Death:

> What were they sick, what did they die of? Lettie Colston, he recited to himself, comminuted fractures of the skull; Godfrey Colston, hypostatic pneumonia; Charmian Colston, uraemia; Jean Taylor, myocardial degeneration; Tempest Sidebottome, carcinoma of the cervix; Ronald Sidebottome, carcinoma of the bronchus; Guy Leet, arteriosclerosis; Henry Mortimer, coronary thrombosis. . . .[39]

This macabre litany attains to almost a kind of poetry because it is not merely a catalogue of Death's victories. Instead it is the sign of a mind trying to realise itself, to break through its own fictions to a reality beyond itself, and in so doing recognise its own nature. The catalogue of Death is a reminder of the Fact, and the fact of Death seems to be an assurance that, since each of us is alone before Death, each of us is thereby assured of uniqueness and value as an individual.

Death makes another appearance in the lyrical novel, *The Ballad of Peckham Rye*,[40] which anatomises the demonic nature of Art. As soon as Dougal Douglas appears on the scene in Peckham, violence and disorder spring up on all sides. It all begins with the memorable incident of Humphrey Place's upsetting the calm procession of the marriage ritual with his 'No, to be quite frank I won't.' This violation of social ritual is not entirely a creative rebellion for freedom on Humphrey's part; in fact it represents the first time he has failed to live up to his belief in the evil of 'absenteeism'. At the marriage ceremony he merely mimics words Dougal had earlier put into his mouth. At one point Dougal had posed as a priest and, with a plate of bacon serving for a Bible, mocked the marriage service:

> Dougal read from the book: 'Wilt thou take this woman,' he said with a deep ecclesiastical throb, 'to be thai wedded waif?'
> Then he put the plate aside and knelt; he was a sinister goggling bridegroom. 'No,' he declared to the ceiling, 'I won't, quite frankly.'[41]

The marriage ritual is only one of the many targets for Dougal's satiric intelligence and the truth about him is revealed in the disparity of his targets: he has no *one* target, no goal. He has an excess of creative energy which goes into his 'poses' but because there is no social use, nor reasonable end for this creativity, it becomes malicious and destructive. Dougal takes to an extreme the suggestion in *The Comforters* that one must never allow any one role to 'stick' and reveals that the extreme, of Art and Imagination, becomes demonic. This portrait of the artist who brings 'vision' to Industry shows that Art can be 'both lyrical and dangerous' and at the end of the story our sympathy is with those common bourgeois people of industry in Peckham, lacking in vision.

It would be difficult to list all the incidents of violence which accrue around Dougal, the book abounds with them, but the major ones include the murder of Merle Coverdale by her former lover Mr Druce who calmly sticks a corkscrew into her throat and 'Then he took his hat and went home to his wife.'[42] Mr Druce has been 'liberated' from his routine life by Dougal's talk of vision, and has developed a homo-erotic love for Dougal, but his old habits still persist and he returns home to his wife. The murder is the central crime of the novel, but we also see Mr Weedon suffer a nervous breakdown because he cannot understand whether 'vision' refers to a matter of optics or to something else. There is a fight on the Rye common between Trevor Lomas, Dougal and their girls which, perhaps symbolically, turns into a dance as the law appears in the form of two constables. Humphrey suffers a gashed face when Dougal sidesteps a broken glass wielded by Trevor. Merle Coverdale is threatened with violence by Trevor, and Nelly Mahone is roughed-up by Trevor and Leslie, because they have been associating with Dougal. The one thing Dougal cannot stand he says is illness, but wherever he goes pain and disorder follow him like a curse. He himself does not escape entirely unscathed and leaves Peckham with a bruised eye. As he is fleeing through a tunnel once used by nuns, he has another fight with Trevor Lomas, 'Trevor caught up with him and delivered to Dougal a stab in the eye with a bone.'[43] Dougal also loses his girl who is offended by his callous attitude to her illness.

To understand this novel, it is necessary to take a closer look at Dougal to discover just how masterful he is at creating illusions. We have already seen how he fascinates Humphrey with his posing as first a cleric and then the bridegroom. When he is being interviewed by Mr Druce for the job of bringing Art into Industry, we discover that he had been in 'University Dramatics' and knows how to 'put all his energy into his own appearance.' He shows himself to be the mercurial master of any number of roles:

Dougal put Mr. Druce through the process of his smile.[44]

Dougal changed his shape and became a professor.[45]

Dougal turned sideways in his chair and gazed out of the window at the railway bridge; he was now a man of vision with a deformed shoulder.[46]

It does not stop there, however, this economy of life, this being able to be all things in one person. While bringing the Arts into Industry for Mr Druce's factory as Dougal Douglas, he is also, as Douglas Dougal, doing 'public relations' and 'psychological research' for Druce's rival Willis. Since Willis is a Scot, Dougal cannily adopts a materialistic approach to his work and hands in reports about the four types of morality prevalent in Peckham. He clinches the job with Willis by telling him that his reason for wanting to come into Industry is his belief that there is money in it. Behind both these roles, as Dougal Douglas and Douglas Dougal, we discover that 'really' he is ghost-writing (posing as the author) an autobiography for Maria Cheeseman, most of which he invents.

Dougal's *tour de force*, though, is reserved for the dance floor.* When the manager interrupts his Highland Fling, which has had the effect of making everybody else stop dancing to watch him, he goes outside briefly and returns with a dust-bin lid:

> Then he placed the lid upside down on the floor, sat cross-legged inside it, and was a man in a rocking boat rowing for his life. The band stopped, but nobody noticed the fact, owing to the many different sounds of mirth, protest, encouragement, and rage. The dancers circled slowly around him while he performed a Zulu dance with the lid for a shield.[47]

There is a brief interruption from several Africans, some of whom disapprove of this, while others cheer him on.

> Next, Dougal sat on his haunches and banged a message out on a tom-tom. He sprang up and with the lid on his head was a Chinese coolie eating melancholy rice. He was an ardent cyclist, crouched over handlebars and pedalling uphill with the lid between his knees. He was an old woman with an umbrella; he stood on the upturned edges of the lid and speared fish from his rocking canoe; he was the man at the wheel of a racing car; he did many things with the lid before he finally propped the dust-bin lid up on his high shoulder, beating this cymbal rhythmically with his hand while with the other hand he limply conducted an invisible band, being, with long blank face, the bandleader.[48]

The creative energy and the comedy make this passage a pure

* One is tempted to think that this novel reflects closely the ideas about the 'dance' and the 'dancer' developed by Frank Kermode in *Romantic Image*.

delight. Its effect is to pile up examples of Dougal's genius until
that very plenitude begins to exact a question: what is it all for?
what does it signify? All of Dougal's poses are effectively done,
but the result of putting all of his energy into his appearance is
that behind the mask there is a sense of emptiness, of absenteeism as a person. The roles themselves seem positive, but because they are not the projection of an inner self, they prove to
be the source of evil.

Dougal encourages absenteeism in the employees of the firms
he works for. He is constantly encouraging Merle to take a day
off and believes that everyone should take Monday off.
Humphrey Place, an ideal trade-unionist, regards this as an
immoral practice:

> 'Now I don't agree to that,' Humphrey said. 'It's immoral.
> Once you start absenting yourself you lose your self-respect.
> And you lose the support of your unions; they won't back
> you.'[49]

Later Humphrey proves that he believes in a form of 'economy'
quite different from that practised by Dougal. He denies the
value of working overtime, since this leads to underproduction
during regular shifts and so to more demands for overtime.
Absenteeism though, becomes an emblem for Dougal's own
form of immorality. Since he can assume any role, he is never
there himself, in any one of them. He disappears into one
mirror and then another. This absenteeism is a refusal to 'be
there' in any one role because he cannot stand to be limited or
to be defined as a person. He wants to be not only himself, but
everybody else as well.

Two images in the novel serve to characterise Dougal for us:
he is cannibal and okapi. We have already seen the cannibal
image in reference to Georgina Hogg of *The Comforters*. It occurs
also in Mrs Spark's poetry:

> A Princedom asked of a Domination
> 'What is Sin?' And he replied, 'The consumption
> Of men by men. They've all got
> An ache to eat what they are not.'[50]

Here the original sin, eating of the apple, is transformed in light
verse into cannibalism. This is the type of macabre shock that

the reader of Spark must begin to expect. Exactly what this cannibalism means is made a little clearer by another section of the poem which describes several animals which failed to adapt to the realities of the world and so became extinct:

> Everyone knows about the Dodo;
> The same goes for the Great Auk.
> The inoffensive Okapi's crime
> Was trying to be other beasts at the same time.[51]

Dougal explains to Merle Coverdale the nature of the Okapi:

'An Okapi is a rare beast from the Congo. It looks a little like a deer, but it tries to be a giraffe. It has stripes and it stretches its neck as far as possible and its ears are like a donkey's. It is a little bit of everything. There are only a few in captivity. It is very shy.'[52]

Dougal has said that Merle is like the Okapi, but when she asks why he thinks so, he can reply only 'Because you're so shy.' Since she has only this one quality Merle cannot possibly be an Okapi, and clearly it is Dougal who tries to be a little bit of everything.

Dougal's playing of many roles may have its comic side, but it is potentially immoral in that it threatens to extend fictions of himself over the lives of others; he threatens by imaginative extension of himself to usurp the individuality of others. This imperialism of the personality, coupled with his absenteeism make of Dougal a potential fascist, and a fore-runner of Jean Brodie. At heart this Okapi quality is the Romantic 'negative capability', which finds its expression as the desire to be completely identified with the other. Dougal is the typical figure of the modern artist, isolated in his society; but he is not isolated because of the evils of bourgeois society (although Peckham is as bourgeois and tedious as possible), but because of the artistic faculty itself. Vision is alienating and, it is suggested, the source of evil. Dougal stands in for Humphrey Place and is the succubus-like author of the infamous refusal at the altar. Also, he substitutes for Merle Coverdale as the object of Mr Druce's affections, and this substitution leads to murder. All of these themes, of supplanting devil, the evils of 'vision' and cannibalism, are united in an image near the beginning of the novel.

Dougal has been telling Humphrey of his research into the history of Peckham:

> 'Fascinating,' Humphrey said.
> Dougal gazed at him like a succubus whose mouth is its eyes.[53]

Humphrey is fascinated like a bird before the gaze of a snake. As succubus Dougal will stand in for Humphrey at the wedding and speak through his mouth. Dougal's eyes become his mouth, and his 'vision' devours other people; 'vision', since it denies the independent reality of other people, is cannibalistic.

The story that Dougal tells Humphrey about Peckham that so fascinates him is of a mermaid exhibited at a fair in 1840 in Peckham. The mermaid, according to the newspaper report dug up by Dougal, 'combs her hair in the manner practised in China, and admires herself in a glass in the manner practised everywhere.'[54] This activity of hair-combing occurs frequently in the novel, notoriously in the scene in which Dougal breaks down in tears in the cafeteria because his girl has left him, and the factory girls console him by combing his hair: 'It calms you down, a good comb' one of the girls remarks. Dougal, then, is associated with another beast of various parts, the mermaid, and it is clear that his ability to play various roles is merely another way of admiring himself in the glass. His protean creativity comes to nothing more than egotism.

Dougal, as artist, brings a new interest, a new taste and freshness to the bourgeois world of Peckham. That is what we have come to expect of the artist: he is the rejecter and leavener of society at the same time. Society itself is a pattern of conformities, a collection of dead gestures, of instinct and passion become habit, lacking in vision. Just as she questions this typical portrait of the artist, so too does Muriel Spark suggest that even in the very depths of the *mauvaise foi* of the Peckham compromises, there is something which is humanly valuable. The clearest example of living in 'bad faith' would seem to be the tepid and longstanding 'love affair' of Miss Coverdale and Mr Druce. Their automatic habits – Druce mixes drinks, changes into his slippers, they have dinner, watch television, undress to the numbers, every time they meet – hint that they may be modelled on the typist and her 'lover' in *The Waste Land*. Under questioning by Dougal Merle Coverdale begins to see into the lack of romance in her life:

'But you feel,' Dougal said, 'that you're living a lie.'
'I do,' she said. 'You've put my very thoughts into words.'[55]

She tells Dougal that 'she had fallen out of love with Mr. Druce yet could not discontinue the relationship, she didn't know why.' Dougal advises her, since she is free, to stop seeing Druce. She replies: 'After six years, going on seven, Dougal, I'm tied in a sort of way. And what sort of job would I get at thirty-eight?' Mrs Spark manages to make Miss Coverdale's plea sound convincing and when she says she is tied we tend to feel that she is tied not out of mere habit or weakness, but by shared experience, even if the experience is not of the Romantic kind. The tie is a human one, and the 'bad faith' inherent in Dougal's vision is that it takes no account of such experience. As Mrs Frierne his landlady says to him, 'You want to learn some experience, son.'[56]

In *The Ballad of Peckham Rye* then, we see that Mrs Spark continues to work for a fictional expression of the meaning of fictions in life, and in particular shows her growing interest in the matter of dramatic role-playing. Like Caroline who was fascinated by Eleanor's dramatic self-presentation, Mrs Spark is fascinated in her fiction by figures given to self-dramatisation, to creating fictions of themselves. No one novel seems able to convey the whole truth of the matter, and each individual novel is like an attempt to discover the meaning of a mysterious and abiding obsession. In *The Comforters* it was found that role-playing contained many dangers, in particular there was a danger of any role, or mask, 'sticking'. The conclusion of that novel, however, seems to toy with the notion that a pattern of life adhered to consistently could bring about a 'cure'. *The Ballad of Peckham Rye* picks up this possibility and shows what happens when the artistic personality refuses to allow any one public presentation or definition of the self to develop a consistency. Such a refusal amounts to never being there for others, and it is seen to be the Devil's choice of life style. Self-dramatisation is still viewed negatively as the natural mode for the man of vision; both 'vision' and 'posing' are cannibalistic and cannibalism turns out to be another word for solipsism:

both deny the reality of others. It must be said, though, that despite the threat of danger and violence which seems to accompany the devil's skill at changing his shape, there is still something appealing and attractive and imaginatively stimulating about the figure of Dougal Douglas. This may be the false charm of Milton's Satan or Cary's Jim Latter, but it also attests to the strength of Mrs Spark's interest in this particular question of protean 'posing'.

The Ballad of Peckham Rye, The Bachelors and *The Prime of Miss Jean Brodie*, all published in the period 1960–1, form almost a trilogy on the subject of demonology. Although it is my intention to pursue the theme of this chapter directly from Dougal Douglas to Jean Brodie and beyond, it is worth having a brief look at *The Bachelors*.[57] The central character is Ronald Bridges and as his name suggests he is a more successful medium – better at building bridges, at overcoming dualisms – than is the spiritualist Patrick Seton, whose name is as close to Satan as he is to absolute evil. Bridges informs us that the theme of the novel is 'all demonology and to do with creatures of the air'. Behind the title is St Paul's bitter consolation that it is better to marry than to burn, and in one way or another the bachelors, the 'fruitless souls, crumbling tinder' are heretics: 'It shows a dualistic attitude, not to marry if you aren't going to be a priest or a religious. You've got to affirm the oneness of reality in some form or another.'[58] So the subject is not really Kensington bachelors as such, so much as bachelorism of the spirit, or dualism, and it is Patrick Seton's unusual attitude to women and marriage that gives us an important clue to the evil inherent in his intense spiritualism.

Seton has some remarkable successes as a seer and at times he seems ready to transcend the body altogether and enter the empyrean. This dualism, however, has its own ironic limitation since Seton's trances are not much different from the epileptic fits – that is, the physical abnormality – of the other 'medium' Bridges. In fact, Seton's trances have on occasion been heightened by physical means. Dr Lyte is under Seton's power and as his pawn 'even went so far as voluntarily to obtain the new drug which had been employed, for experimental purposes, to induce epileptic convulsions in rats, and which, taken in certain minor quantities, greatly improved both the spectacular quality of Patrick's trances and his actual psychic powers'.[59] Despite the obvious ground of his spiritual powers, Seton is the enemy of the flesh and in his pursuit of absolute freedom indulges in the perverse desire to free the woman who would be his wife, Alice, from the confines of her body: 'I will release her spirit from this gross body.' As he half-contemplates the murder he feels 'an acute throb of anticipatory pleasure at the mental vision of Alice crumpled up . . . '.[60]

What keeps Muriel Spark from becoming merely a 'Catholic novelist' is her ability to reveal religious themes at the centre of life as it goes on day by day, for everyone. The 'heresy' of Seton arises from his rejection of dogma, but it has an equal source in his rejection of man-made laws. His heresy is ultimately the attempt to identify himself with God and from this temptation to expand the ego infinitely none is free. This heresy, it is suggested, possibly has its origin in sexual distortions; or else the two disorders are cognate. There is perhaps a more universal spring, however. Patrick Seton likes to have everything going his own way, in his own dreamy, visionary world, and reality is offensive. He is constantly being 'upset by all the disgusting details':

> There is a lot of nasty stuff in life which comes breaking up our ecstasy, our inheritance, I think, said Patrick, people should read more poetry and dream their dreams, and I do not recognize man-made laws and dogmas.[61]

When taken to excess, the virtues of the poetic imagination become regressive (Seton's psychic energy comes from his vaguely remembered childhood), neurotic and destructive. The seance group headed by Seton is called the 'Interior Spiral' – an image to be repeated later in *The Public Image* with reference to the suicidal 'artist' Frederick Christopher – and one can see that as he climbs the interior spiral of his own mind, spirit, or imagination, he must eventually come a cropper against the top of his own skull. Dualism, like solipsism, won't work.

If excessive individuality is one source of evil, the solution is not to be mindlessly sought in 'sociability'. At a Chelsea party Bridges reacts to the excess socialisation:

Isobel's party stormed upon him like a play in which the actors had begun to jump off the stage, so that he was no longer simply the witness of a comfortable satire, but was suddenly surrounded by a company of ridiculous demons.[62]

The suggestion in this passage is that although one cannot live merely like 'automatic animals' making 'sociable noises', there is a dramatic discipline to life, not equal to social place, position or 'role', which one must accept. When one refuses to play a proper part the result is the multiplication of demons. Between demonology on the one hand and 'automatic animals' in Society on the other there is perhaps a dramatic medium, a bridge of some kind.

Patrick Seton is himself addicted to drama of a sort, a very peculiar sort. He relives 'the dream of childhood . . . from which everything else deviates':

He is a dreamy child: a dreamer of dreams, they say with pride, as he wanders back from walks in the botanical gardens, or looks up from his book. *Mary Rose* by J. M. Barrie is Patrick's favourite, and he is taken to the theatre to see it acted, and is sharply shocked by the sight of the real actresses and actors with painted faces performing outwardly on the open platform this tender romance about the girl who was stolen by the fairies on a Hebridean island.[63]

Seton would reduce all external drama to the drama of his own soul and will never get to the stage of mature development achieved by Chester Nimmo who learns to live in the world of public drama. Seton has a defective sense of the role of imagination, believing that romantic, dreamy, visionary self-indulgence is enough. This 'ideal' is shown to be dualistic and destructive. The drama of life requires that the internal, the private, obsessional and fantastic find some way of confronting the external and actual. Ronald Bridges has a brief insight into the value of visions, of fictions or 'creatures of the air':

It is all demonology and to do with creatures of the air, and there are others beside ourselves, he thought, who lie in their beds like happy countries that have no history.[64]

The proper role for imagination is to discover the reality of others and not to aggrandise the self. Ronald Bridges can see that there are others in the world, Patrick Seton cannot; that is the theme of *The Bachelors* in a nutshell.

The Prime of Miss Jean Brodie[65] investigates further the moral ambiguity involved in creative self-expression. Miss Jean Brodie achieves an apotheosis of personality; 'prime' takes on an almost reified existence as if it were a 'calling' rather than a manifestation of potential (in this same semi-religious sense Bridges is a 'confirmed' bachelor). For Miss Brodie, being in her prime means that creative individuality is in full bloom. Her prime gives her the freedom to be assertively and interestingly unconventional. And yet we find that there is a fascistic tendency to Miss Brodie. No matter how impressive she is as a teacher, somehow she carries creative self-expression too far; she over-extends herself (her 'self') and so must be stopped or delimited. Sandy Stranger puts a stop to Miss Brodie and despite the unpleasant nature of Sandy (who is constantly being referred to as the 'pig-eyed' Sandy), one must finally agree that her decision to 'betray' Miss Brodie is right.

Miss Brodie's prime cannot be called a 'pose' perhaps, since she does not seem wilfully or hypocritically to adopt her 'prime' in order to dupe people as Dougal does. Nor is 'prime' a mask or public role which hides a personal emptiness. And yet, one can sense that we are in the same world where these opposites are to be found; we are being confronted again with the nature of the interaction between personal potential and public expression, or realisation of that potential. Miss Brodie's prime is her way of being 'devoted' to her girls. Miss Brodie is the equal of Dougal Douglas in the realm of creative personality. What makes *The Prime of Miss Jean Brodie* differ from *The Ballad of Peckham Rye* is its taking of the discussion a step further by having Miss Brodie 'stick' to one public expression of herself as a devoted teacher. In her prime, mask and self coincide; the public expression is a lucid realisation of potential. Nevertheless, it turns out that the moral ambiguity surrounding the question of 'how to be' is not resolved. Despite the commitment, Miss Brodie still is guilty of the original sin, the 'consumption of men by men'. Although one might think that Miss Brodie's devotion as a teacher would lead her to transcend solipsism, the novel reveals that she does not. What had seemed to be the problem, a lack of coincidence between inner self and the public expression of that self, is found not to be the source of evil in this novel. The source seems instead to be the self itself. Simply being oneself, fully and in the prime, may be the transgression against others, the original sin.

Miss Brodie centres her life around a belief in Art. Her scale of value is clearly expressed on this issue; she says 'Art comes first, and then science.'[66] She falls in love with the school artist, Teddy Lloyd, but refuses to be his mistress, presumably because of a reluctance to interfere with his family life since he is Roman Catholic. She teaches her pupils about Art, in a peculiarly personal way. When she receives the answer that Leonardo da Vinci is the greatest Italian painter she says, 'That is incorrect. The answer is Giotto, he is my favourite.' As David Lodge points out, Miss Brodie teaches her own preferences as if they were facts, and Lodge is essentially correct when he says that she 'exemplifies the defects of the uncontrolled romantic sensibility.'[67] This is true of Miss Brodie, but it must be constantly borne in mind that she also represents the virtues of such a sensibility, and although she has a fascistic influence over her pupils' lives, for the most part they shake off her influence 'as a dog shakes pond-water from its coat'.[68]

Lodge, in his essay on this novel, usefully makes reference to Frank Kermode's discussion of fictions and it is worth repeating here since it is a theme which recurs throughout this study:

> We have to distinguish between myths and fictions. Fictions can degenerate into myths whenever they are not consciously held to be fictive. In this sense anti-Semitism is a degenerate fiction, a myth; Lear is a fiction. Myth operates within diagrams of ritual, which presupposes total and adequate explanations of things as they are and were; it is a sequence of radically unchangeable gestures. Fictions are for finding things out, and they change as the needs of sense-making change. Myths are the agents of stability, fictions the agents of change. Myths call for absolute, fictions for conditional consent . . . literary fictions belong to Vaihinger's category of the consciously false. They are not subject, like hypotheses, to proof or disconfirmation, only, if they come to lose their operational effectiveness, to neglect.[69]

It is on this basis that Lodge defends Muriel Spark's use of 'omniscience' which is one of the devices for making conscious the fictive nature of the novel. Lodge's article is one of the most revealing pieces of criticism about *The Prime of Miss Jean Brodie* and in his use of Kermode's insights into the nature of fictions, he casts a deal of light on her work as a whole. It is a little misleading, however, to consider this one novel in isolation as if it summed up all of Spark's ethic about fictions. With an awareness of *The Comforters* and *The Ballad of Peckham Rye* in mind, one can see that tied in with the question of the consciousness or unconsciousness of fictions is another profound investigation of the ways in which the self can both be completely free in itself, and yet be for others without either diminishing itself nor denying the reality of others. In fact, as we shall shortly see, *The Public Image* continues this investigation by means of a character who is completely unconscious of the fictions she makes and she seems free from any sort of transgression. Miss Brodie's excess is that she commits the crime that seems to cling to all those blessed with a highly creative internal life: cannibalism.

What she tries to do is to substitute her own life for the lives around her. Despite her dedication and apparent self-denial – or perhaps because of that self-denial – she is discovered to be arranging a very strange relationship which would allow her to experience a vicarious love affair with Lloyd. Vicarious experience is a very economical form of experience, in that it allows one to have the benefit of experience without having to submit oneself to the material facts of experience.

> It was plain that Miss Brodie wanted Rose with her instinct to start preparing to be Teddy Lloyd's lover, and Sandy with her insight to act as informant on the affair. It was to this end that Rose and Sandy had been chosen as the crème de la crème. There was a whiff of sulphur about the idea which fascinated Sandy in her present mind. After all, it was only an idea.[70]

The whiff of sulphur will be familiar to those just come from *The Ballad of Peckham Rye*. Sandy is ready to be fascinated (as Humphrey was) by the idea, only so long as the idea is not materially manifested in action. When it is, she 'betrays' Miss Brodie.

The theme of substitution is echoed throughout the novel. Miss Brodie takes on Gordon Lowther as an obvious stand-in for the lover she cannot have in Teddy Lloyd, until Lowther can take the offence no longer and marries Miss Lockhart, the science teacher. In every one of the portraits that Lloyd paints of the schoolgirls he unconsciously substitutes Miss Brodie's face for that of the sitter (she is not substituted, however, in the portraits of his wife and children, her refusal to interfere in the family of her beloved extending even to his unconscious life apparently). Even the minor Misses Kerr repeat this theme in their sewing classes: 'instead of teaching sewing they took each girl's work in hand, one by one, and did most of it for her.'[71] Such a method is obviously highly inappropriate as far as the passing on of traditional skills and information is concerned. What makes Miss Brodie's case more complicated and more interesting is that she is not a teacher at all in the traditional sense. She is 'teaching' her pupils how to be individuals and this can only be done by example and through a period of mimicking, of identification: 'By the time their friendship with Miss Brodie was of seven years' standing, it had worked itself into their bones, so that they could not break away without, as it were, splitting their bones to do so.'[72] There is no escaping the pain in this type of relationship, and although Miss Brodie tries to stuff Lowther with more and more food when she visits him at Cramond, it cannot substitute for the love which she cannot give him. When she is with Lowther she is really 'absent' in her mind, perhaps living out a fantasy of what it would be like with her ideal lover:

> And she made him eat a Chester cake, and spoke to him in a slightly more Edinburgh way than usual, so as to make up to him by both means for the love she was giving to Teddy Lloyd instead of to him.[73]

Her ideal lover, of course, is not actually Lloyd. He is little more than a convenient post to which she can pin her dreams. Her real lover is some impossible romantic ideal which by definition can never be realised in the flesh since the actual kills the ideal. Teddy Lloyd is as close as Miss Brodie dares allow her dream, her fiction, to reality. Individual men in her life tend to melt into one figure and Sandy recalls 'Miss Brodie's variations on her love story, when she had attached to her first, wartime lover the attributes of the art master and the singing master who had then newly entered her orbit'.[74] She then notes that Teddy Lloyd's artistic method is similarly 'economical' and goes on to echo Newman in the phrase referred to earlier: 'it always seemed afterwards to Sandy that where there was a choice of various courses, the most economical was the best, and that the course to be taken was the most expedient and most suitable at the time for all the objects in hand.' Whereas Miss Brodie's economy becomes a fascistic economy in that her individuality replaces that of everyone else and her personal vision becomes cannibalistic, Sandy adopts a different form of economy and goes to the opposite extreme in valuing objectivity. Her view of 'objects in hand' is one way of overcoming the solipsism of personalism, but like the error it cures, it goes too far. If Sandy is like an assassin in the way she puts a stop to Miss Brodie, Miss Brodie herself is apparently more than a ready victim: 'she had elected herself to grace in so particular a way and with more exotic suicidal enchantment than if she had simply taken to drink like other spinsters who couldn't stand it any more.'[75] Once again we see the Narcissus myth at the bottom of one of Muriel Spark's novels; Miss Brodie is another imaginative, inner-directed, personality who wants to see her own face reflected in the faces of others. On the other side of the cannibalist-Okapi syndrome lies the sin of self-slaughter.

Readers have often been bothered about the apparent lack of motivation for Sandy's betrayal, finding in her sudden turning a forced note in the story. Her defection, if that is what it is, can be readily understood, it seems to me, as the inevitable act of one supreme individualist against another. Sandy learns the value of individualism from Miss Brodie and so her eventual rebellion seems unavoidable. It is when Miss Brodie tries to bring her dreams into some semblance of reality that Sandy is moved to rebel. Miss Brodie prepares the vicarious love affair with great precision. We see her with her arm around Rose's shoulder 'as if she and Rose were one'.[76] Sandy guesses the truth about the nature of the relationship with Lowther: 'Sandy assumed that the reason why Miss Brodie had stopped sleeping with Gordon Lowther was that her sexual feelings

were satisfied by proxy; and Rose was predestined to be the
lover of Teddy Lloyd.'[77] Sandy here puts two observations side
by side, but her mind is not yet active enough to connect them
and draw the conclusion. She is very near to doing this, but as
yet her insights are connected by a semi-colon and not by
'therefore'.

When Miss Brodie gives voice to her belief that 'Rose and
Teddy Lloyd will soon be lovers,' the actuality tears Sandy's
mind out of its subjective musings and she becomes capable of
connected reasoning:

> All at once Sandy realized that this was not all theory and a
> kind of Brodie game, in the way that so much of life was
> unreal talk and game-planning, like the prospects of a war
> and other theories that people were putting about in the air
> like pigeons, and one said, "Yes, of course, it's inevitable."
> But this was not theory; Miss Brodie meant it. Sandy looked
> at her, and perceived that the woman was obsessed by the
> need for Rose to sleep with the man she herself was in love
> with; there was nothing new in the idea, it was the reality
> that was new.'[78]

Sandy realises that she must put a stop to the expansive Miss
Brodie because she perceives (even with her short-sighted pig-
eyes) that every personality must have a limit, its internal freedom *must* be objectively delimited by factual reality.

So Sandy puts a stop to Miss Brodie's rampant fiction, and in
doing so scores a victory for Science over Art (although Miss
Brodie believes that Art comes first and then Science, in this
instance the first are last and the last first). If Sandy were
nothing more than a copy of Miss Brodie, it is not likely that she
would ever have had the strength to turn against her. However
Sandy joins to the subjectivity learned from Miss Brodie, an objectivity learned from the science teacher, Miss Lockhart. Miss
Lockhart begins her first lesson with the dramatic an-
nouncement, 'I have enough gunpowder in this jar to blow up
the whole school.'[79] She possesses tremendous power, but she
keeps it responsibly under control, 'she could also blow up the
school with her jar of gunpowder and would never dream of
doing so.'[80] Lodge is perhaps right in suggesting that Miss
Brodie, by implication would dream of doing so, but the novel

shows just how nearly impossible it is for any of Miss Brodie's romantic dreams ever to be realised in fact. The more she dreams, the less power she has. Miss Lockhart, on the other hand, has power, the ability to act in reality with potentially disastrous results, but fortunately she does not dream. Sandy moves between both poles. As the protégée of Miss Brodie she dreams, but she acts as the initiate of Miss Lockhart. It is Miss Brodie herself who will be blown up, and it is Sandy, with a sense of power transmitted to her by Miss Lockhart, who will do it.

The ability to act comes with the attainment of objectivity; that is to say with the clear recognition of the reality of the world external to the self. From the time they enter the senior school – after having left Miss Brodie's class, that is – the girls drop their obsession with sex and fantasy. Their language takes on a scientific cast which can be very humorous, just as their subjective romantic musings in the letter they draft from Miss Brodie to her lover Lowther tend to the humorous:

> By the summer term, to stave off the onslaughts of boredom, and to reconcile the necessities of the working day with their love for Miss Brodie, Sandy and Jenny had begun to apply their new-found knowledge to Miss Brodie in a merry fashion. 'If Miss Brodie was weighed in air and then in water . . .' And, when Mr Lowther seemed not quite himself at the singing lesson, they would remind each other that an immersed Jean Brodie displaces its own weight of Gordon Lowther.[81]

The affection continues, but the mode of perception is changing. The girls are confident that Miss Brodie will continue to be a match for any threat posed to her by the Kerr sisters:

> Miss Brodie was easily the equal of both sisters together, she was the square on the hypotenuse of a right-angled triangle and they were only the squares on the other two sides.[82]

Jenny's mother is of the opinion that Miss Brodie gives her students too much freedom. In the science room it is different: 'All the girls in the science room were doing just as they liked . . . and that's what they were supposed to be doing.'[83] Sandy finds a paradoxical equilibrium in the science room where freedom is given sanction, is somehow equal to duty: 'science class is supposed to be free, it's allowed.' Sandy is fascinated by all the strange apparatus by which Miss Lockhart 'established her mysterious priesthood' and her first conversion is to the clear-sighted objectivity of science.

What Sandy gains from science is a disciplining of subjective impulse in order to pursue truth. She does not arrive at the whole truth about Miss Brodie, of course, and this fact explains her lack of repose in the convent. Miss Brodie lacks any kind of order or discipline to her subjectivity. Her 'prime' and her devotion turn out not to be ordering principles so much as devices for intensifying egoism. The narrator suggests that it is only the Catholic Church that 'could have embraced, even while it disciplined, her soaring and diving spirit, it might even have normalized her'.[84] The novel does not necessarily endorse the solution offered here, and 'normalized' sounds as much like a threat as a promise of salvation. Miss Brodie represents a beautiful, lyrical and suicidal individuality, which is countered by an ugly, objective, expedient ability to act with power in the world. Muriel Spark asks us to choose neither. If a value by which we might begin to assess both Miss Brodie and Sandy does emerge from the novel, it is in the overcoming of the limitations of one's personal vision that it is to be found. Sandy takes a scientific way of doing this and achieves a necessary result. Science though is too small a God, since if it offers an objective look, it also reduces people to objects.* Considering that she takes her principle, apparently, from Newman, and later undergoes a religious conversion, we may be right in suspecting that Sandy is on the right road. From the anxious and tormented way in which she clutches the bars of the grille in the convent we can be sure that at the very least she is not on the primrose path, which leads to the everlasting bonfire. There is, in fact, one brief passage in the novel which reveals precisely what Sandy achieves by being able to move from the Artistic to the Scientific point of view. She muses on what Edinburgh has meant to her: 'And many times throughout her life Sandy knew with a shock, when speaking to people whose childhood had been in Edinburgh, that there were other people's Edinburghs

---

* It is useful to recall Alec Warner's 'scientific' observations in *Memento Mori*.

quite different from hers. . . . '[85] At the very least, Sandy is capable of this shock of recognition which comes when the individual imagination admits that others exist, that there are other sets of eyes in the world which see the same 'facts' with a different ambience and a different meaning. She learns to admit, in George Eliot's phrase, that the *other* has 'an equivalent centre of self, whence the lights and shadows must always fall with a certain difference'.[86]

We can see then, after a close look at what may at first reading seem an over-simple book, that being oneself is not the source of evil after all. Rather it is the Romantic and Artistic idealisation of the imaginative self, and the belief in an undisciplined absolutely free creative self, which is the source of danger. For Muriel Spark, once again, absolute freedom is a fiction; which is not to say that it is not True or that it does not exist. The fiction of freedom, or the freedom of fiction has its own proper realm and rules. What Mrs Spark seems to be trying to make us grasp, by implication and suggestion – by Art and fiction – is that one needs as well as this inner freedom, a clear recognition of the outer world and a disposition to act in the real world without allowing our fictions to violate the uniqueness of other lives – whether the fictions be Artistic or Scientific ones. When private fictions threaten to turn themselves into public realities, there is a noticeable whiff of sulphur.

The Prime of Miss Jean Brodie suggests that it is in overcoming solipsism that the way to reconciling the opposites of inner and outer lies, but it does not really offer a triumphant resolution of the problems with which it confronts us. Perhaps we should take the desperate, bar-rattling Sandy at the end of the novel as an image of her author trying to work her way through the impossible and confusing ideas she has conjured up. One might be tempted to make such a substitution were it not for our knowledge that she believes 'things which are difficult to believe, but I believe them because they are absolute.' If this is her own private solution, it does not obtrude into the novels, unless it can be said to be implicitly given to the reader because of its very absence in the novel. Her concern is the imprisonment of the self within itself and the only safe way out of this imprisonment lies in recognising an external limit to our own view of the world. For her own private uses, this recognition is the recognition of an absolute other. For the novels, it is enough to begin to recognise the reality of another human being. This is all that Mrs Spark's Catholicism means to her fiction, and it certainly does not represent a dogmatic violation of the novels.

With *The Prime of Miss Jean Brodie*, Mrs Spark seems to reach a peak of achievement, and at least a temporary impasse. It is such a good novel in so many ways that what comes after it is in danger of appearing merely secondary, no matter what its merits. *The Girls of Slender Means* (1963) has few enough merits and instead of carrying on a theme developed in earlier novels it is repetitious in an almost mechanical way. Nicholas is a demonic figure reminiscent of Dougal Douglas, without his liveliness, who abandons art and is converted to Catholicism by a vision of evil. One of the girls, Joanna, is burned to death trapped in the May of Teck building in a scene that is a close imitation of the death of Mary Macgregor in *The Prime of Miss Jean Brodie*, who 'ran hither and thither in the hotel fire and was trapped by it'.[87] The vision of evil which so moves Nicholas is a sight of slender Selina who slips back through the narrow window-opening into the burning building, not, as it first appears, to sacrifice herself in a rescue attempt, but just to collect her famous Schiaparelli dress without which her social 'poise' would not be perfect. Selina is famous for poise, but her public propriety and detachment are nothing more than a deceptive surface belying an inhuman interior. 'Poise' as a means of public self-expression is revealed as an inadequate disciplining force; as, in fact, a denial of the very creative, living self which needs mediation before it can appear to the world.

The Mandelbaum Gate (1965) also deals with the inadequacy of strict public roles which serve to repress the self rather than express it. Barbara Vaughan breaks through apparent barriers and draws the highly repressed diplomat Freddy with her. Barbara, by her adventurous willingness to take action – crossing into the Arab half of Jerusalem despite the threat of death from Arabs watching for Israeli spies – finds fulfilment for her passions and also performs a public duty by capturing some actual spies. Both of these novels deny that institutionalised roles, or modes of behaviour which are already highly defined and ready to be adopted like a mask which hides the face rather than reveals it more fully, are adequate. The Eichmann trial which is carried on in the background of *The Mandelbaum Gate* suggests clearly enough the evil inherent in the surrendering of individual freedom of choice and conscience to a social fiction of duty Any evil is possible for the man who can hide his personal responsibility by the claim that he is 'just doing his job'. Although this theme is given interesting embodiment in *The Mandelbaum Gate*, in itself it is nothing more than an elaboration on the theme already well developed in *The Comforters*: the fascination with poses and roles threatens a dehumanisation if any role is allowed to 'stick' and so kill off personal freedom.

Just as Muriel Spark is not content to repeat the achievement of earlier writers, but must always be searching for something new to say and a new way to say it, so too she could not for long be satisfied to repeat her earlier achievements in slightly differing forms. After *The Prime of Miss Jean Brodie* (1961) there is a temporary lull in her creative achievement until the publishing of *The Public Image*[88] in 1968, which sees the addition of a new twist to the set of problems and situations with which Mrs Spark is fascinated and obsessed. In the last three of her novels she has renounced the attractive central character, such as Dougal Douglas and Jean Brodie. One result has been a drastic simplifying of the complexity and ambiguity of the tales and a diminution of the 'entertainment' level of the novels. Her later novels may not be as much 'fun' as her earlier ones, but for the assiduous reader of Spark, they are extremely interesting and important.

One might call Annabel Christopher an anti-heroine, except she does not even have any of the left-handed romance usually associated with such characters. She is descended from Mrs Hogg and Sandy Stranger but, unlike her predecessors, she is a central figure in the novel and not a mere *ficelle*. It is unlikely that *The Public Image* will ever be widely popular with the average reader, precisely because Annabel is unlikeable, unlovely, and victorious. She has none of the usual signs or attributes by which we recognise value, or potential, in a person and yet she achieves remarkable success because, it seems, she has a public image which has been painstakingly constructed by the film industry. Her husband Frederick, on the other hand, exhibits the proper signs of genius; he is introspective, trying to be a creative writer, is very sensitive and vulnerable to the evils of the modern world. But the hard logic of *The Public Image* suggests that unrealised potential is nothing; there are no mute inglorious Miltons. The message is like that of Hopkins's poem: 'What I do is me.' What counts is what gets done in the open public world where people actually live; our secret romantic visions of our potential heroism, like those of Lord Jim, are so much lumber.

Luigi Leopardi, called 'Voo' by his friends, describes the change wrought in Annabel:

> Before I made you the Tiger-Lady, you didn't even look like a lady in public, never mind a tiger in private. It's what I began to make of you that you've partly become.[89]

The 'partly' is an important qualification because, as Annabel later indicates, she has never really cared for 'tiger-sex', in public or in private. Innocently, Annabel suggests that Leopardi has spelled out the theme of Pygmalion. Clearly, Leopardi is not the only magus of transformations, and Annabel's process of change would seem to be as old as history, as old as mythology. There is no doubt though that Leopardi is essentially correct, Annabel changes:

> Annabel was still a little slip of a thing, but her face had changed, as if by action of many famous cameras, into a mould of her public figuration.[90]

By a surprising use of the powers of the omniscient narrator, we are given a look at Annabel's constitutional defect:

> But in those earlier times when she began to be in demand in English films, she had no means of knowing that she was, in fact, stupid, for, after all, it is the deep core of stupidity that it thrives on the absence of a looking-glass.[91]

Ironically, as a defect, stupidity has its advantages; because she is not conscious of her deficiency she acts without reference to it and so overcomes it:

> In those early days when she was working in small parts her stupidity started to melt; she had not in the least attempted

to overcome her stupidity, but she now saw, with the confidence of practice in her film roles, that she had somehow circumvented it. She did not need to be clever, she had only to exist.[92]

The last sentence serves to disparage mere cleverness and indicates that the novel is, in a way, a response to Stein's question in *Lord Jim*: 'How to be?' Annabel is not paralysed, or tempted to suicide like Narcissus, because she has no looking-glass. Also, unlike Jim, she apparently has no imagination, and so she is able to work effectively in the world. The result of this working in the ranks is the transformation of her personality, and the transformation is not for the worse.

There are many instances in the novel of Annabel's self-control and her devotion to duty. The strongest sense of duty she feels is for her baby, but the most striking example of her professional character comes out in the press conference she holds after her husband's suicide, at the time when she was supposedly, and as everyone believes, taking part in an orgy. Annabel denies that there was any party and her stout Italian neighbours stand by her in spite of the fact that they saw the party going on:

> The neighbours were silent, upholding that principle of appearance appropriate to an occasion which they called *bella figura*.[93]

As Annabel's name suggests, it is her capacity for *bella figura*, for putting a good face on circumstances, that is the source of her strength. Leopardi tells Annabel, 'Life is all the achievement of an effect. Only the animals remain natural.'[94] The human world then, is an unnatural, artificial, artful and creative one. To live one must act, and that means one must be an actor. Full integration of the self can only come with self-dramatisation:*

> In practice her own instinctive method of acting consisted in playing herself in a series of poses for the camera, just as if she

* This idea is given full expression in Mrs Spark's play *Doctors of Philosophy*, Macmillan (London, 1963). Leonara, one of the PhDs, overcomes the limitations of her intellectuality by discovering a 'dramatic sense' of herself. The result is that she feels 'like the first woman who's ever been born. I feel I've discovered the world.' (p. 64). She is able to stop playing roles that have been created for her by others, and to create free roles for herself.

were getting her photograph taken for private purposes. She became skilled at this; she became extremely expert.[95]

Whereas Annabel has the uncomplicated idea that when she is 'acting' she is simply 'working', Frederick has a much more sophisticated notion:

> He was firm in his opinion that an actor should be sincere in the part he played, and should emotionally experience whatever he was to portray, from the soul outward. Even in her acting, he thought, Annabel is a sort of cheat, she acts from a sense of manners only.[96]

Frederick prides himself on the integrity of his 'private self-image'[97] but it is Annabel's manners that have more consequence for the world. Unable to force his personal worth on the world, Frederick must watch Annabel climb the ladder of public success while he pursues a more restricted means of ascent:

> His mind took the inward turns of a spiral staircase, viewing from every altitude and point of contortion the unblemished, untried, fact of his talent. In reality Frederick was an untrained intellectual.[98]

Annabel has turned outward, projected herself into the world, and so learned by its corrections how to live. Frederick's interior staircase leads him to commit suicide by leaping from the staircase to the foundation of the Church of St John and St Paul (perhaps the Church could also have tamed and disciplined his 'soaring and diving spirit'). This leap occurs while Annabel is in the process of studying a new script tentatively called *The Staircase*.

Frederick's suicide is not self-punishment; it is a last desperate attempt to force his ego on the world. He hopes to destroy Annabel's public image by having arranged for an orgiastic party to take place at Annabel's flat at the moment of his suicide. He very nearly succeeds in his plan, but it is left to Billy (who hangs around 'like a worn-out something that one had bought years ago on the hire-purchase system, and was still paying up with no end to it in sight'), to pursue revenge. Annabel gives up her career, but she does so by choice. She refuses to

pay Billy's blackmail and so stop his exposing of Frederick's letters which, although faked, will sway public opinion. When
Frederick poses before the public, he is not playing himself; he
is lying in order to destroy a reality which he cannot accept.
Annabel's public image is not destroyed then, it is sacrificed.
Here we see the deficiency of a merely social mode of transcendence of the ego: the roles offered by Society, roles like
'starlet', are tainted by the perverse 'economy' of our times.
Annabel is aware of this deficiency and will not risk herself too
far with a false god:

> She felt a curious fear of display where the baby was con-
> cerned, as if this deep and complete satisfaction might be dis-
> figured or melted away by some public image.[99]

The semi-poetic prose of Frederick's posthumous letters
reflects his wish to make one last impression on the misguided
public world by showing how the sensitive artist has been
driven to death by the evils of Society. He writes:

> You are a beautiful shell, like something washed up on the
> sea-shore, a collector's item, perfectly formed, a pearly shell
> – but empty, devoid of the life it once held.[100]

This is rubbish and Annabel pays scant attention to it. The
image of the shell persists, however, and it concludes the novel:

> Waiting for the order to board, she felt both free and unfree.
> The heavy weight of the bags was gone; she felt as if she was
> still, curiously, pregnant with the baby, but not pregnant in
> fact. She was pale as a shell. She did not wear her dark
> glasses. Nobody recognized her as she stood, having moved
> the baby in a sense weightlessly and perpetually within her,
> as an empty shell contains, by its very structure, the echo and
> harking image of former and former seas.[101]

Unlike Eleanor and Georgina Hogg, Annabel does not need
to fear death by water. Despite Leopardi's claim that only the
animals remain natural, we see, surprisingly, that it is Annabel
herself who is presented to us in images of nature. Just as the
shell is essential to the life of any crustacean, so too it seems the
public side of the self, one's appearance or role, is a necessary
and natural part of an integrated personality. The shell image

suggests the accretion of experience which makes both the history of an individual and of a culture. It evokes the 'harking image' of 'former and former seas', of seas which stretch back into an ancient and mythic past which is made to sound infinitely rich and creative. The shell is like the womb, it has structure and so can contain life. Since Annabel is not pregnant 'in fact', we must understand that she is 'pregnant' metaphorically and is still perpetually capable of bringing forth new life. This creativity stems from an equilibrium of character which neither denies nor gives too much free play to either the private or the public.

The Public Image then can be regarded as Muriel Spark's breakthrough; it is the nearest she comes to offering a 'solution' to the problems which were recurring to her. It represents the closest realisation of the 'antisyzygy' which seems to be her goal. It affirms the possibility of Unity of Being even at a time when the public world is as tawdry and corrupt as that of the film industry. *The Public Image* offers us as a counter to the imaginative romantic visionary ideal of the self, a humbler conception of the average human being as an agent, as an actor in a world which must contain other actors, other unified human beings. Annabel is only at the beginning of the road, and the weakness of the novel is that it does not show her to us in a full and satisfying relationship. There is only the potential relationship to her child which promises that not only is self-fulfilment possible, but that love is also. The novel does not theorise about how such fulfilment is possible, since it is concerned to reveal the possibility as achieved, in action. One is not to theorise, at least not exclusively, since such a resort to the theoretical mind threatens to paralyse action. Annabel has no 'vision' and this has come to mean in Mrs Spark's work that she can see more clearly, since her own imaginative interpretation (or fiction) of the world does not interfere with the matter of optics. Because she lacks imaginative 'vision' she can see others clearly and, as a result, has no difficulty in acting, or in being herself which is the same thing. Because she can see others – which is not necessarily to say that she therefore knows them in any profound way, she merely recognises them as being there – she is willing, without having to think about it, to be seen by others. What is seen is no more than appearance, and is therefore not the whole of the self. What *The Public Image* reveals is that without 'appearance' there can be no 'reality'. Potential must be actualised; what is inner must be outered, or uttered. Even if this transformation of private into public is imperfect – as it must be since the image of a thing must be different from the thing which is imaged – it is a *sine qua non*.

What a novelist these days must be most careful of is to be seen to be presenting a positive 'solution' to anything. The task of literature is conceived to be the revealing of the complexity and impossibility of life rather than as the offering of myths, or modes of acting in the world. It is possibly for some such reason that the positive myth, or 'way', conveyed by *The Public Image* is so much in a minor key and hedged round with internal qualifications. Despite these qualifications, Muriel Spark's next fiction comes almost as a corrective to the distortion of the 'vision' of the earlier novel. They form almost an 'Allegro–Il Penseroso' pair. Lise, the central figure of *The Driver's Seat*[102] makes a public spectacle of herself on every possible occasion. She creates a scene at the dress shop and draws attention to herself at the airport by her loud clothes and obtrusive manner. She is constantly posing, but unlike Annabel who plays herself in her poses, Lise's poses are desperately willed inventions, they are *lies* propagated by someone who insists on being in the driver's seat. At the airport at the beginning of her holiday – perhaps one of those holidays one takes when it is too difficult to face the facts – she tells the clerk, 'I believe in travelling light because I travel a lot. . . .'[103] Shortly, however, another traveller asks her, 'You travel much?' and she replies, 'No. There is so little money.' She tells the garage workmen that she is 'a tourist, a teacher from Iowa, New Jersey' despite the fact that she is on holiday from her office job in the U.K. (at least, somewhere in the north). She tells Carlo: 'I come from a family of intellectuals. My late husband was an intellectual. We had no children. He was killed in a motor accident.' This last is perhaps true, the 'family of intellectuals' part, given her own fluency in languages, but there is no way of being sure. These lying attempts to make an impression on the world outside, to be noticed, lead to her murder; more accurately, she commits suicide by somehow 'coercing' the sex-maniac Richard to kill her. Rather than simply 'being there' so that others can see her, like

Annabel, she is like Frederick, egoistically demanding that the public world stare at her. She has broken hysterically from her role, from her position in an ordered world, but this wilful attempt to be free is ultimately suicidal and she will win for herself no more public existence than can be found in a complicated and mysterious police dossier. At times, the novel itself seems to be pretending to be nothing more than this very dossier.

The novel investigates two possible life styles open to Lise and both are found to be wanting. The first is the sterile and imprisoning world of institutionalised Society and the second is its opposite, which is so often held up as an alternative to the 'established' world, the way of 'personal relationships'. Lise is reluctant to leave the office for a rest because, as she says, 'I've got all this work to finish.' As it becomes clear that she must break her routine, she begins to laugh hysterically. 'She finished laughing and started crying all in a flood.' Lise breaks down because the only public identity she has is that of her role in the office:

> Her lips are slightly parted; she, whose lips are usually pressed together with the daily disapproval of the accountant's office where she has worked continually, except for the months of illness, since she was eighteen, that is to say, for sixteen years and some months. Her lips when she does not speak or eat, are normally pressed together like the ruled line of a balance sheet, marked straight with her old-fashioned lipstick, a final and a judging mouth, a precision instrument, a detail-warden of a mouth; she has five girls under her and two men. Over her are two women and five men.[105]

The apparent equilibrium of her office life is a parody of an ordered society. Her official identity, adopted from the form of a balance sheet is not a sufficient nor satisfactory role. The mask denies the inner life instead of expressing or mediating it. When holidays come, her official face is taken away from her and she must madly invent new faces. To leave her environment is suicidal, she needs the order which would allow her to live with others, but the order of institutionalised Society with its prefabbed identikits is certainly not seen to be a worthy possibility. She must not leave, but she cannot stay either.

The description of her flat indicates again how little Society has to offer in the way of roles suited to personal fulfilment. It is fitted out in a functional and sterile manner. All the chairs stack conveniently out of the way; beds swing out and disappear accommodatingly. Many of the fixtures deceptively change their role; the writing table doubles as a dining table, the bracket lamp can also be a wall lamp. The overall effect of her architect designed flat is inhuman:

> Lise keeps her flat as clean-lined and clear to return to after her work as if it were uninhabited. The swaying tall pines among the litter of cones on the forest floor have been subdued into silence and into obedient hulks.[106]

As the very trees have been betrayed into flats, so too have creative individuals been betrayed into obedient hulks. Except on holiday.

On holiday, Lise encounters a number of people who offer her the very familiarity that seems to be lacking in her daily routine. But Lise does not want, nor need, familiarity. The man she is looking for will not be familiar she says:

> 'Not my man at all. He tried to get familiar with me,' Lise says. 'The one I'm looking for will recognise me right away for the woman I am, have no fear of that.'[107]

Even her murderer disappoints her in this respect, since he insists on the familiarity of sexual intercourse before he will do her will and kill her. Bill, the macrobiotic hipster, is rejected for the same reason. Believing in personal relationships, he is too immediately intimate and has no respect for the appropriate external rituals that Lise needs. Bill has adopted a personal corruption of Taoist belief and dismisses one of the principles, the Yin:

> 'Yin and Yang are philosophies,' he says. 'Yin represents space. Its colour is purple. Its element is water. It is external. That salami is Yin and those olives are Yin. They are full of toxics.'[108]

However right he is about the official airline food, Bill is wrong in his philosophy, or religion, as we can see from this summary by Fung Yu-Lan:

> The *yang* and *yin* are conceived of as two mutually comple-
> mentary principles or forces, of which the *yang* represents
> masculinity, light, warmth, dryness, hardness, activity, etc.,
> while the *yin* represents femininity, darkness, cold, moisture,
> softness, passivity etc. All natural phenomena result from the
> ceaseless interplay of these two forces.[109]

Here is a non-Caledonian source of antisyzygy that Mac-
Diarmid occasionally recognises. It is because the world of *The
Driver's Seat* does not permit the interplay of opposite forces that
the novel ends with the unnatural phenomenon of Lise's sui-
cide-murder.

Neither the coldly and rigidly formal world of Society, nor
the warm and intimate familiarity of personal relationships are
fully satisfactory then. The possibility for life which Lise seeks
and fails to find lies somewhere between the two extremes. Lise
has been stuck in a repressive public role for so long that she no
longer has a personal creative centre left from which to act. As a
result, when she breaks from her office routine, she must habitually seek salvation in a series of appeals to the public, but
her performances are only pathetic parodies of the protean
volatility of Dougal Douglas. Without an inner resource Lise is
destroyed because there is no adequate public world to complete her identity; Society offers no roles adequate to human
needs. After the killing, Richard the murderer has a vision of his
future, he

> sees already the gleaming buttons of the policemen's uni-
> forms, hears the cold and the confiding, the hot and the bark-
> ing voices, sees already the holsters and epaulets and all
> those trappings devised to protect them from the indecent
> exposure of fear and pity, pity and fear.[110]

The uniforms do not serve to project a healthy interior life; they
are 'trappings', meant to repress and imprison, to shut out
human contact. The trappings have usurped the role of
mediator between internal and external, the role that should be
played by ritual. The function of ritual, as Philip Rieff says, is to
'protect the difference between the public and private sectors –

and encourage forms of translation between the two sectors'.[111] That is to say, the role of ritual is to provide a medium for decent exposure. In a way, *The Driver's Seat* is almost overtaken by the disorder it enacts. There is little mediation from the narrator and the novel's sense becomes public only with much effort by the reader. The reader must work to find a myth of order to make sense of disparate facts. The implication – and herein lies the importance of the novel – is that in the absence of ritual and myth, of fictions which provide acceptable human order, chaos and disaster ensue.

In her later novels Muriel Spark has become increasingly concerned with suicide. Miss Brodie is characterised by an 'exotic suicidal enchantment', as are Frederick Christopher and Lise. Suicide is the complement to the theme of 'cannibalism' in the earlier novels. Mrs Spark has investigated the denial of others and the denial of self and they are found to be intimately connected. The artistic pursuit of 'vision' can lead to a solipsism which finds its outlet as 'cannibalism'. This very cannibalism, however, is a highly dubious source of sustenance, since the denial of others turns out to be the denial of self. Narcissus can see only his own face in the reflection, and because he cannot see another reality beyond this self, he dies. Muriel Spark's most recent novel, *Not to Disturb*[112] seems to tie all of her themes together in perhaps her most unusual and most interesting work.

In absolute privacy, secretly, behind locked doors with the warning 'not to disturb' posted, the Baron Klopstock murders his wife and her lover (their secretary) and then commits suicide. The aristocratic figures of *Not to Disturb* 'absent' themselves for their deeds of violence, as if in debased parody of some Greek tragedy, while we watch the antics of the plebeian chorus holding centre stage. That chorus is busy arranging contracts with the film industry and with various scandal sheets to which they are going to sell the lurid story of adultery, murder and suicide. Lister, the immortal butler who can do anything, orchestrates the scene and even arranges a hasty marriage between the servant Heloise (hugely pregnant by she knows not which Abelard) and the 'zealous cretin', the sex-mad brother of the Baron who is kept locked in the attic. The action of this novel gives us no semi-romanticised figures, either good or evil to fascinate us. Instead we are plunged into the grotesque, the human, world of the 'poor naked wretches' that Lear was forced to recognise as a result of his *hubris*.

The novel is littered with the shards of cultures, best exemplified perhaps in Lister who quotes from Jacobean drama, particularly that of John Webster. The whole of the action takes place amid a raging storm reminiscent of the one which swirls round Lear during his 'madness'. Lister's opening speech underlines for us that this background of 'culture' is not merely incidental to the novel:

> 'Their life,' says Lister, 'a general mist of error. Their death, a hideous storm of terror. – I quote from *The Duchess of Malfi* by John Webster, an English dramatist of old.'[113]

When high Art and Culture become the provenance of the servants, we can apparently expect that literary references will be spelled out fully. There will be no erudite and esoteric obfuscation. Lister invites us to inspect his reference and his attitude to Art is that it is a functional source of quotation, meant to serve living men and not dead aristocrats. There is a danger that this novel could be read as a lament for the demise of the ruling class with its demanding code of *noblesse oblige* and Death before Dishonour. One does not really need, however, Mrs Spark's comment that the book is 'very *pro*-servant. They fill nearly the whole picture, and the employers 'hardly appear except as remote figures talked about by the servants'.[114] The reader is soon aware that the grotesquerie of the servants is part of their vitality, and that their ability to carry on living amid the chaos of a culture is a sign of hope.

What then do the absent employers mean? It is perhaps temptingly easy to be satisfied with the idea that they represent the 'rulers' and the novel deals with the suicide of established order amid the vital chaos of the bawdy servants. The opening lines of *The Duchess of Malfi* (not mentioned in the novel, but immediately encountered by anyone who checks up on Lister's allusions) might seem to support such an idea:

> Consid'ring duly, that a prince's court
> Is like a common fountain, whence should flow
> Pure silver drops in general: but if't chance

Some curs'd example poison 't near the head,
Death, and diseases through the whole land spread.

But Webster's play is not really a plea simply for better kings and Cardinals; and *Not to Disturb* is not a plea for the virtues of elitism in society. Webster's play demonstrates the evils which ensue when a system of culture is divorced from the people; when there is a split, that is to say, between society (the people) and culture. The society *has* a culture (possesses it self-consciously), but society *is* not that culture. The form of authority is carried on in the person of the Cardinal and his brother, but it does not serve the love (which is seen as lust) and engaging domesticity of the Duchess, Antonio and her children. People are made to serve culture, and not culture to serve life.

Webster's presence in the novel then serves to remind us of the potential horror of an ideal of Art or Culture which becomes divorced from life. If the servants are meant to be representatives of humanity, such as those that Lear had neglected in his pride of position, then Shakespeare is invoked for the same reason. The novel, however, despite its references to the past, is about contemporary reality, which is seen to be informed by the time of the Renaissance which saw the disappearance of the 'analogous universe' in which the order of the cosmos mirrored that of the State and of the individual man. By the end of the novel, with the Baron and his wife and secretary out of the way, the storm — a conscious use of the pathetic fallacy — which has haunted their end:

> The wind now whistles round the house and the remote shutters bang as another storm wakes up.[115]

has cleared and order in the cosmos is restored:

> The household is straggling up the back stairs to their beds. By noon they will be covered in the profound sleep of those who have kept faithful vigil all night, while outside the house the sunlight is laughing on the walls.[116]

Lister establishes a new order of society by arranging marriages. Prince Eugene is looking for a servant and offers 'a very good wage'. ' "These days," says Lister, "they want more." '[117] 'Accept no other offers.' says the Prince, and the deal, the marriage, is made. The position of servant and master is overturned to start a new order. Similarly, the position of Art and Culture has been changed. The obvious use by Mrs Spark of the pathetic fallacy cannot be ignored. It is not mere lack of invention on her part. What she is suggesting is that the proper role for Art is to serve, to make clear. The conventions of Art, the storm and its clearing are used to indicate the condition of the characters.

We are perhaps now in a position to suggest that the theme of the novel derives from a reaction to Romantic and Symbolist art. Its most likely origin would seem to be that well-known passage from a central symbolist work, *Axel* by Villiers de L'Isle-Adam, which gave its title to Edmund Wilson's *Axel's Castle*. In *Axel* illusion and reality change places, uncompromising ideality replaces reality. For Axel and his companions the external world is merely a source of evil interference with the vision, the ideal vision which each individual can have of the world. Axel and Sara choose the supreme option, to die as a gesture of rejection of the value of the external world. Before they drink poison Axel says:

> What has the Earth ever realized, that drop of frozen mud, whose Time is only a lie in the heavens? It is the earth, dost thou not see? which has now become the illusion! Admit, Sara: we have destroyed in our strange hearts, the love of life – and it is in REALITY indeed that ourselves have become our souls. To consent, after this, to live would be but sacrilege against ourselves. Live? our servants will do that for us. . . .[118]

Muriel Spark is willing to allow the Axels and the Baron Klopstocks to absent themselves from the world in pursuit of their suicidal ideal visions. She has focused her eyes on the servants who get on with the muddy business of living. The world they inhabit is far from ideal, but it *lives* – one of the characters even seems to exude a sort of 'life force'. The servants are alert to the tawdry economies of the films and the flashy magazines. What they sell, now that a new order is to be established, is not themselves as servants, but stories.

To say that Art is to be made to serve is not to say that men, even former servants, can do without Art. When a film director tells Heloise to speak out her fantasies, she is caught short, not having any:

'I didn't know what the hell to say, I thought he meant a fairy story, so I started with Little Red Riding Hood, and Mr. McGuire said "That's great, Heloise! You're great!" So I went on with Little Red Riding Hood and Lister and Irene changed sides. They joined in with Red Riding Hood. Lister was terrific as the grandmother when he ate me up. You can see in the film that I had a good time. Then Irene got eaten up by Lister's understudy. Mr. Samuel is an artist, I'll say that, his prespectives coalesce.'[119]

Several other fairy stories are similarly used and judged: 'Puss in Boots is a big bore.' 'Goldilocks and the three bears is best.' Little Red Riding Hood reveals that the tendency to cannibalism can be exorcised by means of fictionalising the experience. Art, properly employed is a means of transcendence and as such contributes to social and individual cohesion. The practice of mime is not dangerous if one condition is met:

'You should always do your own thing in a simulation. It all works in.'[120]

The message is similar to that of *The Public Image*.

The important truth that appearance and reality are an inseparable pair of opposites, spelled out in *The Public Image*, is expressed very differently, then, in Muriel Spark's most recent novel; and yet the message is the same and it is the insistence that the way to Unity of Being lies through the 'antisyzygy': 'perspectives' must 'coalesce'. She has, it would seem, completed her picture, completed the mosaic of truth to which each of the several novels contributes in its own economical way. At the end of her quarrel with the novel, we see that Muriel Spark is now able to shift freely to subjects quite different from some of her earlier preoccupations. It remains to be seen if the synthesis which she has achieved on the subject of Art and fictions will allow her to produce new and better novels, or if it will mean that her novelistic ground has been fully reaped.* She has at

---

* *Hothouse on the East River* (1973) shows an undiminished inventiveness, facility with language and moments of wild comedy, but it does not seem to extend any of the themes which reach a culmination in *Not to Disturb*. *Hothouse*

least effectively demonstrated that the post-Modern novel is not dead, nor is it a mere orthodox accommodation refusing to ask the significant questions posed by the great Moderns. If the artist is the hero of Modernism, then the post-Modern novelist has asked searching questions about the nature of Art and revealed the dangers of a naive view of fiction, and of reality. Art itself has become a subject for critical consideration and evaluation.

Although the form of his trilogy betrays no active distrust of Art, Joyce Cary significantly moved the centre of action from the artist (Jimson in *The Horse's Mouth*) to the politician and asked what role the artistic power has to play in the lives of ordinary, non-alienated men. His discovery and his revelation is that the artistic power is at the centre of all human activity. It is in solipsistic inactivity and idealistic subjectivity that art and life are both most threatened. Muriel Spark has carried on this implicit questioning. She began with the premise that if fictions are not acceptable in life, then they cannot be accepted in novels. This premise led through a long dialectical investigation of the various possibilities that emerge from such a questioning of Art. She too found that Art is a necessity for life, but in doing so she has given us a profounder understanding of the meaning of fictions. If we understand fictions better, she says, they will work that much more effectively for us. At times the preoccupation with the meaning of the fiction threatens to destroy the interest of the fiction being presented. While at times she comes close to the writing of 'damaged' fictions of the *tel quel* variety, or like those of B. S. Johnson, Muriel Spark remains an artist and so insists that fiction is the best method of exploring the nature of fiction.

The following chapters will be less concerned with the philosophical intricacies of fiction and reality. Although there will be no attempt to show that there is anything like an established 'school' of novelists, we shall be looking at a number of novelists who seem to have responded individually to a central and recurring post-Modern concern: the question of action, and of

focuses on the extent to which psychoanalysis, institutionalised as a secular (or vulgar) form of conversion, has taken over from religion. Mrs Spark's concern with role and identity could be traced to her own conversion, but such an approach is likely to be unrewarding. *Hothouse*, for those clued-in to the shorthand, contains one of the funniest dramatic scenes of all the novels.

self-dramatisation as a means to overcome the solipsism of subjective idealism. Some seem to value 'action' itself at the expense of role-playing or self-dramatisation (Graham Greene, for instance). Others find the question of artificial or artistic action the most important one and their work tends to abound with the metaphor of drama. Still others reflect the central concern of our time by means of fictions which are exoteric, opening out to the world outside and away from the incestuous interiority which is the negative concomitant to the achievements of literature since the Romantic period. There are many novelists, of course, who write with apparently no reference to the achievement of the great Moderns. Many of these novelists counsel 'behaviour' – the passive acceptance of roles created by Society – as the way to the palace of Wisdom, rather than 'action' – the intentional, conscious dramatisation or actualisation of a full subjectivity. They provide answers without ever having asked the right questions. By ignoring the achievements of past literature they can never hope to respond to its challenges. The one thing a sense of tradition insists on is individual talent.

5 Christopher Isherwood's Psychological Makeup

Perhaps the last thing we might expect to find in Isherwood's novels is an expression of hunger for the comforts of a defined position in an ordered society, and yet at times it seems as if his work is imbued with that very sentiment. His main characters give the impression of standing outside society less in the postures of contemptuous rejection or heroic defiance than in those of woeful acceptance that some quirk of personality in themselves makes them isolate and outcast. Yet that impression quickly fades. The wistful desire to belong to an ordered and hierarchical society never becomes more than a vague dream. So troubled are they with the problems of their own inescapable individuality that at times any relief seems appealing. Close though he comes at times to endorsing society, Isherwood's own temperament and trust in individual experience and self-discovery make him forgo the temptation to believe in the *status quo*. Instead, we find at the centre of his work, not Society, but a proliferation of dramatic metaphor. What might at first seem to be a question about the necessity of belonging to a group turns out to be a question of art.

My purpose is to study closely one of Isherwood's recent novels, *A Single Man*, with reference to the meaning in it of dramatic metaphors. A focus on drama is most useful in the investigation in fiction of the dualism of body and spirit (or mind), and the dualism of self and other which centres on the meaning of personal relationships. Briefly, however, I would like to indicate that the subject of drama and the theatre is one that has occurred many times in Isherwood's other writings and in his life. In the recent autobiographical work *Kathleen and Frank*, Isherwood is ostensibly writing the lives of his father and mother,

213

and yet the book, as he says, turns out to be about himself. The book proves to be about the fascinating turns taken by the mind of the child and young man as he tries to build for himself a world that flouts the official version given to him by his parents, but that long and complex story is not of immediate concern here. One thing we learn, between the lines about his parents as it were, is that the theatre had a powerful influence on the young Christopher. We learn from an entry in his mother's diary for 9 May, 1911 that drama is an obsession of the young Isherwood, in fact, 'anything to do with plays he is wild about'. On 27 June she repeats the claim: 'Anything to do with the stage or theatre seems to interest him more than anything in the world.' In recounting his early days in the family seat of Marple Hall, Isherwood describes the privileged theatrical position he sometimes found himself in as a child:

> As long as he was trotting around after them or doing play-jobs which Cook invented for him in the kitchen, he was like a stage-hand behind the scenes in a theatrical production, he was part of the show. But when the curtain finally went up, and some of the maids put on starched aprons and became actresses who served lunch in the Dining-Room, then Christopher was excluded. He had to sit still at the table and be waited on. He was just a member of the audience.[1]

The passage reveals an early prejudice in favour of acting and against mere spectating. The child's passion for drama led finally to his being given a toy theatre which was used for staging plays with Christopher not only as the central actor, but also as a 'deadly serious director'. The adult Isherwood unassumingly says of the young Christopher, 'He wanted to be an actor, like Frank.' There is a sting in the tail of that comment, however. Frank (his father) was *not* famous for being an actor, but was in fact a somewhat reluctant career soldier who used on occasion to take dramatic parts, and once came near to giving up soldiering to become an art student. *Kathleen and Frank* records the situation that led the young Christopher to reject the 'hero father', and the biography of his parents is really his own autobiography because it reveals how he has replaced the myth of the hero father with another myth, that of the sensitive, artistic father who was an 'actor' as well as a soldier. The need to have a father who was an actor, and his own intense interest in things theatrical offer a suggestive clue about what we might watch for in reading the novels themselves.

With Herr Issyvoo in *Goodbye to Berlin* we are in the apparently passive world of 'I am a camera'. Isherwood the narrator says: 'I am a camera with its shutter open, quite passive, recording, not thinking.'[2] Despite his own lack of activity – activity being one of the sacrifices made for Art apparently – the 'camera' focuses as if by instinct on characters remarkable for their theatricality. The charming and dissolute Sally Bowles is like nothing so much as a 'theatrical nun'. While she makes a phone call to her lover of the previous evening, Christopher and Fritz sit 'watching her, like a performance at the theatre'.[3] Another of the fascinating characters of Berlin, the young Otto Nowak, displays the dramatic quality characteristic of his family. When Otto enters to find Christopher waiting for him, he drops his previous sullen manner. '"Why . . . it's Christoph!" Otto, as usual, had begun acting at once.'[4] When his mother Frau Nowak tells a story she acts it out: 'Like Otto, she had the trick of acting every scene she described.' There seems to be no particular thematic significance to the theatricality of these characters; we are asked only to notice that, against the backdrop of Hitler's rise to power, some at least of the pathetic members of 'the lost' still, somehow, reveal a strange streak of mimetic genius in their lives. The point is perhaps simply that: the interesting people one meets are often the best 'actors'.

One of the functions of dramatism, or theatricality, in general is nevertheless the escape from imprisonment inside oneself. The conscious creation and playing of roles is at least a temporary release from a sick and isolated consciousness. Isherwood's more recent novel *Down There on a Visit* deals with the problems of lives that can find no transcendence. As the prefatory note tells us:

Down There refers to that nether world within the individual which is the place of loneliness, alienation and hatred. This novel in four episodes describes characters shut up inside private hells of their own making, self-dedicated to a lifelong feud with The Others. The Author laughs at and with them often – for even hell can be funny – but he is forced to realise that his visits to them are, at the same time, visits to the *Down There* inside himself.[5]

Mr Lancaster, the subject of the first part of *Down There on a Visit*, runs a shipping company office in a town in North Germany. He makes an attempt to establish contact with his nephew, the narrator Isherwood, but fails, having been for too long shut up inside himself:

> If my visit had any decisive effect on him, it can only have been to show him what it was that prevented him from having any close contact with anybody. He had lived too long inside his sounding-box, listening to his own reverberations, his epic song of himself.[6]

As a result of this imprisonment he ends his life by lapsing into a fiction which he does not himself consciously recognise as a fiction. He creates an imaginary nephew to 'play a supporting part in his epic' and often tells extravagant stories about his nephew who is certain to become a famous novelist. One year after the disappointing visit from his nephew, Mr Lancaster shoots himself.

Paul, the subject of the last section of the novel has been *Down There* with the aid of drugs:

> I've been right down into the inside of myself with dope, two or three times – and I know one thing for sure: if, by some wildly unlikely chance, there *is* any afterwards, and I swallow those pills, in the state I'm in now, then I'm going to find myself in a mess which'll be a million times ghastlier than anything that could possibly happen to me here. Because there I'll be really *stuck* with myself. *That* much I *know*.[7]

In an attempt to avoid being 'stuck' with himself, at least in the here and now, Paul adopts Isherwood's routine of meditation and under the influence of Isherwood's *guru*, Augustus Parr, his life is drastically changed. Although he eventually returns to drugs and has to undergo another painful withdrawal treatment, and then reverts to his former non-ascetic life, it is clear that he gains some measure of freedom as a result of what he learns from Isherwood, and more particularly from Parr.

Isherwood describes Parr as perhaps 'studied, theatrical':

But that's exactly *why* he impresses me. I mean, I don't trust these sweet child-like little wide-eyed saints. Augustus is absolutely sophisticated and absolutely aware of the impression he makes. And that reassures me.[8]

Unlike Mr Lancaster who finds himself trapped in a dream he cannot identify or direct, Augustus Parr is altogether conscious of the dramatic effect he produces. He seems even to be given to little games such as purposefully mishearing what one has said to him, 'just in order to make the situation more dramatic'.[9] Even a simple occasion like going to supper 'with Augustus was a dramatic experience. . . .' Like the Nowaks of *Goodbye to Berlin*, he has the habit of miming his statements:

'*Every* moment *is* eternity. And at *any* given moment we can break through the web of time. Or we could, if we weren't strapped down hand and foot –' (Augustus writhed a little, as if straining against his bonds) '– so that we can't move a muscle – '[10]

All in all, as Paul sums him up, 'Miss Parr is still the biggest saint in show business.'[11]

Now, the thematic value of Parr's dramatism is much more obvious than were the theatrical references in *Goodbye to Berlin*. Dramatic action is at the centre of the problem of freeing oneself from the prison of subjectivity, of *down there*. Dramatism allows one to live in the world of other people without having to accept the conformity of any particular definition of society. It is the practice of mimesis in itself which is somehow both potentially curative, and expressive of a state of full health of the personality. The split between self and other is overcome by means of 'symbolic action'. On the subject of another potential split, between 'the active and the contemplative life', Parr 'quotes Bhagavad-Gita on symbolic action' and all 'agreed they are complementary'.[12]

There is reason to believe then, that the general theme outlined in earlier chapters, of the meaning of dramatic metaphors in contemporary fiction, is useful in understanding a central theme in Christopher Isherwood's novels. I would like now to consider in more detail one of his most recent novels, *A Single Man*.[13] *A Single Man* is the story of the way in which George, the aging Lecturer in English at a California

College, comes awake in the morning and gradually during the day assumes the recognisable form of himself. There are four quite clear stages in this daily process of George's awakening and reassuming his identity.* In the morning he is all flesh, mere unrelieved body. At school he has put on his personality and is able to engage in contact with other people. In the third part of his day he enters into a 'symbolic relationship' with Kenny Potter, one of his students. The fourth stage of George's day sees him lift almost entirely free of the body and join with the universal consciousness which is the essence of life. The process of the novel is a movement from complete materiality of the body, to complete release of the spirit from the body. At the centre of the novel then, is the 'symbolic relationship' and the scene which is dominated by the metaphor of drama which precedes it. The two central sections show George at the stages in which body and spirit are working together and reveal the truth of the lines from Hopkins's 'The Caged Skylark':

> Man's spirit will be flesh-bound when found at best,
> But uncumbered: meadow-down is not distressed
> For a rainbow footing it nor he for his bones risen.

In his study of symbolism, *Symbolism: Its Meaning and Effect*, A. N. Whitehead makes the following point about Aristotle: 'Aristotle conceived "matter" . . . as being pure potentiality awaiting the incoming of form in order to become actual'.[14] It is perhaps fair to assume that any study of symbolism might be helpful in understanding a novel which concerns itself with a 'symbolic relationship'. The comment about Aristotle, lifted right out of context, serves as an admirable summary of *A Single Man*, for the novel is precisely about the way in which the mere potentiality of 'matter' is actualised in the 'form' of the human personality. At the beginning of the novel, George does not really exist, 'it' does, his body:

> Obediently the body levers itself out of bed – wincing from twinges in the arthritic thumbs and the left knee, mildly nauseated by the pylorus in a state of spasm – and shambles naked into the bathroom, where its bladder is emptied and it is weighed; still a bit over 150 pounds, in spite of all that toiling at the gym! Then to the mirror.

*There is a good analysis of this part of the novel in Jonathan Raban's *The Technique of Modern Fiction*, pp. 26–32.

What it sees there isn't so much a face as the expression of a predicament. Here's what it has done to itself . . . during its fifty-eight years; expressed in terms of a dull harassed stare, a coarsened nose, a mouth dragged down by the corners into a grimace as if at the sourness of its own toxins, cheeks sagging from their anchors of muscle, a throat hanging limp in tiny wrinkled folds. The harassed look is that of a desperately tired swimmer or runner; yet there is no question of stopping.[15]

The lack of personal identity is driven home by the repetition of the impersonal pronoun 'it' in reference to the body. Only when the body is flooded with the necessity for going outside into an 'outer world of other people' does it begin to be worthy of a personal name:

Obediently, it washes, shaves, brushes its hair; for it accepts its responsibilities to the others. It is even glad that it has its place among them. It knows what is expected of it.

It knows its name. It is called George.[16]

From this point in the narrative George is no longer called 'it' by the narrator. 'It' has been replaced by 'he'. Already the potentiality of matter has begun to be actualised in personal form.

As George drives to the College, there is a brief interval in which he becomes merely 'it', and his body seems to take control of his life once again. As he drives along the freeway his mind is no longer consciously in charge and his body reacts automatically to road situations. The body begins to take on a degree of autonomy:

More and more, it appears to separate itself, to become a separate entity; an impassive anonymous chauffeur-figure with little will or individuality of its own, the very embodiment of muscular co-ordination, lack of anxiety, tactful silence, driving its master to work.[17]

It should be noted that there is no abhorrence of the flesh expressed in this passage. The flesh is disgusting only in that it grows old and is subject to time. The 'master', the conscious self is not subject to such deterioration. The body though, is capable of serving its master well, and it is 'potential' life in that it is capable of action in the world.

There is, however, something potentially very strange and disturbing in this split between body and spirit. The body becomes a fully 'functioning member of society' in that it obeys without question all of the rules of the road. George himself feels that his 'self' is somehow separated from this obedience to law. This schizophrenia gives rise to a strange tension:

> Like everyone with an acute criminal complex, George is hyperconscious of all bylaws, city ordinances, rules and petty regulations.[18]

He has felt on numerous occasions, when his passport has been stamped or his driver's licence accepted as proof of identity, a sense of secret superiority which expresses itself in a gleeful whisper to himself: '*idiots — fooled them again!*' It is as if the body is allowed to fulfil the decrees of the law, but the spirit in its freedom, and its unknowable secrecy, mocks such mechanical signs of obedience.

As he continues his drive to work, the separation of mind and body continues and George, like the characters of *Down There On A Visit*, has 'gone deep down inside himself'.[20] As the reality of the external world fades, George deep inside himself is free to pursue a paranoid fantasy:

> It would be amusing, George thinks, to sneak into that apartment building at night, just before the tenants moved in, and spray all the walls of all the rooms with a specially prepared odorant which would be scarcely noticeable at first but which would gradually grow in strength until it reeked like rotting corpses.[21]

In another version of the same sort of fantasy, he muses on the possibility of a 'kind of virus which would eat away whatever it is that makes metal hard'. The effect of this would be that, during the house-warming party when the house is full of people, 'the whole thing would sag and subside into a limp tangled heap, like spaghetti'.

Even this, however, is not the limit of the viciousness of the subjective mind when it is wrapped up, deep down inside itself, in its 'vision'. He envisions submitting a newspaper editor, the

Police Chief and other figures of authority to psychological torture ('no doubt just showing them the red-hot pokers and pincers would be quite sufficient') until they 'would perform every possible sexual act, in pairs and in groups, with a display of the utmost enjoyment'.[22] The individual mind, when it is absolutely freed from all recognition of the reality of other human beings is not after all an ideal thing; it becomes in fact, more and more the image of Nazism. George goes on in his fantasy world to conclude that mere torture and satire would not be enough since such people understand nothing but 'brute force':

> Therefore we must launch a campaign of systematic terror. In order to be effective, this will require an organization of at least five hundred highly skilled killers and torturers, all dedicated individuals.[23]

This form of the fantasy continues for a long while, and it is not meant in any way to be 'satiric'. It is a genuine expression of the state of the inner soul of a 'single man'. George pretends to himself that he hates the world because it has killed his friend Jim (who was actually killed in a car crash), but this is not a satisfactory excuse:

> But, when George gets in as deep as this, Jim hardly matters any more. Jim is nothing, now, but an excuse for hating three quarters of the population of America. . . .[24]

The separation of body from spirit, then, seems to be a possible event, at least for periods of time, but it does not at all seem to be a desirable event. A single man, conceived only as a subjective consciousness, is motivated not by love and a desire for universal freedom, but by destructive hate.

As George approaches the University he begins more and more to approach a state in which body and spirit are fused into an active unity, so that the soul clothes the body, and the body's activities are nothing more than the expression of the spirit. George 'comes up dazed to the surface' and realises that the 'chauffeur-figure' has been in control for a record length of time. 'And this raises a disturbing question; is the chauffeur steadily becoming more and more of an individual? Is it getting ready to take over much larger areas of George's life?' But this is a somewhat confusing passage in terms of the novel, since it is not the 'chauffeur-figure' who is the most dangerous figure. The mere body, doing its mechanical routine, obeying the laws of the road, does not seem particularly to be feared. Certainly it is not as potentially dangerous as the 'spirit' freed from the body. It is the radical split in the self between mind and body that is the source of the greatest evil – at least this is what the action of the novel seems to indicate. The narrator's comments on this action seem to suggest that it is the body which is evil, and the spirit or consciousness which is good. This discrepancy between the action of the novel and the narrative commentary will be referred to again when the ending of the novel is dealt with.

As George comes out of his sadistic dream, he begins to think consciously of the other people, his students, he is about to encounter. As he does so, he begins to think, and to be described, in dramatic metaphors:

> So now he consciously applies himself to thinking their thoughts, getting into their mood. With the skill of a veteran, he rapidly puts on the psychological makeup for this role he must play.[25]

The body is now to be adorned, but this is no mere mechanical or chemical adjustment that is going to be made to 'matter'. The makeup that is to be applied is psychological. The mind, the spirit is now going to adorn the body, and the result will be a dramatic performance. And once more we see that the dramatic performance emerges from a process not of thinking about oneself, but out of thinking oneself into the lives of others. Drama needs a recognition of a field of action, and the presence of other agents. As he gets closer the impulse gets stronger:

> So now George has arrived. He is not nervous in the least. As he gets out of his car, he feels an upsurge of energy, of eagerness for the play to begin. And he walks eagerly, with a springy step, along the gravel path past the Music Building towards the Department Office. He is all actor now; an actor on his way up from the dressing-room, hastening through the backstage world of props and lamps and stage-hands to make his entrance.[26]

As he walks to the classroom, accompanied by one of his students, he is caught by the sight of a tennis game, in which the more physically attractive player is obviously going to lose. As George says, if this were a fight the dark Mexican player would lose, since his physical capacity is less. The big blond player, however, finds that 'his classical cream marble body seems a handicap to him. The rules of the game inhibit it from functioning'.[27] In order to assert his physical superiority he should 'throw away his useless racket, vault over the net, and force the cruel little gold cat to submit to his marble strength'. Nevertheless the *game* goes on and its 'cruelty' is sensually stimulating to George and seems to reveal something of the meaning of life. The meaning can be summarised as something like: physicality, matter, must be forced into some kind of symbolic form – here the rules of the game – for it to be interesting. The cruelty of the game is not like the cruelty of George's subjective fantasy. It is a symbolic cruelty only. The game reflects what is happening to George as the day progresses. The potential of his own body is being forced into a form of actualisation as a dramatic actor in a world inhabited by other people. The recognition of these others is a painful limitation of individual freedom, and yet playing a role amid others makes more life possible. It is the way for the single man to be fully alive and united in mind and body.

The road to such unity of being is not a simple one and on the way there are examples of false roles which one might be tempted into. George fights against the possibility that the free playing of roles will be reduced by the IBM monster to a series of official identity cards. He 'blasphemes' against this bogus god by threatening to punch extra holes in one of the cards. But he refrains because he recognises that this monstrous system of official 'roles' really hides individual suffering students behind its punch cards. Another danger for the man who plays roles is that the role he plays will become automatic; that the dramatisation of self will cease to be an activity which is freely, consciously and continuously chosen, and will become an imprisoning reflex. George senses this danger when he recognises that, in the classroom, his role has begun to operate without his will and he has become the 'talking head', rambling on habitually in a lecture about English literature. The talking

head is the opposite and complementary danger to the 'chauffeur-figure' body: 'Can it be that talking-head and the chauffeur are in league? Are they maybe planning a merger?'²⁸ The
demonic mind and demonic body threaten an unholy union.
The ideal state is for the mind, the free conscious self, to be
expressed through the body. The 'self' is an actualisation of the
mere potentiality of the body and 'George should be onstage
every second, in full control of his performance!'²⁹ Like the
tennis players, George must play the game consciously and
freely, otherwise he will disappear and only his functions will
remain.

George carries on with his class in response to a 'deeply-
rooted dramatic instinct', having on his entrance created a
'subtly contrived, outrageously theatrical effect'.³⁰ The process
which George has been undergoing can be described in spatial
terms. He tended to go 'deep down' inside himself on the drive
to College, with what results we have already considered. As he
comes up to the surface (like a swimmer) he becomes increasingly theatrical, consciously so, as mind and body work together. Having reached this exciting stage of his day, George
exhibits a tendency to go on transcending himself, to continue
upwards. One sign of this is the lapse into the 'talking-head'
state. In conversation over lunch inspiration strikes him:

> George feels himself racing down the runway; becoming
> smoothly, exhilaratingly airborne. 'My God, you sound like
> some dreary French intellectual. . . .'³¹

He goes into an impromptu lecture on the symbolic nature of
American life: 'We've reduced the things of the material plane
to mere symbolic conveniences. And why? Because that's the
essential first step. Until the material plane has been defined
and relegated to its proper place, the mind can't ever be truly
free.'³² This extreme tendency to become mind and spirit is
grounded, however, when he visits Doris, the woman who had
been Jim's lover, who is dying in hospital. He realises that the
deterioration of Doris's body *has* made a difference to Doris and
that even Jim would not love her now. After he leaves the hospital he rejoices in his bodiliness:

> *I am alive*, he says to himself, *I am alive*! And life-energy surges
> hotly through him, and delight, and appetite. How good to

be in a body – even this old beat-up carcase – that still has warm blood and live semen and rich marrow and wholesome flesh![33]

No longer is the spirit, or mind, soaring beyond the body and the body is no longer merely the decaying material that imprisons the soul. The flesh is now the material expression of the psychological energy of George. This is the spirit flesh-bound and found at its best.

Having reached this balanced state of being a self in a body, George is ready to enter into the 'symbolic relationship' with Kenny Potter which seems to be the goal of the novel. Kenny has arranged to be in a bar which he knows George to frequent. George does turn up, and they find that they have similar attitudes about 'personal relationships'. Kenny, perhaps surprisingly for a modern American youth, cannot abide an easy and too-ready familiarity. He insists on a degree of formality with George, calling him 'Sir' even though they are discussing personal matters, and expressing his regret that he could never call his father 'Sir'. As Kenny puts it:

> 'What's so phoney nowadays is all this familiarity. Pretending there isn't any difference between people – well, like you were saying about minorities, this morning. If you and I are no different, what do we have to give each other? How can we ever be friends?'

He *does* understand, George thinks, delighted.[34]

George, of course, understands the nature of the 'symbolic relationship' much more clearly than Kenny since he has thought the subject out previously and has decided that this special relationship is most like a Platonic dialogue:

> George can't imagine having a dialogue of this kind with a woman, because women can only talk in terms of the personal. A man of his own age would do, if there was some sort of polarity, for instance, if he was a Negro. You and your dialogue-partner have to be somehow opposites. Why? Because you have to be symbolic figures – like, in this case, Youth and Age. Why do you have to be symbolic? Because the dialogue is by its nature impersonal. It's a symbolic encounter. It doesn't involve either party personally. That's why, in a dia-

logue, you can say absolutely anything.[35]

And that is why even the most personal topics can safely be discussed in this impersonal dialogue. The essence of the 'symbolic relationship' is respect for the integrity of the other individual as different, as 'other'. George is ready for such a relationship, at least in part, because of his earlier exercise in donning his 'psychological makeup' and engaging in the dramatic presentation of himself, since it is the essence of self-dramatisation that the reality of the other be recognised. George is capable of his dramatic exercise, only because he has meticulously thought himself into the frame of mind of his audience.

Late at night, when they are both very drunk, Kenny suggests a swim and George agrees. They run down to the beach, stripping as they run. At this point the symbolic relationship takes a turn towards the personal: 'During the descent, their bodies rub against each other, briefly but roughly. The electric field of the dialogue is broken. Their relationship, whatever it now is, is no longer symbolic.'[36] When they return to George's house the change seems to continue: 'This isn't at all like their drunkenness at The Starboard Side. Kenny and he are no longer in the symbolic dialogue-relationship; this new phase of communication is very much person-to-person.'[37] In this more personal situation, George's homosexuality appears in a more demanding form, and yet nothing really changes and he does not allow his bodily desires to interfere with the relationship with Kenny: 'Yet, paradoxically, Kenny seems farther away, not closer; he has receded far beyond the possible limits of an electric field.' Having established one level of relationship with the youth, George cannot be selfish enough to allow his lust to interfere, to turn Kenny into an adjunct to desire rather than an independent and 'other' person.

After George falls drunkenly asleep, Kenny, whose clothes have by now had time to dry, leaves. Once more the swimmer image reappears, and George is submerged in sleep: 'Partial surfacings, after this. Partial emergings, just barely breaking the sheeted calm of the water. Most of George remaining submerged in sleep.'[38] The omniscient narrator now plays freely with the fictiveness of George as a character. We are not told, as we would be in a 'realistic' narrative that 'George died in his sleep'. Instead we are asked to 'suppose': 'Let us then suppose that, at that same instant, deep down in one of the major branches of George's coronary artery an unimaginably gradual process began.' The result of this process 'deep down' inside the body is predictable enough: 'Thus, slowly, invisibly, with the utmost discretion and without the slightest hint to those old fussers in the brain, an almost indecently melodramatic situation is contrived: the formation of the atheromatous plaque.'[39] There is one interesting thing to note about this method of dealing with a character in a novel. Isherwood, or the narrator, is openly admitting that George is not 'real', that he is fiction. And no attempt is made to make the 'illusion' so complete that it could somehow hope to substitute for 'reality'. There are many possible opinions one could have about the value of such a technique. Perhaps it might help in evaluating the technique to note that it is perfectly consistent with the theme of the novel itself. George himself takes part in the creation and publication of dramatisations of himself, which could be called 'fictions' of himself. Suitably enough, since the theme of the novel is the inescapable necessity for such fictions in George's life, the novel itself is justified because it too is consciously and purposefully a fiction.*

It is just possible, however, that the narrator adds an interpretive point of view at the conclusion of the novel that conflicts with the meaning that has emerged from the action of the novel itself. The conclusion seems to suggest that the spirit in George might separate itself from the body and rejoin the universal spirit:

> And if some part of the non-entity we called George has indeed been absent at this moment of terminal shock, away out there on the deep waters, then it will return to find itself homeless. For it can associate no longer with what lies here, unsnoring, on the bed. This is now cousin to the garbage in the container on the back porch. Both will have to be carted away and disposed of, before too long.[40]

One might be tempted to allow one's knowledge of Isherwood's

---

* This advertising of the fictiveness of fiction recalls Muriel Spark, particularly perhaps of *The Driver's Seat*.

interest in oriental philosophy to interrupt here and be led to read the conclusion as a celebration of the release of the spirit from its prison of the body. There is just the faintest suggestion in those closing lines that the spirit is timeless and therefore immortal and the flesh is time-bound and therefore evil. Such a theme certainly occurs in the novel which is the subject of George's lecture at the college: Huxley's *After Many A Summer*. In that novel Propter argues for pages on end the evil of being subject to time. Such a theme, however, seems to be at odds with the theme of *A Single Man*, that 'spirit will be flesh-bound when found at best'. The novel argues for the necessary equilibrium and interaction of body and spirit, and there is a taint of evil whenever either body or spirit takes on the autonomy of the 'chauffeur-figure' or the 'talking-head'.

If the concluding paragraph is in danger of striking a false note and foisting upon the story a moral that it just will not carry, a short passage earlier on perhaps gets the balance right:

> Up the coast a few miles north, in a lava reef under the cliffs, there are a lot of rock pools. You can visit them when the tide is out. Each pool is separate and different, and you can, if you are fanciful, give them names – such as George, Charlotte, Kenny, Mrs Strunk. Just as George and the others are thought of, for convenience, as individual entities, so you may think of a rock pool as an entity; though, of course, it is not. The waters of its consciousness – so to speak – are swarming with hunted anxieties, grim-jawed greeds, dartingly vivid intuitions, old crusty-shelled rock-gripping obstinacies, deep-down sparkling undiscovered secrets, ominous protean organisms motioning mysteriously, perhaps warningly, toward the surface light. How can such a variety of creatures coexist at all? Because they have to. The rocks of the pool hold their world together.[41]

Now this image of the rock pool and the water that fills it does perhaps adequately suggest that both the rock, the solid materiality as of the body, and the water, the consciousness or spirit, are equally necessary for the formation of rock pools, or individuals. But it is still not really adequate for the complexity of meanings that actually occurs in the novel. The image of the rock, for instance suggests that it is the body which gives form to the personality and is not merely potential. This suggestion contradicts the point made in the novel, that it is the spirit, the conscious self that puts 'phychological makeup' on the body and so gives it human form.

For whatever reason, the novel ends with a slightly weak and disturbing disquisition, in somewhat vague metaphor, on the relation of the body to the soul and on the possible immortality of the soul. If the novel has a flaw perhaps this is the source of it, the inconsistency between narrative comment and fictional action. Nevertheless, the novel has a great many merits and the overall effect is that of an honest and thoughtful investigation of an exceedingly complex problem, the nature of an individual, of a single man, and the necessity for the individual to make contact with other selves beyond himself. And at the centre of that attempt to see into the nature of individual life, we have found once again that metaphors of drama have an essential task to fulfil.

6 Inconsistencies of Narration in Graham Greene

In this chapter I wish to look at three of Graham Greene's most recent novels: *Our Man in Havana* (1958), *The Comedians* (1966), and *Travels With My Aunt* (1969).* Many of the themes which have occupied him during his prolific writing career appear little changed in these recent books: the innocent figure around whom disasters multiply (the most familiar character in this mould is Pyle in *The Quiet American*), the Manichean insistence on the necessity of evil and suffering in the world, and a narrative focus on the seedy, disreputable and flagrantly dishonest character who may in fact, at times, reveal an astonishing imaginative ingenuity and even selfless heroism. Of particular interest in these three books are the characters who are in one way or another 'living a lie', or to put it into the terms used thus far in this study: playing a role. The focus in the novels on a character who is presenting a false image of himself to the world is coupled (as we may by now have come to expect) with an interest in the nature of fiction; that is, of the fictiveness of novel-writing. At times there is quite a close echoing of themes we have already looked at in the work of Muriel Spark, and this is not surprising perhaps, since possibly Greene too considers 'fictions' to be economical ways of expressing the truth. Mr Visconti, near the end of *Travels With My Aunt* suggests the idea:

> Any Catholic knows that a legend which is believed has the same value and effect as the truth. Look at the cult of the saints.[1]

Despite Mr Visconti's firm belief in the value of 'legend',

* The dates given are those of original publication in London. To allow for easy access, I shall refer to the readily available Penguin editions.

231

Graham Greene is not always of the same opinion about the value of fictions. Like Muriel Spark, he is at times suspicious of the character who indulges in fictions and presents a critical view of the inauthenticity of 'posing'. Sometimes, though, in his novels dramatic fictions are good; that is, they produce desirable ends. His pursuit of this subject is not nearly so exhaustive as is that of Muriel Spark and he offers little aid to an understanding of *why* fictions produce one end or another. His attitude is almost wholly pragmatic: when dramatic fictions produce desirable ends they are justified, and not when they do not. Such a view leads at times, not surprisingly, to confusing inconsistencies. Nevertheless, a concentration on dramatic action in his work offers a rewarding way in to some very interesting stories.

One possible source for the confusion surrounding the question of role-playing in Greene's novels is the fact that 'dramatic action' can be seen in one of two contexts: either role-playing belongs to the creative realm of fiction and serves as a means of self-transcendence, or alternatively role-playing can be seen as a matter of taking a position in established Society, of accepting the illusion of a code of behaviour rather than seeking self-expression in free creative acts. One type of drama which Greene does not believe in is the playing of conventional roles. Stephen Spender makes the interesting point that the Catholic writer differentiates sharply between the law of God and the law of man. As a result of this, the Catholic writer is preeminently interested in the innocent 'child of nature' who is 'playing a game against man and human institutions, and sharing the secret of his innocence with God'.[2] It is essential for a writer drawing heavily on metaphors of drama in his novels to discriminate clearly between the role-playing which belongs to institutionalised society (which is condemned by Greene) and that which belongs to the realm of justifiable fiction-making, in the special sense developed in this study. If such a discrimination is not made then the negative judgement – made by means of the use of metaphors of drama – against one type of role-playing, will inevitably infect the picture presented of the other type of role-playing – which is presented in precisely the same metaphors. It would appear that Greene has not thoroughly imagined (or thought through) the possibilities of 'dramatic action' because occasionally it looks too much like 'institutionalised acting'. As a result he is often fascinated by romantic, adventurous action – blind action that is to say. Such inconsistencies as arise do so as a result, then, of a failure to think thoroughly about the nature of dramatic fictions, and about the nature of controlled, conscious, ritual action or self-dramatisation. *Our Man In Havana* comes closest to overcoming these deficits.

This novel bears the characteristic Greene qualification 'An Entertainment', and therefore we expect to find the usual Catholic preoccupations set aside in favour of a good story. There is no doubt that the novel is one of Greene's most satisfying achievements, but it is no less meaningful simply because it is 'entertaining'. In fact, it is better than the two that follow it, which do not bear the qualifying subtitle. Wormold is not a Catholic and so has no secret innocence – although he is still an innocent – known only to himself and God. He quite consciously defies the law by posing as a secret agent and inventing fantastic reports for MI5, including drawings of parts of a vacuum cleaner which he claims are military installations in the mountains near Havana. Perhaps the most interesting thing about this novel is that there is no chance of confusing the 'role-playing' of Wormold with passively accepting a codified place in Society. It is because Greene has Wormold play a fictional role which is opposed to 'human institutions' that he is able to point up a moral which has nothing to do with recourse to dogmatic notions of innocence or a differentiation between man's law and God's. Wormold poses as a secret agent not in order to belong to established Society (although that is what eventually happens, since he receives the O.B.E. and a job lecturing on methods of setting up a spy network). He adopts his pose as a result of a selfless perception of the reality of another human being, his daughter Milly. As we have seen, dramatic action on the part of an individual in a novel usually occurs when the reality of the world beyond the self is perceived. Wormold is moved to action in order to give Milly a chance at a better life, away from the attentions of Segura, The Red Vulture with his cigarette case made from human skin. Although Wormold plays a false role, then, he retains innocence not because he believes in God's laws as opposed to man's, but simply because he can love another human being. Of course, this too is one of God's laws, but we do not react badly when the theme of a novel is love, whereas we might tend to react with annoyance if we felt that we were being offered dogma about the workings of 'divine law'.

As Wormold begins to invent a role for himself – a role with which he could never, unlike his superior Hawthorne, completely identify himself – we begin to see that this conscious choice of a public pose is very much like the activity of a novelist. To cover up for his time spent composing reports for London, Wormold tells Milly that he is becoming an 'imaginative writer'. When he feels that he must have one of his invented agents, Raul, involved in a fictional accident because there is a chance that his new secretary Beatrice might see through his game and report him, he begins more and more to act like a novelist. Beatrice is offended by the novelistic attitude to a 'real' man: 'You haven't spoken about him as though he were a living man. You've been writing his elegy like a bad novelist preparing an effect.'[3] Ironically, life begins to imitate art and Raul is in fact killed. This turn of events is disturbing to Wormold since he is not aware that he has given his invented character the name of a real man, and that his code has been broken by the men who have a hold over his friend Hasselbacher. The engineer Cifuentes is shot as well. Wormold can understand this since he had purposely used the name of a real man for agent Cifuentes, but Raul he had thought entirely fictional:

> 'I invented Raul.'
> 'Then you invented him too well, Mr Wormold. There's a whole file on him now.'
> 'He was no more real than a character in a novel.'
> 'Are they always invented? I don't know how a novelist works, Mr Wormold. I have never known one before you.'[4]

It is at this point that *Our Man in Havana* reaches its peak of interest, and it is also the point at which its limits begin to become clear. Mr Wormold can safely play the role of spy because he is betraying only a corrupt organisation. His role is a consciously held fiction, and it is not as corrupting as the roles that MI5 can hand out. To be a 'real' spy, would be to adopt another sort of role, and to accept it completely would be to put an institution before love of individual human beings. Both Hawthorne and Wormold are playing roles, but Hawthorne's whole self has been absorbed into the role, while Wormold is consciously not giving himself up to the role, he is holding back. He is like Beatrice who replies to Wormold's charge that she plays 'the game': 'I don't believe in it like Hawthorne does.' She said furiously, 'I'd rather be a crook than a simpleton or an adolescent.'[5] Wormold's loyalty is first of all to those he loves, and for them he is ready to betray impersonal institutions which offer codified and rigid roles which eliminate the personal element. Simply, the message of the book is the one E. M. Forster so eloquently expressed:

> I hate the idea of causes, and if I had to choose between betraying my country and betraying my friend, I hope I should have the guts to betray my country.[6]

If, however, life does imitate art, and 'real' events in the world can be influenced by fictions – an uninvolved bystander called Raul can be killed, for example – then there must be a danger point beyond which the fiction which Wormold has made will start to become the reality of his own life. And Greene does not make it clear just where or what this point is. If life imitates art, then Wormold's life must begin to imitate his own art. Sooner or later he must be in danger of becoming fully absorbed by his created role. Hasselbacher, who has as little belief in institutions as Wormold, finds that *he* cannot escape total involvement in the fiction created by Wormold, and he too is killed in the 'game'. Wormold is, of course, temporarily in danger at the traders' dinner when his enemies plan to poison him. He escapes readily from this threat, however, and never seems in danger of what befalls Hasselbacher: the loss of his innocence and the radical changing of his everyday life and of his own conception of himself. The end of the novel, then, in which Wormold is given the O.B.E. and a prestigious job (which is obviously temporary, until he can be quietly dismissed) seems rather a wishful, fairytale sort of conclusion. Why should Wormold get off so easily? What is it that can keep him clear of being compromised by the fictions he has created? If they are dangerous enough to corrupt and destroy the lives of others how can they not have any adverse effect on Wormold?

The problem here is similar to the one discussed at length with reference to Muriel Spark's novels. She too expressed the idea that it is necessary to avoid being fully submerged in a role, but she committed herself to a thorough investigation of the powers of fiction and to the dual problem of the ways in which it is possible to play a role and yet keep oneself separate from it, and the degree to which it is justifiable to 'absent' oneself from the roles one plays. The insight that roles and actions do have an effect on the player, that they do 'stick' and become the 'self' leads to the interesting complexity of her fictional world. Graham Greene seems willing to admit that fictions can be all-powerful in the world, and yet by arbitrary fiat allows the maker of the fictions to escape freely from them – and also to escape freely from the fictions made by others. The book has a comic ending as a result of a decision of the author, but the ending, while it sustains the comic spirit of the novel, does have a quality of intervention about it, as if searching questions are to be dismissed rather than looked at too closely. If fictions are powerful and potentially dangerous, then they should have more effect on Wormold and the novel should perhaps come closer to tragedy for Wormold himself than it does.

But such an argument does an injustice to the novel perhaps, by taking it too seriously. We are not meant to look for a fully worked out 'philosophy' in an 'entertainment'. It seems that we have to accept the arbitrary limits within which Greene chooses to work if we are to enjoy him at all. He himself settles for a 'good story', with a mixture of humour and sadness, and a brief, incomplete analogy of 'role-playing' to the novelist's craft. If Greene can play a game with the novel and get away with it, then so too can Wormold.

To compare Graham Greene with Muriel Spark is to be tempted into a somewhat depressing conclusion. Greene can write 'entertaining' adventures but he does so by jettisoning a full look at the question of the meaning in life of 'fictions' and dramatisations of the self. His lack of theory is perhaps made up for by the 'fun' of his stories. Muriel Spark, on the other hand offers much more to our understanding of the way in which life itself works, and the way in which fictions can be acceptable. By concentrating on this task perhaps she has been forced, by a too conscious awareness of a theory of fiction, to give up the entertaining story which cannot bear any (or too much) weight of theory.

In fact, *Our Man in Havana* comes very close to a complete theory of fiction, and it is very similar to the general position we have been tracing throughout this study. It is permissible to indulge in fictions (or lies) so long as one is doing it for love. Dramatic action is both justified and made possible for the individual by means of a clear perception of the needs of an *other* human being. Role-playing is justifiable, that is to say, so long as it does not entail capitulation to the impersonal, codified roles of Society. If we try to push our interest in the nature of fictions further with Greene we are likely to be disappointed. He is willing to admit that 'legends' can have the same value and effect as truth if they are believed, but the role that Wormold plays, that of secret agent, although valuable and effective is permissible precisely because he does not fully believe in it.

Many of the literary allusions in Greene's novels come from Shakespeare, attesting possibly to his own belief that, in some sense, all the world's a stage and all the men and women in it merely players. The code book used by Wormold, for instance, is Lamb's *Tales From Shakespeare*. At one point he gleefully encodes a message by starting with Olivia's line from *Twelfth Night*, 'But I will draw the curtain and show the picture. Is it not well done?'[7] In *The Comedians* there is a similar, almost casual, use of allusions to the drama. The ship which brings the three characters Smith, Brown and Jones to Haiti is called the *Medea*. Smith, the presidential candidate as he comes to be known, hopes to begin a vegetarian centre on the island and one of his plans is to promote a school of vegetarian dramatists. Until local playwrights get underway he intends to fall back on Bernard Shaw. Brown himself once played the part of Father Lawrence in a French production of *Romeo and Juliet*. When Smith corrects Brown's exaggerated worry about the jailing of Jones, Brown notes: 'I felt a little like the player-king rebuked by Hamlet for exaggerating his part.'[8] All of the central figures in the novel are 'comedians' which means, on one level at least, that they are playing parts; their public appearance is in some sense an illusion. This false appearance can at times be regarded as nothing more than a pretence which is meant to obscure the one reality, which is death. As Brown's mother says in her posthumous letter to her lover Marcel (who will hang himself from grief at her death), 'As long as we pretend we escape.' Marcel, however, is not altogether a 'comedian', since he kills himself and 'Death is a proof of sincerity.'[9]

One use of the image of the 'comedian' then is to suggest that playing a part is lying in order to escape reality. The reality which must be escaped is that of Papa Doc, who is no comedian: 'Horror is always real.' Brown's mistress, Martha, seems to emphasise the point that role-playing is merely a pretence, an escape:

> 'For Christ's sake,' Martha said in English, as though she were addressing me directly, 'I'm no comedian.' We had forgotten her. She beat with her hands on the back of the sofa and cried to them in French now, 'You talk so much. Such rubbish. My child vomited just now. You can smell it still on my hands. He was crying with pain. You talk about acting parts. I'm not acting any part. I do something. I fetch a basin. I fetch aspirin. I wipe his mouth. I take him into my bed.'[10]

This seems to be the authentic Greene tone, suggesting that vomiting children, sordid political murders, infidelity, are the reality which demands not pretence, but action. And yet, a few pages further on we discover that Martha is very capable of putting on a false mask in order to deceive her husband with Brown. She calmly tells her husband that she is showing Brown around the rooms when in fact she had just been pulling him down on to the bed: 'There was not a false note in her voice; she was perfectly at ease, and I thought of her anger when we talked of comedians, although now she proved to be the best comedian of us all.'[11] Like Wormold, she can freely engage in 'dramatic action' such as 'playing a part' because she is ready to take 'action'; that is, she is committed by her love and that love makes deception necessary.

It is very difficult to abstract from this novel any clear idea of just what Greene thinks about the question of 'playing a part'. At times it seems to be characteristic of living in bad faith, and at other times it is justified by necessity and love. He seems to be at pains to demonstrate that being a comedian is both good and evil at the same time. 'Playing a part' is a deceptive action, but it is at least action, and action is positive in that it leads to commitment and involvement. Lack of involvement in the struggle against evil is the greatest of sins. But 'playing a part' is in itself a lack of involvement; it is pretence which keeps the personal element hidden behind a mask. There is a circle of confusion surrounding this question of 'play acting' and 'comedians'. The confusion seems to stem from Greene's Manichean belief that evil is not only inevitable in every human activity, but that it is necessary.*

There is of course nothing wrong with a novel which is built around a moral ambiguity, so long as it is ambiguity and not confusion which is at the centre of the work. A novel does not need to resolve every moral question it raises. The conclusion of *The Comedians*, however, does seem to be an attempt to resolve the ambiguity. Jones's pretence leads him into the leadership of the rebels against Papa Doc. He is committed to the lies he has spread about himself – that he was one of Wingate's key men in Burma, for instance – and so he is committed to carrying on in his role as guerilla fighter and as result attains almost heroic status. Role-playing has a positive effect for Jones since it leads him into a good action, the active opposition of an evil regime. Brown continues to act out of jealousy, however, and his role-playing is a degrading refusal to be there himself. Why, one might ask, does the fiction not have a curative effect for Brown if it does for Jones? The answer seems only to be that Greene has decided that that is the way it will be in this novel. One is forced to conclude that confusion and not ambiguity underlies the use of metaphors of drama in this novel.

One can go some way to understanding why Brown's posing is not positive and transforming; he is not capable of seeing the *other* as *other*. He constantly projects his own idea of what his friends are like onto them; his 'vision' of them distorts them:

* Once wonders if Brown might be speaking for the author when he replies to the comment of the cashier in the casino that ambassadors are a 'necessary evil': 'You believe that evil is necessary? Then you're a Manichean like myself.' (*C*, p. 82). In Greene's essay on Dickens there is further evidence of the fascination with evil. He identifies the true theme of Dickens in 'the eternal and alluring taint of the Manichee, with its simple and terrible explanation of our plight, how the world was made by Satan and not by God, lulling us with the music of despair. . . .' See Penguin *Collected Essays*, p. 86. To simplify, one could regard Manicheeism as an extreme exaggeration of the belief in original sin.

'You should have been a novelist,' she [Martha] said, 'then we would all have been your characters. We couldn't say to you we are not like that at all, we couldn't answer back. Darling, don't you see you are inventing us?'[12]

In the earlier chapters we looked at the way in which an imaginative vision can be a denial of external reality. One concomitant of this 'vision' was separation from the external world, a refusal and an inability to take action. The denial of others and inaction or lack of involvement seemed to belong together. We might expect then that Brown, who 'invents' his friends, will also be distant and uninvolved. Martha leaves no doubt that Brown is an 'idealist' who risks being a 'solipsist':

'My darling, be careful. Don't you understand? To you nothing exists except in your own thoughts. Not me, not Jones. We're what you choose to make us. You're a Berkeleyan. My God, what a Berkeleyan. You've turned poor Jones into a seducer and me into a wanton mistress. You can't even believe in your mother's medal, can you? You've written her a different part. My dear, try to believe we exist when you aren't there. We're independent of you. None of us is like you fancy we are. Perhaps it wouldn't matter much if your thoughts were not so dark, always so dark'[13]

Perhaps. If so, then it is not being a Berkeleyan that is so contemptible, it is being a gloomy Berkeleyan? But why are Brown's thoughts always so gloomy? Because the novelist Greene has decided that they should be. His characters are what he chooses they will be. Is Greene too then a 'novelist'? a Berkeleyan who escapes whipping because at least he is not gloomy – at least not all of the time?

Such questions may seem flippant, but they are intended to point to an inconsistency between what goes on inside the novel (which is presented to us in terms of the arts of drama and the novel) and Greene's own activity as a novelist. The confusion about the theme of being a 'comedian' inside the novel, could well be a function of severe doubts on the part of the novelist himself about the meaning of appearing to the world as a novelist. It is perhaps worth noting in passing that the fictions that Brown creates do not have the same value and effectiveness in the world as do those of Wormold. Wormold too is a 'novelist' whose fictions remake the world (or at least part of it). Brown's fictions are merely his delusions, and they do not make Martha wanton, nor Jones a seducer. What this means is that Greene does not have a thoroughly consistent idea of what 'fictions' are for, and yet the subject of fictions is at the centre of some, his best work.

If Brown is the idealist Martha claims he is, then we might expect that he would be capable neither of action, nor of dramatic action. We find, however, that Brown is capable of action because his 'idealised' version of Martha and Jones (that is, his jealousy of his 'invented' characters) leads him actively to aid Jones's escape from Port au Prince and to arrange his meeting with the rebels in the hills. He does this in order to get Jones out of the way and have Martha all to himself once again. Somewhat surprisingly he seems also to be one of those who engage in 'dramatic action'. When he first meets his mother in their hotel, she says to him, 'You really are a son of mine. What part are you playing now?'[14] The implication of her question is that Brown characteristically 'plays a part'. Brown himself says of his 'cuckolding a member of the diplomatic corps' that 'the act belonged too closely to the theatre of farce'.[15] We must conclude then that Brown is one of the 'comedians' referred to in the title, and that to be a comedian is to risk being a man like Brown, which is to risk the greatest of evils: the denial of the independent reality of others.

Such a conclusion is at odds, however, with the meaning that attaches to the word comedian as it is used in association with Jones. Jones freely engages in 'dramatic action', in that he plays the part of a guerilla fighter with experience in the Congo and Burma. When Brown calls his bluff, he is consistent in the part he plays, and allows his dramatic self-presentation to lead to a commitment to *action* in the Haitian jungle. When the Tontons Macoute Captain Concasseur nearly captures him, he is saved by the intervention of Philipott who kills Concasseur. Jones is physically ill as a result of the killing and confesses to Brown, ' "I'm sorry, old man. One of those things. Please don't tell them, but I've never seen a man die before." '[16] He has allowed his fictionalised presentation of himself as a guerilla fighter to lead him to a confrontation with the horror. The fiction, the 'part', leads to a confrontation with reality and not an escape

from it. He consistently plays his role, and so is capable of
heroic action in the fight against unmitigated evil. This comedian then, is not blind to the realities of life, he is willing even
to sacrifice himself – that is, he is drastically unlike the Berkeleyan Brown who denies the reality of others. Jones offers his own
life in the service of others. He does it not out of any theoretical
understanding, nor out of any conviction that he is doing the
right thing. He simply acts in accordance with the appearance
he has put abroad. He exemplifies the quotation from the poem
by Hardy which appears under the title:

> '. . . Aspects are within us,
> and who seems
> Most kingly is the King.'

Which is to say, that what we appear to be, is what we are.
Since what we pretend to be is what we appear to be, then the
roles we adopt as dramatisations of ourselves amount to what
we are. All this is perfectly well exemplified in the life of Jones.
Only, Brown pretends to be the lover of Martha, he appears to
be the lover of Martha, and yet he somehow holds back, he is
not really the lover of Martha.

What is potentially an extremely significant exploration of
appearance and reality then, is vitiated by the inconsistencies
which surround the narrator Brown. It may be that Greene has
a rooted suspicion of the character who narrates the novel and
must make him a less than admirable character in order to be in
tune with the trend of the so-called 'anti-hero' of the twentieth
century. More likely, however, he has not fully worked out for
himself, the meaning that a private fiction has for the public
world. Unlike Muriel Spark, he does not clearly distinguish
between a 'lie' and a 'fiction' and this lack of distinction lends a
confusing note to his most significant theme.   ·

In *Travels With My Aunt*, Graham Greene seems willing to try
to confront this very problem by focusing closely on the character of Henry Pullings's Aunt, who is another character who is
like a 'novelist'. At first it might seem difficult to see just how
this novel is unified. When one realises that it is little more than
a series of adventures strung together around the person of the
Aunt we see that it is her character which provides the unity. It
is her adventures in the present which are so fascinating and

amusing, and even more, it is her narratives of her past adventures which we are to look at. For instance, Henry earns her long-lasting anger by saying that he does not wish to hear the story of Charles Pottifer and Boulogne. He finally has to plead with her to tell him the story before he is once more restored to her favour. She is a narrator who will not be denied. An evaluation of Aunt Augusta should lead us then to Greene's evaluation of the art of narration. If the effect of the Aunt's narration is good then we may assume that the novel endorses the creation of fictions. If the effect is deleterious then of course we make the opposite conclusion. The implied judgement of the novel, once again, comes somewhere confusingly between these two possibilities.

We might note that since the Aunt herself is telling her own stories, we have no way of checking the objective truth of what she says. She does seem capable of bold lies, however, which Henry cannot see through. For instance, to his comment that he hopes she has not planned anything illegal on their first trip abroad together, she pleads absolute innocence: 'I have never planned anything illegal in my life,' Aunt Augusta said. 'How could I plan anything of the kind when I have never read any of the laws and have no idea what they are?'[17] However, a few pages further on we discover something quite different. She explains to Henry that she does not trust to luck when passing through immigration and customs:

'Only a fool would trust to luck, and there is probably a fool now on the Nice flight who is regretting his folly. Whenever new restrictions are made, I make a very careful study of the new arrangements for carrying them out.'[18]

Surprisingly, Henry makes no comment on her inconsistency. Aunt Augusta's claim to be 'innocent' of the laws may well have struck a responsive chord in the reader. We are willing to be anarchists of the mind so long as we are reassured that the whole thing is essentially innocent. But what are we to make of the woman who contradicts herself? Is she unaware of her own inconsistency? Is the author? Is the reader meant to respond to the Aunt's entertaining lawlessness only to be brought up short by the chastening reality? The questions begin to multiply, but the novel offers little help in answering any of them.

There is little doubt, however, that most of the novel is entertaining to read; that is, Aunt Augusta's stories are stimulating.
Certainly Henry Pulling is stirred by them and he gives up his
comfortable retirement to join his Aunt in a smuggling operation in Paraguay. That he makes no comment on the obvious
untruth about customs is perhaps an indication that tempera-
mentally he too prefers fiction to Truth (there are enough hints
to establish the fact that his Aunt is really his mother and so
possibly he has inherited her tendencies). After hearing from
his Aunt the story of his uncle Jo Pulling, Henry says:

> Without breaking the silence I took a reverent glass of Cham-
> bertin to Uncle Jo's memory, whether he existed or not. The
> unaccustomed wine sang irresponsibly in my head. What did
> the truth matter? All characters once dead, if they continue
> to exist in memory at all, tend to become fictions. Hamlet is
> no less real now than Winston Churchill, and Jo Pulling no
> less historical than Don Quixote.[19]

The truth of this particular passage is qualified by Henry's
drunkenness, but it is not clear if his drunkenness makes him
more insightful, or less. The *effect* of the fictions, however, is to
begin to make Henry take action. His putative uncle Jo dies like
a character from a Beckett novel, refusing to accept immobility
caused by a heart attack. He continues on his pilgrimage from
room to room in his house – he spends one week in each of the
fifty-two rooms; the movement is somehow a denial of time and
makes life longer – and dies as he drags himself towards the
bathroom, the fifty-second room. Henry is obviously intended
to follow his heroic example.

The Aunt herself of course believes in adventurous action.
Her narratives are not simple accounts, they are enactments.
Her method is dramatic. Henry unfavourably compares his
father's narrative technique: 'I am sure my father – the admirer
of Walter Scott – would not have told the story of the Curlews
nearly so dramatically; there would have been less dialogue
and more description.'[20] Henry and his Aunt seem to agree that
the essence of Art is not to describe but to enact, that is, to
mime. As Henry thinks of the figures he has come to know from
his Aunt's stories, he realises that they have been brought
mimetically to life:

I thought of Curran and Monsieur Dambreuse and Mr Visconti – they lived in my imagination as though she had actually created them: even poor Uncle Jo struggling towards the lavatory. She was one of the life-givers.[21]

She gives life to characters who may or may not be real, and she also gives new life to her nephew-son Henry. The source of her dramatic method would seem to be her early association with the theatre. At least, when Henry asks if she has been in a theatre company she says that the 'description will serve'.[22] There are many suggestions in the novel that the theatre in which she served was in fact a brothel. She hints at this other form of dramatic calling when Henry again asks her if she had been in a theatre:

> 'I can't think why you persist in calling it a theatre. "All the world's a stage", of course, but a metaphor as general as that loses all its meaning. Only a second-rate actor could have written such a line out of pride in his second-rate calling.'[23]

And her anger may well be the pique of one producer of dramas at the superior talent of another.

Despite the apparent contempt she has for Shakespeare, she seems to have attended performances of his plays in such out of the way places as Tunis. She recalls this experience when trying to explain how the average policeman is firmly set in the pattern of his role:

> 'No,' she went on, 'the mind of a policeman is set firmly in a groove. I remember once when I was in Tunis a travelling company was there who were playing *Hamlet* in Arabic. Someone saw to it that in the Interlude the Play King was really killed – or rather not quite killed but severely damaged in the right ear – by molten lead. And who do you suppose the police at once suspected? Not the man who poured the lead in, although he must have been aware that the ladle wasn't empty and was hot to the touch. Oh no, they knew Shakespeare's play too well for that, and so they arrested Hamlet's uncle.'[24]

Now, once again, this is a very comic anecdote, but it is hard to see just what it could mean. It does not by any means indicate that policemen are set in their grooves. It does, however, suggest that a 'legend' if it is believed has the power of Truth. In this case the police are mistaken because they take an artistic fiction for reality – not the sort of error of which we might ordinarily suspect any policeman who is stuck in the groove of his job. One could speculate for a long time on the possibilities of meaning in this little story, and it does seem to invite such speculation since it looks like one of those small narrative incidents which can so readily reveal character as well as theme. But, in the novel nothing is made of it. Henry limply responds to this comic story by saying, 'What a lot of travelling you have done in your day, Aunt Augusta.'[25] And that is that.

If we accept that the apparent meaning of the passage is the real one – that is, that one should never allow oneself to act as a result of believing in fictions – then we must conclude that one of the aims of the novel is to show us the decline and fall of Henry Pulling as the result of his Aunt/Mother's dramatic narrative genius. Her stories of adventure stir him to give up his 'static character'. To conclude that, of course, would also be to decide that we must not ourselves believe in Graham Greene's fictions. Such a conclusion is damagingly at odds with the feeling of *Travels With My Aunt*. If the novel is a consistent, work of art we can only say that while it is entertaining, exciting at times, it offers us nothing in which we can believe. But we must believe in the narrative adventures before we can be at all entertained or excited by them. The heart of the matter would seem to be that in this novel, as we have seen, Greene is not fully in control of his material. He allows apparently interesting and significant events and images to get out of control and to interfere with one another. One would hesitate to call Greene an amateur, but one is tempted to say that Aunt Augusta's strictures on the lack of discipline in modern sexual affairs as compared to the old brothel system, can be applied to Greene's novels: 'An amateur is never in proper control of his art.'

Aunt Augusta, like Prospero perhaps, renounces her art once she has rejoined the love of her life, Mr Visconti:

'This is my journey's end,' Aunt Augusta said. 'Perhaps travel for me was always a substitute. I never wanted to travel as long as Mr Visconti was there.'[26]

Once again, it is futile to try to follow the logic of this decision, since it contradicts what has already been said about the value of activity, of travelling in her story about Uncle Jo Pulling. She disappears with Mr Visconti into the 'deep incurable egotism of passion'. Henry is to marry the sixteen year old daughter of the Chief of Customs: 'There is, of course, a considerable difference in our ages, but she is a gentle and obedient child, and often in the warm scented evenings we read Browning together.' And the novel concludes with two lines from Browning:

> God's in his heaven –
> All's right with the world!

Is this marriage to a gentle and obedient child meant then to represent some sort of moral and courageous victory for Henry, who has been able to break out of the static pattern set by his thirty years in a bank? Or does the conclusion show that Henry has been so degraded by his conversion to a life of danger and action that he is willing to submit a child to his lusts? Is he too now, like his Aunt, one of the devotees of the 'incurable egotism of passion'? And if so is that a good thing or not? Henry's own conclusion is the scarcely credible one that there is 'nothing so wrong as thirty years in a bank'. Some of his discoveries, however, make one suspicious about his scale of values. For instance, he is hit by the police when he mistakenly blows his nose on a politically significant red handkerchief:

> When I said '*Ingles*' for the third time and 'Ambassador' for the second he hit me but without conviction – a blow which hardly hurt me at all, I was discovering something new. Physical violence, like the dentist's drill, is seldom as bad as one fears.[27]

Now, on one level this is a heroic discovery. No longer will Henry shy away from commitment because he is physically afraid. For the passive recipient of violence the message is encouraging. The problem arises when one wonders what are the implications of such an insight for a Henry who has now become active in the world. It is fatalistic realism for the helpless recipient to accustom himself to violence. For an active Henry there is a less satisfying implication that if physical violence is not so bad after all, one is justified in using it on others (perhaps even impersonally, institutionally and 'without conviction' like the policeman) in order to make them come round to a different point of view. In an extreme form it is a justification of torture.

What then, does one make of the novel as a whole? The number of confusing and unanswered questions that crop up around every potentially interesting and significant passage suggest that there is no one 'message' to the book. The confusion stems from the question of whether or not fictions are justified. Greene offers no solution to this problem, since he seems to want it both ways – and I do not mean that he has a perception of some creative paradox or antisyzygy – : fictions are good and they are also bad. This too seems to be the only conclusion one can come to about Henry Pulling and his Aunt. They are good when they are vital and life-giving, and this vitality is closely related to the Aunt's ability to make interesting fictions. They are bad (if the novel really does make such a criticism of them) because even in fictions there is no transcendence, no escaping one's egotism. All man has to choose between is being in a 'groove', which is not to live; or being actively involved in the world, which is a corrupt and corrupting place. If this is true of fictions, however, we are never able to place any trust in any apparent Truth we see in a novel because it is a mixture of good and evil and there is no way of distinguishing between the two – fiction corrupts as it enlightens. This may account for the feeling one often has in reading a novel by Graham Greene that, while it is fun, it is in some way demoralising.

The subject of dramatic action, then, is once more the centre of interest in a contemporary novelist. We find that metaphors of drama recur in Greene's novels and often seem to indicate a subject of compelling interest. In the earlier analyses of Muriel Spark, Joyce Cary, Christopher Isherwood, the use of metaphors of drama was found to be more or less consistent throughout a large body of work. The 'content' of the novels is the way in which the characters in the novel cope in their own lives with dramatic, active fictions of themselves; and the novels themselves in their 'form' reflect the need for fictions to be consciously and freely chosen. Graham Greene seems not to have a fully worked out and consistent theory of the way in which his characters should respond to fictions, and this confusion inside the novel is reflected in the reader's confusion outside the novel. He is unable to decide what the fiction is 'for'. Greene's own arbitrary role as novelist is unfortunately at odds with the doubts raised in the novels themselves about the value of making fictions. In the case of Graham Greene then, a study of dramatic metaphors has shown the limits of his art. That he is hovering around subjects of central interest to our time is one reason for his popularity. The other is that he himself, like Aunt Augusta, is capable of telling a good tale. Enough virtues for any man perhaps. It is as well to know, however, what challenges he seems not to have met, and to know also that others have taken the subjects that he is interested in and found a valuable way of unifying 'form' and 'content'.

7 John Fowles's Sense of an Ending

I wish to select one particular aspect of Fowles's work for consideration. His two novels since *The Collector: The Magus* and *The French Lieutenant's Woman*, are both very long works (perhaps needlessly long) and deal with a great many topics; far too many for me to attempt to comment on them all in this discussion. One can get an impression of the range of subjects which interest Fowles by taking a look at the presentation (on the whole disappointing) of his personal 'philosophy' in *The Aristos*.[1] A man may have a great many ideas, good or bad, and his novels may be vehicles for those ideas, but that does not guarantee that his fiction will therefore be any more interesting or any more valuable. So it is not his 'philosophy' as it appears in the novels that I am interested in, but what might at first sight seem a much less important affair, the use of scenes of ritual drama at crucial points in *The Magus* and *The French Lieutenant's Woman*. Although these scenes are very short in comparison with the great length of the novels in which they occur, they are the focal points of the fiction, the points towards which the novels seem to be moving. Their occurrence is, I believe, a significant event for the novel in our time.

Fowles's most recent book, *The French Lieutenant's Woman* shows that he has come a long way in his short career. It is both very readable and interesting as an evocation of the Victorian period, fully deserving the praise Walter Allen gives it as 'a remarkably solid historical novel in which Fowles recreates a large part of the ferment in English life a century ago, the intellectual ferment, the class ferment, the shifting of classes, the shifting of power, and the effects of these on the assumptions by which men and women live. It is a quite considerable achieve-

251

ment.'² Although one may not finally be able to understand why Sarah, the woman of the title, chooses to tell Smithson the elaborate fabrication of her deflowering by Varguennes, nor quite why it is necessary for her to wed herself to shame and suffering in order to achieve a sense of identity, the story has a satisfying old-fashioned sentimentality about it and it is told well enough to keep one reading. This is certainly a great step forward since *The Collector*, which now causes one to wonder why it ever became as popular as it did.

The Collector suffers to an extreme degree a fault common to all three of Fowles's novels: the characters in *The Collector* are so tedious and uninteresting that the novel cannot recover from such an integral deficit. The collector himself, Clegg, is a character that we feel to be so far beneath us that he hardly seems to have human status at all. We read about him with the grudging curiosity we might give to a case study in a subject which does not interest us. Clegg, however, seems at times almost preferable to the vapid Beauty which he, the Beast, collects and ultimately kills. Fowles suggests in his preface to the new edition of *The Aristos* what it is that mars *The Collector*. He explains that *The Collector* has a 'deeper message' which concerns the threat of the 'Many' to the 'Few' (Clegg representing the Many and Miranda the artistic Few – the elite who partake of the *aristos*):

> Clegg, the kidnapper, committed the evil; but I tried to show that his evil was largely, perhaps wholly, the result of a bad education, a mean environment, being orphaned: all factors over which he had no control. In short, I tried to establish the virtual *innocence* of the Many. Miranda, the girl he imprisoned, had very little more control than Clegg over what she was: she had well-to-do parents, good educational opportunity, inherited aptitude and intelligence. That does not mean that she was perfect. Far from it – she was arrogant in her ideas, a prig, a liberal-humanist snob, like so many university students. Yet if she had not died she might have become something better, the kind of being humanity so desperately needs.³

Unfortunately Miranda's imperfections stand out so much in the book that one begins to hunger for the reappearance of Caliban Clegg; perverse and ugly evil quickly seems preferable to hollow and superficial Beauty. That, however, is not what the book 'means'. It means so much more. In fact, it is overburdened with 'ideas' and 'profound insights', the very flaw that makes *The Aristos* all but unreadable. One reason that *The French Lieutenant's Woman* is so much better a book is that it is not made to carry such a heavy load of 'meaning'. It is content to be a good historical novel – at least, it is *almost* content to be that – and escapes the pretentiousness of being 'thought-provoking'.

The Magus occupies somewhat of a middle ground. Nicholas Urfe threatens to be like Clegg, too far beyond human redemption to be at all interesting. Nevertheless one begins to get a feeling, once he has reached the Greek island and encountered the mysterious Maurice Conchis that the story has possibilities. Indeed much of the writing about events on the island, and about many of the minor characters with which the book abounds – including Urfe's Australian girlfriend Alison, whose name means, we are told, 'without madness', and she stands for Sanity, Reason, Reality – is very well done. The novel, then, is more readable than *The Collector*, but it has not yet become limited to the class of 'historical novels'.

Nicholas is an opportunist and amoral young man who feels the existential *angst* of being 'nothing': 'I felt myself filled with nothingness; with something more than the old physical and social loneliness – a metaphysical sense of being marooned.'[4] His suffering, that is to say, is highly fashionable and worn for effect, as he himself comes to realise when he 'attempts' suicide:

All the time I felt I was being watched, that I was not alone, that I was putting on an act for the benefit of someone, that this action could be done only if it was spontaneous, pure, isolated – and moral. Because more and more it crept through my mind with the chill spring night that I was trying to commit not a moral action, but a fundamentally aesthetic one; to do something that would end my life sensationally, significantly, consistently. It was a Mercutio death I was looking for, not a real one.[5]

The rather interesting point made in this passage is that Urfe is living on the first of Kierkegaard's levels, the aesthetic, and has not progressed to the higher stage of moral action.* The reference to Mercutio indicates that Urfe is attempting some kind of inauthentic 'drama' which is false because it operates on the level of art for art's sake. Such drama is merely aesthetic, or selfish, and not yet moral. The whole long and complicated action of the novel is intended to bring Urfe to a full realisation of his moral inaction, to an acceptance of the fact that he stands for 'something passive, abdicating, English, in life'.[6] What is interesting is that he is brought to the moment in which he can perhaps transcend the merely aesthetic by means of an elaborately staged *masque* under the direction of Conchis (whose name obviously is meant to suggest 'consciousness' and responsibility for one's actions).

The question one is forced to ask of *The Magus* is, does it really need quite so much elaboration and mystification in order to get its point across? One soon tires of the endless transformations of Lily and Rose (or June and Julie). The defence one can offer for the masque is that it is not merely aesthetic, but has as its goal the bringing of Urfe to the point at which he can move from the aesthetic to the moral level. Nevertheless, the extreme and endless artificiality of Conchis's undertaking is one of the gravest weaknesses of the novel, despite any excuses one might make for it. If, as I think it does, the novel repudiates fictions at its conclusion in favour of open confrontation between an 'I' and a 'Thou', then it is hard to understand the justification of all of Conchis's prestidigitations, let alone those of Fowles himself. Perhaps that is why one quickly forgets much of the elaborate plot of the novel while the concluding scene stubbornly sticks in the mind.

One of the stories that Conchis tells Nicholas is of the time he spent in the trenches in the first World War. He says:

I experienced the very opposite of what the German and French metaphysicians of our century have assured us is the truth: that all that is other is hostile to the individual. To me all that is other seemed exquisite. Even that corpse, even the squealing rats. . . . The word 'being' no longer passive and

* This Kierkegaardian terminology is suggested also in *The Collector*, but there it seems only to confuse matters more, since the girl Miranda is living on the aesthetic level and at times the Caliban-like Clegg seems almost to belong on the moral level.

descriptive, but active . . . almost imperative.[7]

It is to some such recognition that he is trying to lead Nicholas, who cannot recognise the otherness of the world beyond himself – Narcissus-like he sees his own face reflected in the face of others, see p. 270 – and therefore cannot actively engage in 'being'. To this end, Conchis has conceived of a particular kind of dramatic production, in which the script is written in order to suit the characteristics of the available players, and can be changed according to the actions and decisions of those involved. This new drama is:

> One in which the conventional relations between audience and actors were forgotten. In which the conventional scenic geography, the notions of proscenium, stage, auditorium, were completely discarded. In which continuity of performance, either in time or place, was ignored. And in which the action, the narrative was fluid, with only a point of departure and a fixed point of conclusion. . . . You will find that Artaud and Pirandello and Brecht were all thinking, in their different ways, along similar lines. . . . Here we are all actors. None of us are [sic] as we really are.[8]

The goal of all this is to attempt to overcome the gap between art and life. If 'aesthetic' living is inferior and inauthentic, then Art itself must not be simply beautiful or well-made. It must somehow carry directly over into life so that the artistic action becomes part of, or instigates, moral action on behalf of the participants; and all are participants since the distinctions between actors and audience are done away with: Art is something that is 'done' and not something that is intended to be passively perceived.

There are a number of indications of this idea in the novel. For instance, Conchis announces – and it can hardly come as a surprisingly new idea to any reader – that the novel is dead, and claims that he once burned all the novels he possessed since words are not for 'fun': 'Words are for truth. For facts. Not fiction.'[9] One never knows, of course, whether Conchis is telling the truth or merely playing a role in his own drama in order further to mystify Urfe. Nicholas sees Conchis 'as a sort of novelist sans novel, creating with people, not words. . . .'[10] It

becomes almost impossible to decide what value to give to any
of these statements since they are all contained in the novel we
are reading and the novel itself, apart from its over-elaborate
mystification, is very little unlike any other novel, at least so far
as being made of words is concerned. It is perhaps not worth
trying to work one's way through all the complexities of the fictions within fictions to see what is really taking place or being
said, for Fowles seems to believe that mystification (he would
call it mystery) is its own justification and reward. One of the
themes of the novel is that the attempt to be a 'detective' and
rationally work out the reason of experience is to be on the
wrong track. Life is mysterious and one must accept that the
mind is not adequate to experience. Instead of trying to unravel
Conchis's purpose, Nicholas must accept that he will never
know all, and he must act, that is, he must choose Alison and
commit himself. Supposedly then, the reader also is meant to
act and not try to unravel the mystifications of the text. This
suggests however – to the persistently rational mind, it must be
admitted – that the text of the novel in front of us is not important. The attitude to Art and the Novel which is implicit in *The
Magus* is perhaps very modish and up-to-date, but it is finally
unsatisfactory. Fowles has his way with us, leading us into what
is – at least at first reading – a readable mystery, only to tell us
that *we* should not bother our minds about artistic mysteries
since it is acting in life that is important.

If one is tempted to disregard much of the bulk of the novel
because of its flirting with theories of fiction and the need for
thoughtless or mindless acts, one cannot avoid being impressed
by the implications of the final confrontation between Nicholas
and Alison. Nicholas has been made to prove himself by means
of a long period of waiting, much like a lover of the *amour courtois*
tradition (Charles Smithson is made to go through a similar
period of proving himself by his unattainable lady Sarah).
When he has waited faithfully for long enough, a meeting is
arranged between himself and Alison in Regent's Park.
Nicholas is being brought to the moment at which his mental
choices must be externalised in action. His period of waiting
has given him the opportunity to think long and thoroughly
about his decision, so it will not be characterised by blind or
spontaneous action. He must, if he is to succeed in winning his

love, no longer simply 'decide, and still not enact the decision'.[11] The parallel with a would-be novelist is perhaps illuminating here. Many people at some time or another decide to write a novel. Very few of such 'decisions' are enacted, however. For those who do write a novel, the feeling must occur that while in one sense they must 'pretend' as they write a novel – that is, the writing of a novel is 'play-acting' since one does not appear in one's own immediate guise – in another sense the writing of the novel is an *act* rather than a mere mental decision. For the man who produces a finished product, a choice must be acted out, and the choice leads to play-acting.

It is perhaps for some such reason that the scene in which Nicholas enacts his choice is openly and pointedly a dramatic scene. Nicholas responds immediately to the setting:

> I looked round. There were other seats a few yards away. Other sitters and watchers. Suddenly the whole peopled park seemed a stage, the whole landscape a landscape of masquers, spies.[12]

The last comment indicates that Nicholas has still not learned to trust fully and he is still seeing spies everywhere. During the scene with Alison the truth suddenly dawns on him, Conchis is no longer watching him, the 'godgame' is finished and the gods have 'absconded'. There is no one watching him and he is in the existential situation of freedom in which he must choose and act on his own resources. There is no source of help beyond him in the shape of a God or a Society worth waiting for or trying to please. Alison seems to have learned this truth from Conchis – and one notices that she apparently has not needed the extreme mystification process that Nicholas has required, yet another reason for believing that while the bulk of the novel may be 'fun' it is not strictly 'necessary':

> She was not crying, I leant forward and looked. In some way I knew she was acting, and yet not acting. Perhaps she had rehearsed the saying this; but still meant it.[13]

When Nicholas says that Alison is acting and yet not acting, he means that she is pretending, or not acting spontaneously, and yet at the same time she is 'sincere'; the artificial and rehearsed manner do not belie what she says so much as give it a force and at the same time keep her integrity. She offers to commit herself and waits to see if the drama she proposes will be joined by Nicholas.

Nicholas makes his choice for Alison, but he must involve her in a drama of his own making in order to be sure that she is not still carrying out Conchis's orders:

> You now have a choice. You do as I say. Or you don't. This. In a few seconds I am going to walk away from you. You will look after me, then call my name. I shall stop, turn round. You will come up to me. I shall turn and start walking away again. You will come after me again, and catch my arm. I shall shake myself free. Then. Then I shall slap you as hard as I can over the side of the face. And believe me, it won't hurt me half as much as it hurts you.[14]

The directions continue, Alison is to meet him at Paddington Station, in the waiting room, which echoes his own wait in Conchis's *salle d'attente*. Nicholas will then join her:

> You know damn well what this is. But you don't say yes or no. You do yes or no.

They carry out the drama and as they are in the midst of it, fooling as Nicholas thinks, Conchis and his spies, the truth comes to him:

> There were no watching eyes. The windows were as blank as they looked. The theatre was empty. It was not a theatre. They had told her it was a theatre, and she had believed them, and I had believed her. To bring us to this – not for themselves, but for us.[15]

The fact that there is no audience does not mean that the drama enacted by Nicholas and Alison is needless. It is a formal and ritual confrontation between 'I' and 'Thou' and must partake of the nature of dramatic action. Only the dramatic action can do two things at once: preserve the sense of being a subjective, deliberative and free individual, and simultaneously admit the reality of another person beyond oneself. The ritual is creative and it is mediative as well. This last play lives up to Conchis's idea: 'No good play has a real curtain, Nicholas. It is acted, and then it continues to act.'[16] This is true also of Fowles's novel, at least of its ending, it is acted and it continues to act. It may be that the reader is 'intended' to find fault with the earlier part of the novel, but such an intention does not really save it from being unsatisfactory. The conclusion of the novel is so good that one wishes the rest of the book could have had its dramatic simplicity and much less of topical play on theories of fiction.

It seems that Fowles achieved some kind of significant breakthrough at the end of *The Magus*, and the coincidence of the two types of acting in the dramatic action suggests possibilities for further exploration. This expectation is for the most part disappointed by *The French Lieutenant's Woman*. It does not take up this question of the nature of dramatic action, but is, as has been noted, centred on the creation of period atmosphere. Nevertheless, there is a brief scene, again at the end of the novel, which is similar to that at the end of *The Magus*. After his period of purifying waiting, Smithson finds Sarah living in the house of Swinburne and Rosetti. She does not immediately leap into his arms on the discovery that he has broken off his engagement with Ernestina, but remains aloof and cool, finally claiming that there is 'another'. In fact, she has long known that the engagement had been broken, but she did nothing; she has been putting him to the test (and the other is their daughter). Harsh words ensue; Charles says:

> 'You have not only planted the dagger in my breast, you have delighted in twisting it.' She stood now staring at him, as if against her will, but hypnotized, the defiant criminal awaiting sentence. He pronounced it. 'A day will come when you shall be called to account for what you have done to me. And if there is justice in heaven – your punishment shall outlast eternity.'
>
> Melodramatic words; yet words sometimes matter less than the depth of feeling behind them – and these came out of Charles's whole being and despair. What cried out behind them was not melodrama, but tragedy.[17]

The purpose of this drama which Sarah has engineered is the revealing of their true feelings for each other and the purging of any spleen that Charles may still feel about the way Sarah had 'used' him.

This scene comes from the first ending of the book; there are two as in some Victorian novels. The second ending is not provided in order to give a happier ending, but in order to point out that a separation was as likely as a reconciliation between the two lovers and that Fowles is not so concerned that the two choose each other as that they choose. As a device, the double ending does not fail and the two endings do both appear to be plausible, but one wonders if much is gained by such toying with the form of the novel. All of *The French Lieutenant's Woman* seems directed towards this final scene between Charles and Sarah, just as most of the bulk of *The Magus* is justified, if at all, because it leads up to the dramatic action of the ending. Fowles is very skilful, too skilful and tricksy at times, and this facility may lead him into yet more experiments with the form of the novel. It may be possible, however, that he will turn his serious (or comic) attention to one of the most exciting and central concerns of modern fiction: the nature and value of dramatic action.

8 Conclusion: A Quick Look Around

The one thing it would be impossible to conclude after this study is that there is anything like a 'school' of novelists at work in the post-Modern period and it has not been part of my purpose to try to show that any such school exists. Except for the possible pairing of the co-religionists Greene and Spark, between whom one can see some evidence of interaction, that writers I have focused on are very much unlike one another, and indeed the mere listing of their names would be unlikely to produce any immediate intimation of how they might be related. There is perhaps a strong element of Catholic, or at least Thomistic and Aristotelian philosophy common to all in that they all make use of a notion of mimesis derivable from Aristotle, and the notion of the self as agent occurs in Joyce who gets it from Aquinas, and it is expressed also by Hopkins. But the two Catholic writers included here are not typical of 'Catholic novelists' nor, one suspects, typical of Catholics. I have tried to pay scant attention to religious beliefs held by any author for which there is no adequate expression in the text of their novels. Where such dogmatic belief seems to interfere with the validity of the novel, as perhaps it does in the case of Isherwood, I have commented on the fact. So far as religion goes, the five novelists here considered might in fact have something in common: they are all religious writers in so far as they ask fundamental questions and are not content to define man by the position he can play in an ordered Society. So far as the question of established religion is concerned, they represent the full spectrum, from the highly individual and imaginative non-conformism of Cary on the one hand to the Catholicism of Greene and Spark on the other. Isherwood at times seems to hover overhead in the realm

261

of Vedanta Buddhism and Fowles expresses a post-Exis-
tentialist yearning after sacramental mystery.

How then can one account for the grouping together of these
writers; or more specifically, what is it that has prompted them
all to use (whether consciously or unconsciously is of no concern) allusions to drama and a concept of dramatic action repeatedly in their work? The answer I propose is that they, each
individually, have maintained a sense of the continuity of the
literary enterprise and, fully aware of the achievements of the
traditions of Modern literature, have attempted to do something new without jettisoning what others before them have
achieved. They represent, then, the value of a lively sense of tradition and the exercise of individual talent. In using 'tradition'
in this way, I do not mean to subscribe to the letter of T. S.
Eliot's doctrine so much as to borrow the spirit of his phrase.
When I say that writers such as Muriel Spark do not deny the
tradition of the Modern, I mean that they have steeped themselves in the literature of the time (and of earlier times) and
their work is as much an extension of themes implicit in that
earlier work – and at times a revelation of the inadequacies of
certain postures current in that work – as much as it is a creation of something totally new to express their own sense of life.

For this reason, the use of metaphors of drama in recent fiction can only be fully exploited by writers who are not by nature
antipathetic (have no *a priori* objection) to the works of the revolutionary Modern writers and have no crippling adulation for
them. Similarly a critical exposition of the use of such allusions
to the drama in the post-Modern period can only hope to attain
to any completeness if it considers the meaning for the Moderns
(and for the Romantics as well) of action and 'dramatic action'.
The ground occupied by the Moderns is that of the inner man;
they are the explorers of consciousness, and explorers also of
the unconscious. In the attempt to answer the sphinx's question: What is man? they turned their attention to what the
inside of the individual is like, in contrast to their predecessors
who paid more attention to the value of externals and abstractions such as Duty, Society and so on. As they occupy this
ground, however, they do not fail to express a sense that a single
man is in some way deficient. They are aware that the gaze
turned inward is narcissistic and potentially suicidal. As a

result of this realisation they express a need for appropriate rituals of externalisation; they do express the beginning of an awareness of the necessity for rituals of 'decent exposure'. This expression takes the form of a recognition of a need for the *act* to overcome the potential solipsism of *consciousness*. Blind action in itself is no answer however, since it finally denies the validity of the free internal world altogether. Yeats's conception, then, of ritual or dramatic action and the ideal of the 'antithetical' man, is of central importance to an understanding of the literature of the twentieth century. Dramatic action permits the ritual expression of subjectivity, that is, the actualisation and realisation of the individual self, yet it does not deny the reality of the world of others beyond the self. There is a tendency for the post-Modern British writer to be 'superficial'; that is, to turn away from excessive internality and return to the 'ordinary universe'. Those writers I have considered are part of this trend, but their investigation of life in the ordinary universe is particularly commanding because it recalls the exploration of the depths by earlier writers. Their subject is the interaction of inner and outer. They too, then, have a natural call on all the potential of the concept of dramatic action. There is another sort of writer, however, who also is aware of the need for a renewed sense of the value of the external world, who uses the metaphors of drama in a limited sense and assumes that the only alternative to narcissistic, solipsistic Individuality is accommodation to Society. They assert the necessity for 'working in the ranks' without Conrad's sympathetic, if critical, investigation of the rich inner life of the subjective imagination. One is tempted to suggest that only those who can conceive of a Lord Jim have any claim to authority in their assertion that the meaning of life is to be found in working in the ranks. It might also be fair to say that only those writers who are initially anti-Social can in the long run provide us with a convincing argument that life must be social, that is must be lived in an 'outer world of other people'.

One of the important developments of literary history is the gradual change of focus from inner to outer in the shift from Modernism to post-Modernism. Metaphors of drama have an important task in expressing the essential interplay of inner and outer. There are many other places, of course, where one can find allusions to the drama aside from the novels I have studied here. I have tried to restrict my choice of novelists for analysis to those whose work provides a useful correction as well as exemplification of the theory outlined in the first two chapters. The theoretical concepts developed there are meant to make the reading of the novels a little easier, and the readings of the novels are meant to correct any tendency to ethereal abstraction in the first two chapters. To that extent then this book tries to imitate the themes developed in the novels under consideration: a primarily mentalistic (and perhaps also subjective) theory is meant to be fully realised only in the act of criticism. The theory is not necessarily meant to stand on its own, but is justified, if at all, in that it gives rise to more comprehensive acts of practical criticism. Therefore, I have not tried to explicate every occurrence of metaphors of drama in the current scene.

Naturally this must lead to certain glaring omissions, such as the case of Henry James. One should perhaps have begun such a study with a consideration of the nature of dramatic action in Shakespeare, and then have gone on to consider Fielding, Dickens, Thackeray, George Eliot, Henry James and then every important novelist after him.* Such a task is beyond my capacities and I believe it to be beyond the limits of necessity for a useful study. I do not think that the element of dramatic action is unimportant in James, nor do I think that the method of analysis developed here would fail to reveal significant truths about Henry James's fictional world. It is simply that James is too big a fish to be caught in this net and he needs a book all to himself. On the question of Shakespeare, there can be little doubt that he has had a significant influence on almost all English literature written since his time. Even the objection raised in Greene's novel *Travels With My Aunt* that 'all the world's a stage' is a metaphor so vague that it could only be invented by some second-rate playwright puffed up with pride in his skill, belies Greene's fascination with the potential meanings of dramatic action. The interesting question one would want to ask of Shakespeare's plays is do they reveal a conscious use, and a conscious pointing to the use of dramatism? Do characters in

* See for instance: Robert Garis, *The Dickens Theatre* (Oxford, 1965); Brian Swann, 'George Eliot and the Play: Symbol and Metaphor of the Drama in *Daniel Deronda*', *Dalhousie Review* (Summer, 1972), 191–202; Adeline R. Tintner, 'Hyacinth at the Play: The Play Within the Play as a Novelistic Device in James', *Journal of Narrative Technique*, (Sept. 1972), 171–85.

the plays consciously and artificially play roles and do the
plays, does Shakespeare, call attention to the artificiality of the
play as it is being presented?

To one question we can easily give an answer. The adopting
of disguises is an integral part of so many of Shakespeare's plays
that it is essential to his method. The plays abound with
'posers' like Olivia and Orsino in *Twelfth Night* and with characters like King Hal who plays at being a drunken roustabout
and then begins to understand that there is another more
important role for him to play. The device of the play within the
play suggests that Shakespeare made his audience conscious of
the way in which plays can work on their audiences. A revealing
study of *Hamlet* by David Pirie shows that Shakespeare is in fact
a direct source for many of the ideas of dramatic action developed by the novelists we have considered. It is Pirie's claim
that Hamlet refuses to identify himself completely with any one
of the pre-fabricated roles that he is confronted with:

> Hamlet's own fascination with actors who have 'strutted and
> bellowed' their way across a stage (III. ii. 32) grows from his
> bitter appreciation of the analogy. The 'real' world of Elsin-
> ore is too vile to be comfortably believed in, too absurd to be
> taken seriously. It signifies nothing more than a number of
> bad plays. The ghost has cast Hamlet for the role of ruthless
> hero in a conventional revenge tragedy. Claudius expects
> him to pursue the plots of an ambitious claimant to the
> throne in a political drama. Polonius sees him playing
> Romeo to Ophelia's Juliet in a tragedy of star-crossed lovers
> parted by their fathers. Fortinbras – less consciously of
> course – challenges the Prince to accept the role of a Danish
> Henry V, and play out a military epic of the kind performed
> by old Fortinbras and old Hamlet. Hamlet's instinct is to
> reject all these scripts as morally and intellectually
> unworthy. The audience is asked to enjoy the tension created
> by the leading player's refusal to act in the play.[1]

Hamlet's disengagement from the play is given expression by
his frequent recourse to soliloquy:

> The soliloquy is an implied denial of the pointfulness of
> trying to share oneself or one's life with another person. The

audience will obviously understand why Hamlet failed to see
Ophelia in time as someone worth more concern than a character in a play. But they will be led by her mad scene, as
much as by the king's soliloquy, to see that Hamlet's withdrawal though at first amusing is ultimately pathetic. His
disengagement is based not only on a despairing knowledge,
but also on a tragic ignorance. *Hamlet* without the prince is
not only a comedy of intellectual detachment. It is also a
tragedy of waste.[2]

Pirie perhaps overemphasises his claim that the play 'has to
stagger through its five acts without the prince becoming responsibly involved', since Hamlet's 'character' does seem to
undergo a maturing and ripening process during his absence
from Denmark. On his return he is capable of a much more
'committed' reflection on the fates of the other characters
involved in the action of the play. On the whole however, Pirie
successfully indicates the way in which playing roles is something which must be rejected by the worthy individual, and also
the way in which the refusal to play roles, the retreat into soliloquy and subjectivity is the denial of the independent reality of
others. Ultimately Hamlet accepts a role in the tragedy and the
play is the thing which mediates between self and other; if playing is artificial, the artfulness of it at least transcends solipsism.

Shakespeare then, may be one source for the notion of dramatic action with which so many writers have been concerned.
But the question of sources is an endless one; from where did
Shakespeare get the device?* The ultimate source for a literary
device is not necessarily some previous writer. An equally likely
'source' of the device is an individual writer's sense of what is a
necessary response to his own times. The post-Modern scene
was ripe, one might say, for the use of 'dramatic action'. It
could be made to suit a whole host of interconnected problems
and situations of life and art. It is interesting to note that Shakespeare seems to make similar use of dramatic action to that
employed by many modern writers, but that does not exhaust
the matter nor does it make their works any less creative or
unique, or any less worthy of careful reading.

What though of other current writers? Where else can one
find the use in fiction of metaphors of drama, or of dramatic

---

* Ernst Curtius in *European Literature and the Latin Middle Ages* traces the
theatrum mundi metaphor back to Classical times.

action and the idea of role-playing? I shall consider the special case of Iris Murdoch at greater length in a moment. First though, one might consider a minor though competent novelist who does *not* fully explore all the complex possibilities of dramatic action. Elizabeth Taylor is a much praised English novelist whose books receive quietly complimentary reviews praising her skill and clarity. Her recent novel, *Mrs Palfrey at the Claremont*[3] touches on some of the issues raised in the course of this study. She does not, however, focus on the meaning of dramatic action, but urges the necessity for adopting, or attaining, a strict code of behaviour; an external and demanding code of discipline is found to be a very valuable asset. Mrs Palfrey (who is described as 'a dark horse'), now alone in the world moves into the Claremont Hotel, which is obviously a gathering place for those who are waiting to die but still have the ability to finance and take care of themselves. The young man, Ludo, who befriends and is befriended by Mrs Palfrey, is inspired by the woman and the hotel to write a novel called 'We're Not Allowed to Die Here'. At the end of Miss Taylor's novel, Mrs Palfrey dies 'beautifully' and tastefully in a hospital. While in the Claremont she behaves according to the demands of the situation, refusing the temptations to escape the reality of her circumstances by means of gossip, drink, sex or marriage, or self-pity.

Mrs Palfrey sets her own course, and her ability to stick to it gives her a measure of dignity in a situation tending to elicit disintegration of the personality, and the novel is a successful picturing of the dignified and significant end of a life. At times though one feels that there may be a larger theme lurking somewhere in the mind of Miss Taylor, as the following passage suggests:

> She was a tall woman with big bones and a noble face, dark eyebrows and a neatly folded jowl. She would have made a distinguished-looking man and, sometimes, wearing evening dress, looked like some famous general in drag.[4]

This humorous, almost surrealist tone is not sustained and the Shakespearean suggestion of transvestism and changed roles is pursued no further than one other indication that old men might as well be old women, and vice versa. The type of role-playing hinted at by the phrase 'like some famous old general in drag' is of no interest here since Miss Taylor has her mind focused on the value for the individual of an adopted code of behaviour:

> I shall be able to watch the lilacs coming out, she thought. It will be just like the garden at Rottingdean. The setting could scarcely have been more different; but she felt a determination about the lilac trees. They were to be a part of her rules, her code of behaviour. Be independent; never give way to melancholy; never touch capital. And she had abided by the rules.[5]

Mrs Palfrey's private code (and it is private only in that she has made a personal selection from the readily available list of public rules for correct behaviour) is adopted in an attempt to overcome the limitations of her single self. All her life she has tried to think of herself with reference to a real external world:

> In spite of long practice she found that resolution was more difficult these days. When she was young, she had had an image of herself to present to her new husband, whom she admired; then to herself, thirdly to the natives (I am an Englishwoman). Now no one reflected the image of herself, and it seemed diminished: it had lost two-thirds of its erstwhile value (no husband, no natives).[6]

There is almost a hint of capitalistic quantitativeness in the way Mrs Palfrey phrases her estimation of the value of a fixed role. The image she had of herself was, in a sense, a conception of a role for herself; and she is clear that without such a role, and without a clear perception by oneself of others, and of oneself by others, one's 'self' is diminished. This is similar to the themes we have been considering with reference to other novelists; one could for instance, usefully compare Mrs Palfrey, a single woman, to George of Isherwood's *A Single Man*. Within the limits she sets herself, Elizabeth Taylor is a very skilful novelist. Her choice not to use, or to explore the potential of metaphors of drama and the concept of dramatic action, inevitably limits the subject matter she can deal with. She never moves beyond the concept of role-playing appropriate to the 'primary man' who gains strength from a social code of behaviour; she cannot therefore explore the rich territory of the 'antithetical man', which is perhaps hinted at in the person of that 'famous general in drag'.

One might consider *Lucky Jim* as a study in the life of an antithetical man. Certainly the novel is enlivened primarily by the fantastic roles and faces that Jim invents for himself in order to offset the horror of his particular Body of Fate: that of a junior lecturer in a repressive university history department headed by a booby distinguished by neither publications nor teaching genius. In face of a badly run, rigid institution upon which he has found himself dependent, he fantasises outrageous and hilarious anarchistic retributions against his bureaucratic oppressors. His prime target is the Professor, Welch:

> He pretended to himself that he'd pick up his professor round the waist, squeeze the furry grey-blue waistcoat against him to expel the breath, run heavily with him up the steps, along the corridor to the Staff Cloakroom, and plunge the too-small feet in their capless shoes into a lavatory basin, pulling the plug once, twice and again, stuffing the mouth with toilet-paper.[7]

As he is trapped in his job as lecturer in medieval history (which he had chosen as a soft option at school) so too is he trapped in a relationship with the insipid Margaret Peel, a relationship which continues because of his respect for the conventions of courtship and because of his politeness: he just cannot do anything which would hurt Margaret and so their association drags on. If he cannot *do* anything, he can certainly imagine doing things. In her usual soap-opera manner she asks: 'Do you hate me, James?':

> Dixon wanted to rush at her and tip her backwards in the chair, to make a deafening rude noise in her face, to push a bead up her nose. 'How do you mean?' he asked.[8]

Part of the humour of this response derives from the anarchistic violence which Margaret seems so to deserve, this coupled with the knowledge that Jim could not do what he imagines. The humour comes from the contrast between what Jim wishes he could do, and what he actually says. His vicious fantasies are sanctioned as humour partly because he himself is a 'nice guy' who would not really do that sort of thing. That is to say, he lives by convention because he can find no other adequate way of living. The modes of behaviour which he strives for seem desirable because of the extreme lack of freedom of his present situation, but they would not, if acted out, fully express the 'real' Jim Dixon.

In a similar way we can understand the 'faces' that Dixon is always making. He has a 'shot in the back face', a 'mandarin face', and many others, none of which are made when they might be seen by others. These masks of his are a purely private means of release and are not satisfactory 'roles' for use in face-to-face encounters. He also engages in impromptu dramatic demonstrations when he thinks he is not observed. The following passage perhaps recalls Dougal Douglas of *The Ballad of Peckham Rye* (or more accurately, perhaps Dougal is a distant relative of Dixon). Very drunk he finds himself locked out of the bathroom in Professor Welch's house:

> The bathroom was evidently occupied; perhaps Johns had decided to blockade the bedroom allotted to the defacer of his periodical. Dixon stood well back, straddling, and raised his hands like a conductor on the brink of some thunderous overture or tone-poem; then, half-conductor, half-boxer, went into a brief manic flurry of obscene gestures. Just then somebody opened a door on the other side of the landing. There was no time to do anything at all except adopt the attitude of one waiting outside a bathroom, a stratagem vitiated to some extent by the raincoat he still wore.[9]

Jim acts out in private what he would not express in a social situation, and then he finds that he is exposed before another watcher and the result is very comic. His role becomes so convoluted that he must pretend to be doing what he really is doing, waiting to get into the bathroom. With all of his faces and private dramas, Jim is attempting to find a ritual means of self-expression which does not derive from the rigid 'roles' offered him by his situation. As he searches for this private means of self-dramatisation, he simultaneously denies its validity by obeying the conventional demands of the situation. Whereas Muriel Spark pursued this idea of non-institutional, free drama to a significant end, Amis uses it as a comic device but denies that such a device can become a valid replacement for institutional, publicly validated roles. As Jim later 'realises' he has not been doing what he really wished to do when he made his faces:

> Dixon felt that his role in this conversation, as indeed in the whole of his relations with Margaret, had been directed by something outside himself and yet not directly present in her. He felt more than ever before that what he said and did arose not out of any willing on his part, nor even out of boredom, but out of a kind of sense of situation. And where did that sense come from if, as it seemed, he took no share in willing it?[10]

His attempts at private drama are not then, we are told, valid attempts at ritual self-expression, they are neurotic denials of freedom and in fact merely an inverted form of imprisonment to his situation. When he is finally rewarded with the girl Christine and finds himself really in love, he finds that he has no faces and no need of them:

> Christine began laughing noisily and blushing at the same time. Dixon laughed too. He thought what a pity it was that all his faces were designed to express rage or loathing. Now that something had happened which really deserved a face, he'd none to celebrate it with. As a kind of token, he made his Sex Life in Ancient Rome face.[11]

It can be seen then, that the conclusion of the novel is in fact quite consistent with the rest of the book. Jim gives up his face-making (or almost, except for token faces) and his private dramas, and is rewarded with a different kind of role, the job of personal secretary to the financier Gore-Urquhart. Jim is perfectly happy with this job, with this public role, but why will life in this job be any different from the one he has had as a lecturer in the red-brick university? Because Urquhart is a better man than Neddy Welch. Which is to say that the novel is not really an attack on institutionalised roles at all, so much as a critique of the people who fail to fill these roles. There is ample evidence in the novel to indicate that Jim is as much to blame for his discomfort at the college as is the college itself. He is not a fit teacher. So Jim's story is not really that of an 'angry young man' in rebellion against repressive institutions, so much as it is the extremely comic tale of a man in the wrong job. Like so many other writers, Amis is alert to the fact that 'dramatic action' is very important both in life and in art. Instead of exploring all the potentials of dramatic action, however, he is content to grab the laughs and run, turning, in step with Jim himself, to the right.[12]

Another, and less successfully comic, 'angry young man' novel appeared about the same time as *Lucky Jim*, John Wain's *Hurry On Down*. Like Jim, Charles Lumley has 'just come down from the University with a mediocre degree in History.' Rather than face a predictable future, predictably a continuance of his own already unadventurous history, he wonders if he cannot 'cast up and be rid of his class, his *milieu*, his insufferable load of presuppositions and reflexes?'[13] So he becomes first a window-washer, then a heroin runner and finally a radio joke-writer. That is to say, he rejects the codified role that society offers him and he rapidly fills a series of other social roles in the search for some kind of personal fulfilment. Wain takes the idea of dramatic action no further than this simple one of social, prefigured 'roles' (in fact he does not have as subtle a sense of the potentiality of dramatic action, nor of comedy, as does Amis). Lumley ends his battle with society in the belief that his role of comedian is some sort of allowable middle ground, like that of the fool at court, which permits him to be neutral so far as society is concerned, neither alienated nor committed:

> Neutrality; he had found it at last. The running fight between himself and society had ended in a draw; he was no nearer, fundamentally, to any *rapprochement* or understanding with it than when he had been a window-cleaner, a crook, or a servant; it had merely decided that he should be paid, and paid handsomely, to capitalize his anomalous position.[14]

So Lumley too gets the job with the big pay-off, and eventually he gets the girl. If there is a danger that the ending of the novel will look too much like an expression of 'virtue rewarded' or the return of the prodigal, Wain tries to defuse this reaction by drawing attention to it in the final pages with a pointed reference to Moll Flanders who 'turns respectable and repents, but you knew that from the beginning'. To offset the potentially Moll Flanders-like ending, the acceptance of the love of the girl is seen as a dangerous move for Lumley, one that will upset the equilibrium, the neutrality, he has achieved:

> If an animal who was tame, or born in captivity, went back to what should have been its natural surroundings, it never survived. If it was a bird, the other birds killed it, but usually it just died. Here was his cage, a fine new one, air conditioned, clean, commanding a good view, mod. cons., main services. And she had snapped the lock and was calling him out into the waving jungle. When he got there, he would die.[15]

Probably he goes, although the pair stand at the close of the novel looking at each other 'baffled and inquiring', which could suggest anything or nothing. What this jungle call of love does suggest is that the neutrality Lumley has achieved is not such a moral victory after all. It is not clear either, just in what way 'love' will be an escape from the 'cage' of society, since the pair, if they do choose the dangers of the jungle will presumably get married, perhaps have children, and find themselves living in a dense net of institutional commitments. It seems then that the book ends despairingly unable to transcend the condition of society, and yet its premise seems to be that the only struggle worth fighting is the attempt to free oneself from history (or from history teaching) and the rigidity of society. The novel cannot progress any further because its metaphorical terminology is limited by the conception of 'role-playing' as something that can go on only inside society. The other themes which pertain to the concept of dramatic action, in particular the complex interplay of 'inner' and 'outer' are beyond such a book. With novels like *Lucky Jim* and *Hurry On Down* one can see why the claim that the recent English novel is Social has some validity.

Throughout I have been somewhat arbitrarily limiting myself to the discussion of British fiction. This has been done because the current British novel allows one to consider the two types of role playing side by side. I do not wish, however, to be thought to be asserting that writers or novels are somehow national. The Anglo-Irish Cary, peripatetic Greene, expatriates Spark and Isherwood should terminate any such speculation. Perhaps novelists must reflect their national culture to a certain extent (they use its language after all), but the best writers do speak to a human condition which, as Joyce suggests with his use of the Homeric myths, transcends time and place. One can find that the metaphors of drama are at the centre of novel writing in countries other than those of the U.K. Two that I would like to mention here are the Polish novelist Witold Gombrowicz and the American Saul Bellow.*

Much of Bellow's work is an intelligent and impassioned urging of the necessity for civilisation. He often relies on the Schopenhauerian concepts of Will and Idea. He is aware of the tendency of the man of intellect to abstract from and so distort experience, but the man of compassionate intelligence is the potential hero who can keep the world from reverting to the nasty, brutish and short life of the state of Nature. His idea, at least as it is expressed in *Mr Sammler's Planet*[16] (which is the moon, cool distanced and serene) is disinterestedness – and it is almost an act of courage for an American writer to use the word, which has all but lost its original meaning in common usage. This intellectual and spiritual man cannot, however, escape being embroiled in the world of action, nor can he avoid having organs of sex, the seat of the Will; and Bellow's characters do not gain their measure of serenity without struggle and suffering.

In *Herzog*,[17] a number of allusions to the drama occur around a central event, Herzog's desperate and jealous attempt to shoot his former wife Madeleine and her lover Gersbach. Gersbach is one of those who pretend to literate culture. He dresses himself up with all the best things he can find in books, 'just as certain crabs are supposed to beautify themselves with seaweed'. It becomes clear that 'the fellow is an actor, and . . . Madeleine is an actress'.[18] Although Herzog really understands the forms of culture which these underlings pretend to, he too cannot avoid involvement in the theatre of everyday life.

---

* A recent article by A. J. Hansen, 'The Celebration of Solipsism: A New Trend in American Fiction', *Modern Fiction Studies*, XIX, 1 (Spring 1973), 5–15, indicates that the ideas we have been considering are widely embodied in the new American novel. Hansen mentions Vonnegut and Brautigan, among others, as practitioners of a 'new solipsism' which accepts fictions, denies the determinism of Society but admits the reality of the other person.

As he is about to turn his 'idea' of killing into a reality by acting, he is stopped by the reality of the people he is confronted with:

> As soon as Herzog saw the actual person giving an actual bath, the reality of it, the tenderness of such a buffoon to a little child, his intended violence turned into *theater*, into something ludicrous.[19]

The emphatic use of *theater* (*sic*) here indicates that Herzog's action is that of a fanatic who has confused illusion with reality; *theater* is illusion, but it is better than real violence.

There is a suggestion in *Mr Sammler's Planet* that all human attempts at action must partake of this ludicrous taint of theatre; it is equally clear however that theatre is the result of an Idea trying to make itself a reality and so theatre can have a part to play in the attempt to transcend mere Will. Mr Sammler, although he aspires to disinterestedness and serenity finds himself involved in the most fleshly of worlds. The novel opens with his sighting a pickpocket at work on a New York bus. Knowing that he has been spotted, the thief follows Mr Sammler and in a dark corner displays himself to him, apparently as a primitive warning that the flesh can conquer the man of Ideas any day:

> But make Nature your God, elevate creatureliness, and you can count on gross results. Maybe you can count on gross results under any circumstances.[20]

The thief seems to be a good disciple of Schopenhauer: 'He took out the instrument of the Will. He drew aside not the veil of Maya itself but one of its forehangings and showed Sammler his metaphysical warrant.' Despite the tendency for the world to divide either into paralysing and alienating intellectuality (Herzog) or into the disordered actions of the Will and flesh, Mr Sammler holds out some belief that man's ideas can be given the ordered and expressive forms necessary for civilised, that is human, life to continue. Although he has seen action in person – he had been buried by a Nazi execution squad and then dug up by a friend before he died, and he had killed a man face-to-face – and has been disgusted by it, he is still fascinated by the possibilities of action:

Objectively I have little use for such experiences [of the exhibitionist], but there is such an absurd craving for actions that connect with other actions, for coherency, for forms, for mysteries or fables. I may have thought that I had no more ordinary human curiosity left, but I was surprisingly wrong. And I don't like it. I don't like any of it.[21]

Despite his dislike of the messy world of doing, Sammler cannot escape into the world of pure abstraction (he has given up his belief in Wellsian scientific rationalism, for instance). It is not action in itself that he objects to, but it is actions which do not connect, which obey no kind of causality whatsoever, and so provide for no responsibility of action. He ultimately confesses:

I am of course deformed. And obsessed. You can see that I am always talking about play-acting, originality, dramatic individuality, theatricality in people, the forms taken by spiritual striving.[22]

Although it may be, then, that action, particularly dramatic action such as that of Herzog's attempt to murder, can be the imprisonment of the veil of Maya, Sammler suggests another possibility, that dramatic action is the ordered expression of subjectivity, or it represents the beautiful prospect of 'the forms taken by spiritual striving'. The comprehensiveness, the inclusiveness and discriminating ability of Bellow's fiction is closely allied to his ability to differentiate between the variety of meanings that one can give to *theatricality*.

I wish to do no more with the novel *Pornografia*[23] by Witold Gombrowicz than to indicate that it too makes extensive use of metaphors of drama to achieve narrative unity. It is a nightmarish story of political liquidation in a repressive state, and the stage is littered with three corpses at the end. In Nazi-occupied Poland, a Resistance leader refuses to carry out an order received from Warsaw and a small group of people in a county house feel they must execute him to protect themselves, but the action is tawdry and not at all heroic. This story is intertwined with that of the complex erotic relationship which builds up between two old men (one of whom is called Witold) and two young lovers in the group of assassins. The point of the tale seems to be that disaster results because none of the actors can live alone, none has sufficient self-reliance nor individuality and so must always be playing up, falsely, to the expectations of others. The greatest and most demanding expectations are those made by the 'cause', of course, and when Witold is told of the necessity for liquidating Siemian, he reflects on the 'theatrical quality of patriotic conspiracy'. The tale of the loss of individual identity and of complicity in fantasy and externally contrived plots, develops in a fascinatingly horrifying way. Witold realises that he is trapped in an 'old melodrama' and that the result will be the spilling of real blood, but he is helpless to escape, because he has sacrificed his individuality (which is identified with masculinity, manhood); he has been seduced by the charms of the young, who have themselves been seduced by the opportunity to display theatrically their youth to the old. They are all impotent because 'we were not for ourselves, we were for that other, younger sensitivity – and this plunged us into ugliness.' Against the background of roles which are enforced by history, metaphors of drama will tend to be used to suggest illusion and loss of will in the 'play' of external forces, and this is the use made of them by Gombrowicz.*

In the British novels that we have considered in detail, the full range of meaning of dramatic action is explored. This full exploitation is possible because certain novelists were aware of the problems presented by the fictiveness of their own art, and also aware of the problems bequeathed to them by those of their predecessors who had explored the inner self and found themselves on the borders of solipsism. One further element adds to the potential meaning of dramatic action, and that is the tradition of the British novel to speculate about the position of the individual with respect to established 'roles' in Society. When all themes combine together, great subtlety can be achieved by means of the agency of a single set of metaphors. One novelist whom I have not considered extensively in the body of the study is Iris Murdoch and this might seem a notable exception since she is a novelist of considerable skill and her work is often built around allusions to the drama. Her interest in this subject was

---

* Mention should be made also of V. S. Naipaul's *The Mimic Men* (1967) which at times is more of an essay on the meanings of dramatic action than it is an altogether successful novel.

foreshadowed in her first novel *Under The Net*, much of which takes place in theatres or on sound stages. The reason that Iris Murdoch was not included for extensive consideration is that although she uses the subject of drama, she has her own particular meaning for drama which is quite unlike the one herein developed. She is one outstanding exception among the group of writers I have considered and since she so tellingly tests the rule she deserves some consideration here.

Iris Murdoch is known as a 'philosophical' novelist and it is partly because I have not had a great sympathy for her novels that I would like to look primarily at some of the philosophical statements in her essays on aesthetics and morality – which she often seems to identify; the Beautiful and the Good are equal. Whereas the novelists studied in the body of this work could all in one way or another be related to an Aristotelian conception of *mimesis*, Iris Murdoch is best understood, as a thinker and perhaps also as a novelist, by seeing her as a Platonist. She often makes reference to the Platonic myth of the cave in order to explain the progress of the soul and the writer's task.[24] Also she has announced that she believes, and believes that it is necessary for one to believe, in an ideal of Goodness which is almost Platonic. Briefly, she believes that it is necessary to offer the individual a means of self-transcendence by restoring the validity of the concept of the Good, since contemporary philosophy in the guise of existentialism and linguistic analysis does not offer a sufficient paradigm for man (they deny either the subjective inner self or the fact that common sense and reason are limited). Her work, then, can be seen as a search, in Art, for a 'sufficient man' or for an answer to the question, How to be? It may be that her novels suffer at times from a Platonic tendency to be the vehicle for huge abstractions and from the absence of a counterbalancing Aristotelian particularity. In an interview with Frank Kermode she herself points to this possibility when she speaks of the tendency of the 'form' of the work to obtrude on the freedom and 'reality' of the characters: 'The satisfaction of the form is such that it can stop one from going more deeply into the contradictions or paradoxes or more painful aspects of the subject matter.'[25]

The reason why Iris Murdoch is so worried about the 'consolation of form' is that her central theme is the necessity to admit the reality of the other person;[26] that is, she repeats the warning about the dangers of solipsism that has been one of the recurrent themes of this study. She says:

> Existentialism shares with empiricism a terror of anything which encloses the agent or threatens his supremacy as a center of significance. In this sense both philosophies tend toward solipsism. Neither pictures virtue as concerned with anything real outside ourselves. Neither provides us with a standpoint for considering real human beings in their variety, and neither presents us with any technique for exploring and controlling our own spiritual energy.[27]

She has great praise for the nineteenth century novel because there one finds 'a plurality of real persons more or less naturalistically presented in a large social scene, and representing mutually independent centers of significance which are those of real individuals'.[28] The morality of admitting the reality of others is the prime requisite of the novelist: 'A great novelist is essentially tolerant, that is, displays a real apprehension of persons other than the author as having a right to exist and to have a separate mode of being which is important and interesting to themselves.'[29]

She believes, that is to say, that Art itself is Truth and not fiction out of which a 'kind of truth' emerges. To be Good is finally to be an Artist:

> The artist is indeed the analogon of the good man, and in a special sense he *is* the good man; the lover who, nothing himself, lets other things be through him. And that also, I am sure, is what is meant by 'negative capability'.[30]

What is a little puzzling about this passage is that it apparently denies that there is any distortion by artistic 'form', and yet Murdoch would never deny that the essence of Art lies in the achievement of form. The artist may be the analogon of the good man, but it is not clear how any artistic creation, which is the creation of a single man, can negate itself and present the other unmediated. Nor does it seem a practicable, or necessary, ideal to insist that the self must 'negate' itself in order to let the other be. What is needed is a way for the self to be, which does not negate the other. Murdoch points up her dilemma nicely in her conversation with Kermode:

> Another way of putting it would be just that one isn't good
> enough at creating character. One starts off – at least I start
> off – hoping every time that this is going to happen and that a
> lot of people who are not me are going to come into existence
> in some wonderful way. Yet often it turns out in the end that
> something about the structure of the work itself, the myth as
> it were of the work, has drawn all these people into a sort of
> spiral, or into a kind of form which ultimately is the form of
> one's own mind.[31]

I would like to suggest that the inevitable distorting tendency of
'form' in her work is a result of her identifying Art with Truth;
that is, denying, or attempting to deny, the 'fictionality' of the
novel and trusting the art she displays to carry something
'other' than the contents of her own imagination. Only if the fictiveness of her own work were more fully admitted would one
expect the reality of the other to begin to show through the fiction as a kind of unsummoned truth. There is a conflict between
the subject she wants to convey and the form she chooses to do it
with.

It is interesting to note that her recent novel, *The Black
Prince*,[32] a novel which I believe to be not only her best but the
equal of any of the novels we have considered in detail, faces the
question of form directly. There is a narrative presented by
Bradley Pearson, which is enclosed by comments by the 'editor'
and 'publisher', P. Loxias* (who is to be identified as Apollo
the god of clarity and form) and there are post-scripts written
by four of the *dramatis personae* giving their comments on the
story told by Pearson. This breaking up of the narrative focus,
and abandoning her own preference for omniscient narration
has resulted in the achievement of her aim: the characters in the
book seem to be independent of Iris Murdoch and yet we are
made aware all along that Bradley Pearson is in fact the *persona*
(his name is an obvious anagram) of the author herself. If this
novel represents the achievement I believe it does for Iris Murdoch, it results from an act which seems at first sight quite alien

---

* Loxias is a Nabokov-style 'publisher' who has been given Pearson's
manuscripts, written in prison. He is also Pearson's constant companion in
prison, unseen by others.

to her, the conscious adopting of a mask. So far from denying herself and attempting some absolute 'negative capability', she is there all the time bodying forth the fiction of Bradley Pearson and yet Pearson seems one of the few characters in the Murdoch world who is free of the manipulations of the author, he is both *persona* and pe(a)rson.

Why should such mimetic self-presentation seem so foreign to one's conception of Iris Murdoch? One possible answer is that she has not previously seemed to believe in the validity of play-acting. In fact, *drama* is a word which she has used almost pejoratively in the past. Drama is a word which she associates with the Hegelian concept of the Spirit's struggle with itself in the internal dialectical attempt to reach a higher state. She refers to the Hegelian, 'clear, dramatic, solipsistic picture of the self at war with itself and passing in this way through phases in the direction of self-knowledge'.[33] Here, almost surprisingly, 'dramatic' is identified with solipsism. This is so because 'dramatic' means for Murdoch the internal struggle of self with itself; the dramatic therefore takes no notice of what is without. The dramatic soul seeks perfection and justification within itself: 'the self locked in struggle with itself and evolving as a result of the struggle.' The paradigm of man she seeks in her fiction is quite different, quite undramatic:

> Whereas the man that I have in mind, faced by the manifold of humanity, may feel, as well as terror, delight, but not, if he really sees what is before him, superiority. He will suffer that undramatic, because un-self-centred, agnosticism which goes with tolerance.[34]

This passage clearly indicates that 'dramatic' is equal to 'self-centered', and it is self-centeredness which is the greatest evil in Murdoch's world.

This distrust of the dramatic is closely connected with her distrust of action itself. She sees the concept of action as the centre of existentialist 'self-will' and she denies that an idea of spontaneous will and *l'acte gratuit* can yield a picture of a man both free and moral. And yet she is not anxious to accept the consequences of inaction. Her ideal seems to be silence and self-containment until the appropriate moment for considered action arises. So we find her making the following statement, which is very close to the theme I have been trying to develop:

> I would not be understood, either, as suggesting that insight
> or pureness of heart are more important than action: the
> thing which philosophers feared Moore for implying. Overt
> actions are perfectly obviously important in themselves, and
> important too because they are the indispensable pivot and
> spur of the inner scene. The inner, in *this* sense, cannot do
> without the outer. I do not mean only that outer rituals make
> places for inner experiences; but also that an overt action can
> release psychic energies which can be released in no other
> way. We often receive an unforeseen reward for a fumbling
> half-hearted act: a place for the idea of grace.[35]

Here is another attempt to define what I have called 'dramatic
action'.

This concept of dramatic action – and Murdoch would not
fully accept my formulation of it perhaps, nor does her work
before *The Black Prince* exemplify the theory I have drawn – is
one which seems to have been emerging slowly from Miss
Murdoch's work. In an interview with Ronald Bryden and A.
S. Byatt, she spoke of her favourite writer:

> I suppose the writer I owe most to is Shakespeare. That prob-
> ably sounds rather presumptuous: What I mean is that I'd
> like to be influenced by Shakespeare, that I constantly read
> him and pray that some kind of influence will descend on me.
> It's his extraordinary ability to combine a marvellous pattern
> or myth with the expansion of characters as absolutely free
> persons, independent of each other – they have an extra-
> ordinary independence, though they're also kept in by the
> marvellous pattern of the play. It's a sort of miracle that
> Shakespeare manages to pull off, which makes one think,
> whenever one re-reads one of the great plays: 'Good hea-
> vens, it's so short, and yet these enormous people have come
> out of these few pages'.[36]

What is interesting about the context of this remark is the
effect it had on the two interviewers (and Byatt is the author of
one of the few books about Murdoch), who expressed surprise,
almost shock, at the idea that Shakespeare could be the ideal of
an author whom they obviously must have thought to be so un-

Shakespearean. Her attention – attention is a word of supreme importance to Murdoch – to Shakespeare has obviously paid off in *The Black Prince*. The black prince is Hamlet (and also Eros) and a discussion of the meaning of *Hamlet* is at the centre of the work. Perhaps the key word throughout the text is drama; the whole novel is a study of the possible meanings of the word. The novel achieves almost a perfect balance between acts and introspection, and this balance of interplay between inner and outer must be related to Murdoch's decision to sanction the playing of dramatic roles, to use *personae* consciously and to find in dramatic action the way in which the other can be realised without denying the self. The novel deals adequately with the problem of the tendency of the fiction to distort – by pointing to it openly – and yet it remains a readable novel about apparently real characters. Iris Murdoch promises to be the novelist who will make the most significant achievement in the novel form in the near future. She has at least found a way through some very difficult ground by turning her attention fully to *mimesis*.

One can conclude, then, that attention to the subject of mimesis and the concept of dramatic action as the external fulfilment of inner subjectivity will repay the reader of twentieth century fiction. One can also safely say that the novel, far from being moribund, is only yet scratching the surface of its mimetic possibilities. Throughout this study I have insisted (as have the writers I have focused on) that theatricality must of necessity be differentiated from the playing of Social roles if the full possibilities of the metaphor are to be set free. I have tried to show that this opposition to Society did not die out with the last of the great Modern writers but has been carried on in some of the best of contemporary writing. I have tried to show also that such opposition to Society is not (or need not be) anti-social or solipsistic. I have said that the Novel has an ur-motive in the question How to be? It is time to admit that this motive is a social motive and that the search in the novel for a dramatistic ideal of man is ultimately a search for a *possible* society which would allow a man to be both citizen and individual (or Artist if the artist is the highest type of the individual, as in *Ulysses*). Since I have relied heavily on the Aristotelian term *mimesis* (although I have not necessarily used it in its strictest limitations), it might perhaps be permissible to borrow another term from the same source to replace that troublesome word society. Then we might say that the modern novel is using *mimesis* (not in the sense of realist copying, but of creative imitation) in the search for an open society; that is, for the realisation of the *polis*.

To the extent that the Novel is concerned with miming – which is to say enacting in a symbolic form – the *polis* or ideal city in which membership is not in conflict with full individuality, it will *not* be content with the painstaking factual representation or 'realistic' copying of existing societies. The subject matter of the Novel is social in that the achievement of Unity of Being means primarily the recognition of the reality of the *other* person. It is not enough for this recognition to be merely perception, or conscious cognition although that is an important first step. It is equally necessary, however, for 'consciousness' to be realised in action; that is, to be *actu*alised. The self is completed, fulfilled, and the integrity of the other fully granted when impulse becomes action – an act of speech, of friendship, or of love. Acts can of course be good or bad, in the ethical sense. They have this advantage over mere intentions, however, that they are public and a public expressive act invites public reaction and criticism. Realised action leaves open the possibility of human improvement. A bad action can lead to better ones, whereas an unexpressed subjectivity, refusing to submit itself to the world of experience or to bind its theoretically limitless potential to mere definitive actuality tends, in the novels here considered, to be destructive either of self, or other or both: to be, that is, either cannibalistic or narcissistic. And as Muriel Spark shows, cannibalism *is* narcissism; the denial of others *is* suicidal. There is no blind devotion to the cult of activity in the modern novel, then, and there is a clear recognition that individual acts can be evil in effect. Sins of commission are preferable to those of omission, however, and further, if an act is 'dramatic', that is free and yet controlled and directed by the free individual, ritualised, even fictional and yet not altogether false, the danger of bad acting is even further diminished. One can see that the modern novelist has achieved a significant unity of 'form' and 'content' and that the technical question raised by fictions about fiction is in fact a matter of *substance* since the fictions that characters make of themselves in the world of the novel, and the ones that we make for ourselves in the 'real' world reflect the novelist's concern with the effect and meaning of his own fictional acts. It is not surprising, after all, that a novelist, whose Art is also his Act, should be in love with the possibilities of ordered action

List of Abbreviations

Frank Kermode	*RI*	*Romantic Image*
Joyce Cary	*PG*	*Prisoner of Grace*
	ETL	*Except the Lord*
	NHM	*Not Honour More*
Muriel Spark	*MG*	*The Mandelbaum Gate*
	R	*Robinson*
	PMJB	*The Prime of Miss Jean Brodie*
	TC	*The Comforters*
	MM	*Memento Mori*
	BPR	*The Ballad of Peckham Rye*
	TB	*The Bachelors*
	PI	*The Public Image*
	DS	*The Driver's Seat*
	NTD	*Not to Disturb*
C. Isherwood	*GTB*	*Goodbye to Berlin*
	DTOV	*Down There on a Visit*
	ASM	*A Single Man*
Graham Greene	*OMIH*	*Our Man in Havana*
	C	*The Comedians*
	TWMA	*Travels With My Aunt*
John Fowles	*FLW*	*The French Lieutenant's Woman*
Saul Bellow	*H*	*Herzog*
	MSP	*Mr Sammler's Planet*
E. Taylor	*MPC*	*Mrs Palfrey at the Claremont*
Kingsley Amis	*LJ*	*Lucky Jim*
John Wain	*HOD*	*Hurry on Down*
Iris Murdoch	SBR	'The Sublime and the Beautiful Revisited'

287

Notes

INTRODUCTION

1. Peter Mercer, 'The Culture of Fictions; or the Fiction of Culture?', *Critical Quarterly*, XII, 4 (Winter 1970), 293.

2. Philip Thody, ' "The Sociology of Literary Creativity": A Literary Critic's View', *International Social Science Journal*, XX, 3 (1968), 490.

3. F. R. Leavis, 'Sociology and Literature', *The Common Pursuit*, 2nd imp. (1953), p. 198.

4. Coleridge, *Biographia Literaria*, Chap. XV. Walter Allen uses this same passage in his discussion of Joyce Cary in the *Writer's and Critics* pamphlet.

5. J. Huizinga, *Homo Ludens: A Study of the Play-Element in Culture* (1949), pp. 173, 5.

6. Aaron V. Cicourel, *Cognitive Sociology* (Harmondsworth, 1973), p. 9.

7. I draw on: Raymond Aron, *Main Currents in Sociological Thought, Vol. II* (Harmondsworth, 1970); Peter L. Berger, *Invitation to Sociology: A Humanistic Perspective* (Harmondsworth, 1966); R. P. Cuzzort, *Humanity and Modern Sociological Thought* (New York, 1969).

8. Berger, *Invitation*, p. 108.

9. Berger, *Invitation*, p. 113.

10. From the introduction by Charles W. Morris to George H. Mead's *Mind, Self & Society* (Chicago, 1934), p. xxiv.

11. See Maurice Natanson, *The Social Dynamics of George H. Mead* (Washington D. D., 1956) for the limits of this aspect of Mead's thought.

12. See Henri Bergson, *Two Sources of Morality and Religion*, trans. Audra & Brereton (London, 1935).

13. Berger, *Invitation*, p. 159.

14. Berger, *Invitation*, p. 162.

15. Erving Goffman, 'Role Distance', *Where the Action Is* (London, 1969), p. 73. The most widely known of Goffman's works, and the one that makes most thorough use of the analogy with drama, is *The Presentation of Self in Everyday Life*, Penguin (1972; orig. 1956). Readers of Goffman should also look at the critique by Alvin W. Gouldner in *The Coming Crisis of Western Sociology* (London, 1971). Gouldner is particularly good on the capitalist implications of seeing human interaction in terms of 'transactions'.

16. Berger, *Invitation*, p. 123.

17. R. S. Downie, *Roles and Values* (London, 1971); particularly p. 132.

18. Peter L. Berger and Thomas Luckmann in *The Social Construction of Reality* Penguin (1967), draw attention to Arnold Gehlen's theory of the

biological necessity of externalisation (note 16, Chap. 2).

19. Elizabeth and Tom Burns, *Sociology of Literature and Drama*, Penguin (Harmondsworth, 1973).

20. Simmel, in Burns, p. 308.

21. Simmel, in Burns, p. 310.

22. The American poet Charles Olson uses the phrase as the title of an essay which, in its more lucid moments, is worth reading.

23. I am not really thinking here of old novels, which can of course remain current despite their date of production. I am alluding forward to the discussion of the 'social construction of reality' which follows.

24. George Lukacs, an extract from *The Historical Novel* as quoted in Burns, p. 295.

25. Cuzzort, *Humanity in Modern Sociological Thought*, p. 212.

26. Lionel Trilling, *Sincerity & Authenticity* (London, 1972).

27. Trilling, pp. 30–3.

CHAPTER 1

1. Katherine Lever, *The Novel and the Reader* (London, 1961), p. 75.

2. Erving Goffman, *Relations in Public* (London, 1971), p. xii.

3. Alain Robbe-Grillet, *Snapshots and Towards a New Novel*, translated by Barbara Wright (London, 1965), pp. 138–9.

4. See Hans Vaihinger, *The Philosophy of 'As If'* (London, 1924). Frank Kermode draws on Vaihinger's category of the 'consciously false' in his discussion of literary fictions in *The Sense of an Ending*. Also relevant is W. J. Ong's 'The Myth of Myth', in *The Barbarian Within* (New York, 1962).

5. David Riesman, *The Lonely Crowd* (New York, 1953).

6. Rémy de Gourmont as quoted by Eugène Bencze in *La Doctrine Esthétique de Remy de Gourmont* (Paris, 1928). The phrase comes from de Gourmont's *Les femmes et le langage*.

7. John Wain, 'A Salute to the Makers', *Encounter* (Nov. 1970), 51–9.

8. Virginia Woolf, 'The Narrow Bridge of Art', *Granite and Rainbow* (London, 1958), p. 18.

9. W. B. Yeats, *A Vision*, 2nd ed. reprinted (London, 1969); all quotations in this passage are from p. 84.

10. Stephen Spender, *The Creative Element* (London, 1953), p. 14. Although Spender presents a much more comprehensive study of the period in *The Struggle of the Modern* (1963), it is my intention to focus on *The Creative Element* since his underlying assumptions are spelled out more obviously in this book, and they remain essentially unchanged in the later work.

11. Ibid, p. 198.

12. Ibid., p. 11.

13. Ibid., p. 14.

14. Ibid., pp. 11–12.

15. Karl Miller, 'Introduction' to *Writing in England Today: The Last Fifteen Years* Penguin (1968). Miller quotes from Richard Ellmann and Charles Feidelson, *The Modern Tradition*, O. U. P. (New York, 1965).

16. Lionel Trilling, 'Manners, Morals and the Novel', *The Liberal Imagination* (London, 1955), p. 212.

17. Lionel Trilling, *Beyond Culture* (London, 1966), p. 30.

18. Ibid., p. 30.

19. Jonathan Raban, *The Technique of Modern Fiction* (London, 1968), p. 35.

20. Ibid., p. 90.

21. See Edmund Wilson's *Axel's Castle* (New York and London, 1931), p. 258.

22. From *Axel* as quoted by Wilson in *Axel's Castle*, pp. 262–3.

23. Ibid., pp. 19–20.

24. Charles Feidelson, *Symbolism and American Literature* (Chicago, 1953), p. 51.

25. Rémy de Gourmont, as quoted by A. G. Lehmann, *The Symbolist Aesthetic in France 1885–1895*, 2nd ed. (Oxford, 1968), p. 40. (Originally published 1950).

26. Lehmann, p. 45.

27. Frank Kermode, *Romantic Image*, Collins Fontana Books (London, 1971–originally 1957), p. 181.

28. *RI*, p. 181.

29. *RI*, p. 18.

30. *RI*, p. 33.

31. *RI*, p. 81.

32. *RI*, p. 17.

33. Wyndham Lewis, *Time and Western Man* (London, 1927), p. 36.

34. *RI*, p. 41.

35. *RI*, p. 54.

36. Frank Kermode, 'Poet and Dancer before Diaghilev', *Partisan Review*, xxviii, I (Jan.–Feb., 1961), p. 75.

37. Denis Donoghue, 'The Human Image in Yeats', *The Ordinary Universe* (London, 1968), p. 119.

38. Ibid., pp. 119–20.

39. W. B. Yeats, *Explorations* (London, 1962), p. 163.

40. Donoghue, p. 135.

41. W. B. Yeats, *Autobiographies* (London, 1955), pp. 469–70. My italics.

CHAPTER 2

1. Graham Hough, *The Dream and the Task* (London, 1963), p. 51.

2. George Steiner, *In Bluebeard's Castle: Some Notes Towards the Redefinition of Culture* (London, 1971), p. 31.

3. D. H. Lawrence, 'Why the Novel Matters', *Phoenix* (London, 1936; reprinted 1967), p. 535.

4. Roy H. Pearce, 'Foreword', *Experience in the Novel*, English Institute Essays (New York, 1968), p. v.

5. J. Hillis Miller, 'First-Person Narration in *David Copperfield* and *Huckleberry Finn*', in *Experience in the Novel*, p. 31. My italics.

6. Ibid., p. 47.

7. Raymond Williams, *The Long Revolution*, Pelican Books (1965), pp.

313–14. (Originally published 1961).

8. D. H. Lawrence, 'John Galsworthy', *Phoenix*, p. 541.

9. Ian Watt, *The Rise of the Novel*, Penguin ed. (1970, originally published 1957), pp. 95–6.

10. Ernest Hemingway, *A Farewell to Arms*, Cape (London 1966, originally 1929), pp. 161–2.

11. James Joyce, *Ulysses*, Random House Modern Library ed. (New York, 1961), p. 667.

12. Ibid., p. 683.

13. Ibid., pp. 671–2. My italics.

14. Ibid., p. 673.

15. S. L. Goldberg, *The Classical Temper* (London, 1961), p. 217.

16. Ibid., pp. 97–8 and 114–15.

17. Ibid., p. 92. My italics.

18. Ibid., p. 72.

19. Ibid., p. 73. My italics.

20. Stuart Hampshire, *Thought and Action* (London, 1959), p. 74. My italics.

21. John MacMurray, *The Self as Agent*, Faber (paper ed. 1969; first published 1957, delivered originally as a series of lectures at Glasgow University 1953–4). The sequel to this volume is *Persons in Relation* and the overall title for the two volumes is *The Form of the Personal*.

22. Ibid., p. 73.

23. Ibid., p. 23.

24. David Lodge, *Language of Fiction* (London, 1966).

25. Ibid., p. 62. See also J. M. Cameron, 'Poetry and Dialectic', in *The Night Battle* (London, 1962).

26. Samuel Beckett, *Waiting for Godot*, Faber (1956), p. 76.

27. D. W. Lucas, *Aristotle's Poetics*, O. U. P. (1968), p. 258.

28. Aristotle, *Poetics* as translated and edited by Butcher, see next note.

29. S. H. Butcher, *Aristotle's Theory of Poetry and Fine Art*, including a translation of the *Poetics*, 2nd ed. (London, 1898), pp. 122–3. My italics.

30. Ibid., p. 160.

31. Kenneth Burke, *The Philosophy of Literary Form: Studies in Symbolic Action*, Vintage Books (1961), pp. 9 and 51. Originally published in 1941 by Louisiana State University Press. All italics are Burke's own.

32. H. D. Duncan, *Language and Literature in Society*, University of Chicago Press (1953), p. 5.

33. Kenneth Burke, *A Grammar of Motives* (New York, 1945), p. 227. Burke is quoting from a dictionary of philosophy.

34. J. P. Sartre, *The Age of Reason*, Penguin, translated by Eric Sutton (first published 1945), pp. 172–3. The two other volumes of the trilogy *Les Chemins de la Liberté* are: *The Reprieve* and *Iron in the Soul*.

35. Philip Rieff, 'The Impossible Culture', *Encounter* (Sept. 1970), 38–9.

CHAPTER 3

1. Robert Bloom, *The Indeterminate World: A Study of the Novels of Joyce Cary* (Philadelphia, 1962), p. 200.

2. See *The Horse's Mouth* (London, 1944).

3. *NHM*, p. 220.

4. Bloom, p. 198.

5. *PG*, p. 9.

6. *ETL*, p. 5.

7. *NHM*, p. 5.

8. See Henry James, 'The Novel in *The Ring and the Book*', *Notes on Novelists* (London, 1914).

9. Robert Browning, *The Ring and the Book* (Oxford, 1940), Book x, ll. 228–31. Further references will be made in the text by Book and line numbers.

10. *NHM*, p. 220.

11. *ETL*, p. 5.

12. *NHM*, p. 104.

13. *NHM*, p. 67.

14. *NHM*, p. 68.

15. *ETL*, p. 284.

16. Moore makes this faddish comment in his introduction to *The Changing Face* by Vida E. Markovic (Southern Illinois, 1970).

17. Letter to Andrew Wright, quoted by Wright in his *Joyce Cary: A Preface to his Novels* (London, 1958), p. 154.

18. Bloom, p. 197.

19. *NHM*, p. 222.

20. *NHM*, p. 222.

21. Bloom, p. 132.

22. *PG*, p. 400.

23. *PG*, p. 86.

24. *PG*, p. 114.

25. *PG*, p. 13.

26. *PG*, p. 14.

27. *PG*, p. 9.

28. *PG*, p. 14.

29. *NHM*, p. 221.

30. *NHM*, p. 223.

31. *PG*, p. 364.

32. *PG*, p. 365.

33. *PG*, p. 364.

34. D. H. Lawrence, 'Love', in *Phoenix* (London, 1936–reprinted 1967), pp. 151–2.

35. *PG*, pp. 315–16.

36. *PG*, p. 47.

37. *PG*, p. 230.

38. *PG*, p. 402.

39. 'Love', *Phoenix*, p. 151.

40. *PG*, pp. 16–17.

41. *PG*, p. 222.

42. *PG*, p. 245.

43. *PG*, p. 296.

44. *PG*, p. 378.

45. *PG*, p. 296.
46. *PG*, p. 17.
47. *PG*, p. 79.
48. *PG*, p. 145.
49. *PG*, p. 160.
50. *PG*, p. 160.
51. *PG*, p. 215.
52. Cary's Preface to *Prisoner of Grace*, p. 5.
53. *PG*, p. 205.
54. *PG*, p. 238.
55. *PG*, p. 389.
56. *PG*, p. 390.
57. *PG*, p. 392.
58. *PG*, pp. 392–3.
59. *PG*, p. 67.
60. *PG*, p. 237.
61. *PG*, p. 267.
62. *PG*, p. 71.
63. *PG*, p. 239.
64. *PG*, p. 340.
65. *PG*, p. 341.
66. *PG*, p. 344.
67. *PG*, p. 238.
68. *ETL*, p. 52.
69. *ETL*, p. 287.
70. *ETL*, p. 74.
71. *ETL*, p. 24.
72. *ETL*, p. 126.
73. *ETL*, p. 144.
74. *ETL*, p. 162.
75. *ETL*, p. 162.
76. *ETL*, p. 161.
77. *ETL*, p. 192.
78. *ETL*, p. 261.
79. *ETL*, p. 140.
80. *ETL*, p. 279.
81. *ETL*, p. 284.
82. *ETL*, p. 275.
83. *ETL*, p. 93.
84. *ETL*, p. 93.
85. *ETL*, p. 83.
86. *ETL*, p. 84.
87. *ETL*, p. 111.
88. *ETL*, p. 118.
89. *ETL*, p. 279.
90. *ETL*, p. 94.
91. *ETL*, p. 94.
92. *NHM*, p. 33.

93. *NHM*, p. 67.

94. *PG*, p. 39.

95. *NHM*, p. 46.

96. *NHM*, p. 53.

97. *NHM*, p. 58.

98. *NHM*, p. 69.

99. *NHM*, p. 132.

100. *NHM*, p. 223.

101. *PG*, p. 365.

102. *NHM*, p. 127.

103. *NHM*, p. 191.

104. *NHM*, p. 219.

105. *NHM*, p. 189.

CHAPTER 4

1. See *Selected Essays of Hugh MacDiarmid* (London, 1969), p. 58.

2. Muriel Spark, 'Edinburgh-born', *New Statesman*, LXIV (10 Aug. 1962), 180.

3. Muriel Spark, *The Mandelbaum Gate* (London, 1965), p. 173.

4. *MG*, p. 169.

5. *MG*, p. 169.

6. Muriel Spark, *Robinson* (London, 1958), p. 176.

7. Muriel Spark, 'Bang, Bang, You're Dead', *Collected Stories I* (London, 1967), p. 90. My italics

8. David Lodge in his essay, 'The Uses and Abuses of Omniscience', reprinted in *The Novelist at the Crossroads* (London, 1971), discusses the attitude to Romanticism that emerges in *The Prime of Miss Jean Brodie*.

9. Muriel Spark, *The Prime of Miss Jean Brodie*, Penguin edition (1971), p. 101.

10. John Henry, Cardinal Newman, *Apologia Pro Vita Sua*, Longmans (New York, 1947), p. 311 (Note F: 'The Economy').

11. Frank Kermode, 'The House of Fiction', *Partisan Review*, XXX, 1 (Spring, 1963), 79 and 80.

12. Joseph Conrad, 'Preface' to *The Nigger of the 'Narcissus'*.

13. Interview with Kermode, 80.

14. B. S. Johnson, *Albert Angelo*, as quoted by Lodge, *The Novelist at the Crossroads* (London, 1971), p. 13.

15. *Crossroads*, p. 13.

16. See Max Black, *The Labyrinth of Language* (London, 1968), p. 86, and C. K. Ogden (ed.), *Bentham's Theory of Fictions* (London, 1932), p. 12.

17. Max Black, *Models and Metaphors* (Ithaca, N.Y., 1962), p. 16.

18. B. S. Johnson, *The Unfortunates* (London, 1969), p. 6 of the section called 'Last'. My italics. The peculiar typographical arrangement is Johnson's. If the joke in his last sentence is intentional, it may be that Johnson's rejection of fiction is fictional itself, but this is not the place to pursue such apparently unrewarding obscurities.

19. Muriel Spark, interview with Philip Toynbee, *The Observer* (7 Nov.

1971), colour supplement, pp. 73–4.

20. W. B. Yeats, *Autobiographies* (London, 1955), p. 477.

21. Muriel Spark, *The Comforters*, Penguin edition (London, 1969), originally published by Macmillan (1957).

22. *TC*, p. 181.

23. Cf. Sartre's strictures on Mauriac in 'François Mauriac and Freedom', *Literary and Philosophical Essays* (London, 1955).

24. *TC*, p. 156.

25. *TC*, p. 147.

26. *TC*, p. 82.

27. *TC*, p. 82.

28. *TC*, p. 87.

29. *TC*, p. 87.

30. *TC*, p. 87.

31. Muriel Spark, *Robinson*, Macmillan (London, 1958).

32. Carol B. Ohmann, 'Muriel Spark's *Robinson*', *Critique: Studies in Modern Fiction*, VIII (Fall, 1965), 71.

33. Derek Stanford, *Muriel Spark* Centaur Press (Sussex, 1963), p. 127. Stanford does not give the title of the poem and it does not appear in *Collected Poems I*.

34. *R*, p. 186.

35. Muriel Spark, *Memento Mori*, Penguin edition (1963); first published by Macmillan (1959).

36. *MM*, p. 175.

37. *MM*, p. 184.

38. *MM*, p. 214.

39. *MM*, p. 219.

40. Muriel Spark, *The Ballad of Peckham Rye*, Penguin edition (1970); first published by Macmillan (1960).

41. *BPR*, p. 112.

42. *BPR*, p. 136.

43. *BPR*, p. 140.

44. *BPR*, p. 15.

45. *BPR*, p. 16.

46. *BPR*, p. 17.

47. *BPR*, p. 59–60.

48. *BPR*, p. 60.

49. *BPR*, p. 49.

50. Muriel Spark, 'The Nativity', in *Collected Poems I* (London, 1967), p. 81.

51. 'The Fall', *Collected Poems I*, p. 55.

52. *BPR*, p. 30.

53. *BPR*, p. 28.

54. *BPR*, p. 27.

55. *BPR*, p. 31.

56. *BPR*, p. 19.

57. Muriel Spark, *The Bachelors* Penguin edition; first published by Macmillan (1960).

58. *TB*, p. 85.

59. *TB*, p. 61.

60. *TB*, p. 157.

61. *TB*, p. 155–6.

62. *TB*, p. 108.

63. *TB*, p. 155.

64. *TB*, p 214.

65. Muriel Spark, *The Prime of Miss Jean Brodie*, Penguin edition; first published by Macmillan (1961).

66. *PMJB*, p. 25.

67. David Lodge, *The Novelist at the Crossroads*, p. 132.

68. *PMJB*, p. 119.

69. Frank Kermode, *The Sense of an Ending* (New York, 1967), pp. 39–40.

70. *PMJB*, p. 109.

71. *PMJB*, p. 54.

72. *PMJB*, p. 115.

73. *PMJB*, p. 92.

74. *PMJB*, p. 101.

75. *PMJB*, p. 109.

76. *PMJB*, p. 70.

77. *PMJB*, p. 113.

78. *PMJB*, p. 119.

79. *PMJB*, p. 75.

80. *PMJB*, p. 114.

81. *PMJB*, p. 84.

82. *PMJB*, p. 87.

83. *PMJB*, p. 25.

84. *PMJB*, p. 85.

85. *PMJB*, p. 33.

86. George Eliot, *Middlemarch*, Zodiac Press (London, 1967), p. 205.

87. *PMJB*, p. 127.

88. Muriel Spark, *The Public Image*, Macmillan (1968); all references will be to the Penguin edition (1970).

89. *PI*, p. 34.

90. *PI*, p. 35.

91. *PI*, p. 9.

92. *PI*, p. 11.

93. *PI*, p. 72.

94. *PI*, p. 34.

95. *PI*, p. 10.

96. *PI*, p. 17.

97. *PI*, p. 21.

98. *PI*, p. 10.

99. *PI*, p. 35.

100. *PI*, p. 92.

101. *PI*, pp. 124–5.

102. Muriel Spark, *The Driver's Seat*, Macmillan (London, 1970).

103. *DS*, p. 27.

104. *DS*, p. 114.

105. *DS*, p. 12.
106. *DS*, p. 20.
107. *DS*, p. 11.
108. *DS*, p. 48.
109. Fung Yu-Lan, *A History of Chinese Philosophy*, vol II (Princeton, 1953), p. 7.
110. *DS*, p. 160.
111. Philip Rieff, 'The Impossible Culture', *Encounter* (Sept. 1970), 38–9.
112. Muriel Spark, *Not to Disturb*, Macmillan (London, 1971).
113. *NTD*, p. 5.
114. *Observer* interview.
115. *NTD*, p. 121.
116. *NTD*, p. 121.
117. *NTD*, p. 158.
118. From *Axel*, as quoted by Edmund Wilson in *Axel's Castle*, pp. 262–3.
119. *NTD*, p. 93.
120. *NTD*, p. 93.

CHAPTER 5

1. Christopher Isherwood, *Kathleen and Frank* (London, 1971), p. 220.
2. Christopher Isherwood, *Goodbye to Berlin* (London, 1952; originally 1939), p. 13.
3. *GTB*, p. 45.
4. *GTB*, p. 165.
5. Christopher Isherwood, *Down There on a Visit* (London, 1962). This paragraph appears on an unnumbered end paper at the front of the text.
6. *DTOV*, p. 63.
7. *DTOV*, p. 237.
8. *DTOV*, p. 227.
9. *DTOV*, p. 244.
10. *DTOV*, p. 250.
11. *DTOV*, p. 335.
12. *DTOV*, p. 301.
13. Christopher Isherwood, *A Single Man* (London, 1964).
14. A. N. Whitehead, *Symbolism: Its Meaning and Effect* (Cambridge, 1927), p. 42.
15. *ASM*, pp. 7–8.
16. *ASM*, p. 8.
17. *ASM*, p. 27.
18. *ASM*, p. 25.
19. *ASM*, p. 26.
20. *ASM*, p. 28.
21. *ASM*, p. 29.
22. *ASM*, p. 29.
23. *ASM*, p. 30.
24. *ASM*, p. 31.
25. *ASM*, p. 32.

26. *ASM*, p. 35.
27. *ASM*, p. 43.
28. *ASM*, p. 44.
29. *ASM*, p. 44.
30. *ASM*, p. 45.
31. *ASM*, p. 75.
32. *ASM*, p. 76.
33. *ASM*, p. 87.
34. *ASM*, p. 133.
35. *ASM*, p. 130.
36. *ASM*, p. 137.
37. *ASM*, p. 147.
38. *ASM*, p. 153.
39. *ASM*, p. 157.
40. *ASM*, p. 158.
41. *ASM*, p. 155.

CHAPTER 6
1. *TWMA*, p. 261.
2. Stephen Spender, *The Creative Element* (London, 1953), p. 164. The remark is made with more immediate reference to Waugh but Spender applies the same brush to Greene.
3. *OMIH*, p. 109.
4. *OMIH*, p. 141.
5. *OMIH*, p. 109.
6. E. M. Forster, 'What I Believe', *Two Cheers For Democracy* (London, 1951), p. 78.
7. *OMIH*, p. 73.
8. *C*, p. 104.
9. *C*, p. 253.
10. *C*, p. 134.
11. *C*, p. 140.
12. *C*, p. 229.
13. *C*, p. 229.
14. *C*, p. 72.
15. *C*, p. 103.
16. *C*, p. 269.
17. *TWMA*, p. 62.
18. *TWMA*, p. 66.
19. *TWMA*, p. 62.
20. *TWMA*, p. 149.
21. *TWMA*, p. 159.
22. *TWMA*, p. 59.
23. *TWMA*, p. 107.
24. *TWMA*, p. 54.
25. *TWMA*, p. 54.
26. *TWMA*, p. 255.

27. *TWMA*, p. 229.

CHAPTER 7

1. *The Collector* (London, 1963); *The Magus* (London, 1966); *The French Lieutenant's Woman* (London, 1969); *The Aristos* first published London (1965), references will be to the revised edition published in 1968 by Pan Books.
2. Walter Allen, 'The Achievement of John Fowles', *Encounter*, XXV, 2 (Aug. 1970), 67.
3. *The Aristos*, p. 10.
4. *Magus*, p. 48.
5. Ibid., p. 51.
6. Ibid., p. 405.
7. Ibid., p. 121.
8. Ibid., pp. 370–1.
9. Ibid., p. 87.
10. Ibid., p. 228.
11. Ibid., p. 607.
12. Ibid., p. 609.
13. Ibid., p. 613.
14. Ibid., p. 615.
15. Ibid., p. 617.
16. Ibid., p. 407.
17. *FLW*, p. 433.

CHAPTER 8

1. David Pirie, '*Hamlet* Without the Prince', *Critical Quarterly*, XIV, 4 (Winter, 1972), 294.
2. Pirie, p. 313.
3. Elizabeth Taylor, *Mrs Palfrey at the Claremont* (London, 1971).
4. *MPC*, p. 2.
5. *MPC*, p. 9.
6. *MPC*, p. 3.
7. Kingsley Amis, *Lucky Jim* (London, 1954), p. 10.
8. *LJ*, p. 160.
9. *LJ*, p. 56.
10. *LJ*, p. 190.
11. *LJ*, p. 255.
12. The phrase is Amis's; see 'Why Lucky Jim Turned Right', in *What Became of Jane Austen?* (London, 1970).
13. John Wain, *Hurry on Down* (London, 1953), p. 23.
14. *HOD*, p. 239.
15. *HOD*, p. 241.
16. Saul Bellow, *Mr Sammler's Planet* (London, 1970; originally 1969).
17. Saul Bellow, *Herzog* (London, 1964; originally 1961).
18. *H*, p. 217.
19. *H*, p. 258. Bellow's italics.

20. *MSP*, p. 55.

21. *MSP*, p. 120.

22. *MSP*, p. 230.

23. Witold Gombrowicz, *Pornografia*, trans. Alastair Hamilton (London, 1966). Gombrowicz is Polish but has lived for much of his life in Argentina.

24. See *The Sovereignty of Good* (London, 1970) for instance

25. See Frank Kermode, 'The House of Fiction', *Partisan Review*, XXX, 1 (Spring, 1963), 63.

26. See Frederick J. Hoffman, 'Iris Murdoch: The Reality of Persons', *Critique*, VII (Spring, 1964), 48–57.

27. Iris Murdoch, 'The Sublime and the Beautiful Revisited', *The Yale Review*, XLIX (Winter 1960), 225.

28. SBR, p. 257.

29. SBR, p. 257.

30. SBR, p. 270.

31. Interview with Kermode, pp. 63–4.

32. Iris Murdoch, *The Black Prince* (London, 1973).

33. SBR, p. 251.

34. SBR, p. 269.

35. Iris Murdoch, 'The Idea of Perfection', *The Yale Review*, LIII, 3 (Spring, 1964), 379.

36. Iris Murdoch in 'Talking to Iris Murdoch', *The Listener*, 79 (4 Apr. 1968), 434.

Index